"Dawson Church has given us a fascinating, practical synthesis of cutting-edge science, medicine, psychology, and spirituality. Through stories, metaphors, research reports, and really good writing, he takes us on a journey into the future of healing, helping us to grasp the inseparability between spirit and matter. Reading it can inspire us toward full co-creative participation in building a healthier world."

—Susan Campbell, PhD, Author of *Saying What's Real*

"A brilliant amalgamation of the complexities of quantum biology and physics that form the basis of energy psychotherapies in language that is easily understood by us all. This groundbreaking book captures the essence of the problem in health care and beckons us to rise up as one to usher in the quantum leap needed in our society."

—Greg Nicosia, PhD, Past President, Association for Comprehensive Energy Psychology (ACEP)

"I'm compelled to say that The Genie in Your Genes *is in my view the most complete and lucidly written book on medical science and alternative medicine. I have never read a single book that so eloquently uses science to practically and concretely validate the long frowned upon power of metaphysical concepts like faith, belief, prayer, meditation, yoga, acupuncture, etc. With mountains of research at his disposal, Dawson Church shows that contrary to the long-held belief by the medical establishment that our genes dictate our destiny, it's actually the other way around. Our consciousness and external environment actually exert much more influence on the genes than vice versa, literally switching genes on and off moment by moment at the speed of thought. It is evident that Church goes to painstaking lengths to bring this profound work to the layperson, and does a phenomenal job in the process. I've barely skimmed the surface—the rest is for you to explore—but I close by making this bold statement. Humanity unequivocally needs this brilliant work. For a single work,* The Genie in Your Genes *is absolutely the most empowering and enlightening scientific work I've ever read. This is one for the ages."*

—The Worderer

T0112703

"The Genie In Your Genes *is a revolutionary book that reveals why your genetic code doesn't determine your fate. Instead, your mind (and your behavior) has extraordinary control over the expression of your genes, determining your level of health, prevention of disease and much more."*

—Market Watch

"Defining destiny through DNA has been a standard medical practice for decades. The Genie in Your Genes...*challenges this fatalistic theory.... Citing more than 300 medical studies, [Dawson Church] proposes that DNA can be altered through the power of belief. Weaving his way through physics, genetics and biology, Church explores how emotions and difficult experiences can affect health. Negative feelings and painful life experiences can create sickness.... The correlation between health and consciousness has been missing the scientific evidence to back it up. Perhaps Church's book will open up a few minds to the possibilities of alternative medicine."*

—Laura Axelrod, *Birmingham News*

"First of all, if you are a newcomer to Dawson Church's writing, you need to know that his facts are unimpeachable—they were stringently peer-reviewed before publication. What is more, when Church makes categorical statements, he provides research to corroborate them. This is a book that needs to be read more than once. For one thing, it is jam-packed with information. First-time read, it inspires. After that, the book becomes a first-class reference manual for "You, the ultimate epigenetic engineer" as Church puts it. I don't usually use superlatives in my reviews, but this book deserves them. It can prove life-changing for those who take it seriously."

—Chemistry Bookshelf

"Fascinating reading with powerful treatment possibilities for health-care practitioners, as well as revolutionary philosophical implications for the causal interrelationships among genes, the brain, consciousness, and healing. Highly recommended!"

—Richard de la Chaumiére, PhD, Author of *What's It All About?*

"*Faith, prayer, thoughts, emotions, intentions, and beliefs are vital components to creating a space for healing and balance to occur. For those who have questions on the science of this emerging field, numerous studies are cited—there are nearly 400 endnotes—and dozens of researchers, doctors, and practitioners reviewed the manuscript. Well-researched, fast-moving, grounded in credible science while fancifully speculative,* The Genie in Your Genes *offers tantalizing proof that we are on the verge of a spectacular breakthrough in our understanding of how optimal health is achieved and maintained. For those who feel that the future of medicine will be energy- and consciousness-based, this book will become a dog-eared friend.*"

—*Shift* magazine, Institute of Noetic Sciences

"*Challenges the long-held notion that genetic structure is determined at birth and its role in developing different traits remains stable after birth. Besides explaining cogently the complex interplay of electromagnetic energy, body chemistry, and physiological healing from disease,* The Genie in Your Genes *explores several less-known phenomena like: mirror neurons, piezoelectricity in our bodies, changes in DNA influenced by one's intention, healing frequencies of therapists, entanglement, and much more. So exhaustive is Dawson Church's coverage of his case for energy healing that the question of 'Why use alternate healing?' changes to 'Why not try energy medicine first?' Coming fully referenced and listing many important healing techniques as well as useful sources of information,* The Genie in Your Genes *is a commendable read for all educated readers, particularly for science buffs and, of course, a must read for those millions of people who are suffering from some form of stress.*"

—Ernest Dempsey, *The Audience Review*

"*Dawson Church provides a far-ranging survey of the leading edges of research in alternative medicine—especially energy medicine—and synthesizes research from many fields to provide practical guidelines for personal health.*"

—Berney Williams, PhD, Dean of Graduate Studies, Energy Medicine University, Sausalito, California

"Covers a complex subject, yet is written in a way that makes the topic clear. It is well researched, well referenced and at the end is an appendix that gives you further information on how to find a practitioner and some exercises that you can do on your own. This book should be read by practitioners of medicine, alternative therapists, science students and people who have psychological stress or chronic health problems believed to be caused by genetic defaults. The Genie in Your Genes *will open your eyes and give you hope that you can control your life."*

—Reader Views

"To counter the invasive nature of allopathic therapeutic techniques, currently forming the bulk of mainstream treatment, alternate healing experts are knuckling down on scientific research that validates noninvasive, simpler, safer, and less expensive treatment methods. Part of the groundbreaking work in this direction comes from Dawson Church, founder of the National Institute for Integrative Healthcare (NIIH), a nonprofit education and research institute that focuses on consciousness and energy as primary modalities. In his recent book The Genie in Your Genes, *Dawson Church probes into the complex processes that switch on, or turn off, the genes in our bodies, a process that determines whether or not certain healing responses will be triggered. The pages of the book are filled with some of the most amazing findings on genes and illnesses, and their connection with the flow of electromagnetic energy in the body."*

—Bookpleasures

"This book builds a bridge between genetics and health care, and lays the critical scientific foundation for alternative and complementary medicine. Dawson Church gathers and synthesizes new information at the frontiers of science and medicine, putting it all together in a most enjoyable, readable, and provocative book—complete with practical information including exercises for daily life that promote greater health and well-being. It is sure to facilitate the health care revolution under way—one leading us toward sustainable medicine and enhanced self-care."

—Beverly Rubik, PhD, President, Institute for Frontier Science

"Put simply, epigenetics is the study of how environment works to turn genes on and off. Our genes are not our destiny. Rather, they're like the first draft of a movie script. Lots of changes are possible all throughout the creative process we call life. The people, places and circumstances we deliberately or "accidently" find ourselves in the midst of, actually work to change genetic expression within us; as do the things we think, feel and believe on a moment-by-moment basis. Whether we know it or not, or believe it or not, we are constantly performing epigenetic engineering on our own cells. So is the outside environment in a dynamic, lifelong interplay. Dawson Church has written a very readable account of this growing medical research field."

—Brady on the Brain

"Though this book is not an easy read, it offers a wealth of information on coming to terms with a person's health and ability to rely on his own consciousness to direct his well-being. Dawson explains his theory of epigenetic medicine, the notion that there are healing techniques each person can employ to override the effects of the genes that we think control our bodies. This overriding or correcting of errant genetic expression is not a matter of 'wishful thinking' or 'good thoughts' but an active control of our consciousness. In fact, the pivotal chapter between the scientific explanation of genetics and the 'how to's' of putting consciousness into action is called 'Consciousness as Medicine.'"

—MyShelf

"In The Genie in Your Genes, Dawson Church reveals, in a most powerful, practical, and hopeful way, the extraordinary link among body, mind, and spirit, and the undeniable impact of our thoughts and emotions on our everyday experiences. Anyone who reads this book and takes its remarkable information to heart will be equipped to draw to themselves a level and degree of health, abundance, and joy that far surpasses anything they could have imagined."

—Susan Schachterle, Author of The Bitch, the Crone, and
   the Harlot

"The Genie in Your Genes *is an astonishing look at how our beliefs, thoughts, and emotions impact every aspect of our very being. If you want to know where medicine and psychology are headed in the next hundred years, and how to create extraordinary well-being in your life—right now—this is the book to read.*"

—Ray Dodd, Author of *Belief Works* and *The Power of Belief*

"*Dawson Church has done an amazing service by providing an integrative scientific foundation for Energy Psychology and energy medicine. The* Genie in Your Genes *is on my list of required readings for all health and mental health professionals.*"

—Fred P. Gallo, PhD, Author of *Energy Psychology*

The Genie in Your Genes

Epigenetic Medicine
and the New Biology of Intention
Third Edition

Dawson Church, PhD

www.EpigeneticMedicine.org

Energy Psychology Press
Santa Rosa, CA 95403
www.EnergyPsychologyPress.com

Cataloging-in-Publication Data

Church, Dawson, 1956-
The genie in your genes: epigenetic medicine and the new biology of intention /
Dawson Church. 3rd Edition

p. cm.

ISBN: 978-1-60415-243-2

1. Energy psychology. 2. Genetic regulation. 3. Epigenesis. 4. Healing—Psychological
aspects. I. Title.

RC489.E53C48 2007

616.89—dc22

2007009305

Typeset in Hoefler Text and Capitals
Printed in USA
Third Edition
Illustrations by Karin Kinsey
Cover Design by Robert Mueller and Victoria Valentine
10 9 8 7 6 5 4 3 2 1

Contents

Acknowledgments

Many times a day I realize how much my own outer and inner life is built upon the labors of my fellow men, both living and dead, and how earnestly I must exert myself in order to give in return as much as I have received.

—Albert Einstein

This book has been the biggest single project of my life, and I appreciate all who made it possible. I would first like to express my deep appreciation to several brilliant authors, researchers, and doctors who provided the insights that fueled the development of the ideas in the following chapters.

First, to Norman Shealy, MD, PhD, I am indebted for an education in *the critical role that electricity and magnetism play in all healing.* This is the first of several insights that led to the writing of this book. Norm is an expert in the subject; I coauthored a book with him called *Soul Medicine,* which stimulated my curiosity about the links between faith healing and electromagnetic conduction. Norm also chaired my dissertation committee, and has contributed mightily to the professional development of alternative medicine in many ways: through his insistence on rigorous documentation of "miraculous" cures, through his establishment of Holos University, through his founding of the American Holistic Medical Association (AHMA) and cofounding of the American Board for Scientific Medical Intuition (ABSMI), through the development of the SheliTENS treatment machine, and through his many books. He has also mentored me, encouraged me, listened patiently (well, at least stoically) to me during my explication of ideas in process, and even—surely the supreme test of human courage—suffered through being a passenger in my car on the freeways of Los Angeles, California.

I would also like to thank Ernest Rossi, PhD, for his amazing book *The Psychobiology of Gene Expression.* Until I read his book, I did not realize *just how quickly genes may be activated by memories, feelings, thoughts,* and other aspects of the internal environment—some genes

17

in *under two seconds*. This was the second great insight that motivated me to complete this book. Rossi applies these findings to psychotherapy in general and clinical hypnosis in particular, in ways that explain many mysteries of the therapeutic process. In his book, Rossi laid a foundation for a whole generation of researchers to investigate the effects on genes of mental and emotional shifts in the individual. Rossi's book gave me many research pointers and great inspiration.

Another book that contains stunning implications for medicine and research is *Energy Medicine in Therapeutics and Human Performance*. Written by James Oschman, PhD, this book synthesizes much other research in the field in a way that presents a compelling picture of some of the mechanisms by which energy creates healing. To Jim, I am especially indebted for the third insight: that *the body's connective tissue system is a giant liquid crystal semiconductor.* Oschman's comprehensive survey of research in the field makes further research much easier. He has also done duty as a friend, cheerleader, and critical thinker in the development of this book, reviewing and correcting the chapters on connective tissue and its role in the transmission of information in the human body.

I would also like to thank those who have instructed me in Energy Psychology (EP). To these wise instructors, I owe the discovery that *emotional trauma—even deep, ingrained, long-standing trauma—can be alleviated very quickly, often in just a few minutes.* I had great trouble believing this when I first heard about it, and my logical belief system still has trouble wrapping itself around the idea that a neurosis or psychopathology for which a patient might have spent an unsuccessful decade in psychotherapy can be permanently resolved in just a few sessions with EP. Yet there are thousands of case histories, and a growing number of clinical studies, that show that this is often possible.

Therefore, I believe that EP has a potential for the alleviation of human suffering that rivals any advance in psychology or medicine in the last five centuries. That's a huge claim, but it is not hyperbole. Try it for yourself by downloading the free mini-manual at www.

DawsonGift.com. You'll be a convert within an hour—and it will change your life thereafter!

I deeply appreciate David Feinstein, PhD, who coauthored a clear and compelling guide to these exciting new techniques called *The Promise of Energy Psychology*. Thanks, too, to David for suggesting the title of this book at a time when I was having trouble seeing the forest for the trees. I also appreciate the inspiration I derived from his seminal papers defining the field (see www.HandoutBank.org), and for his valuable feedback and friendship. David has also done a great deal to encourage professional standards of competence in the field, and to collect the science behind these methods into a coherent whole. The book *Energy Medicine,* which David wrote with Donna Eden, is a best-seller, and one of the foundational texts for this field.

Fred Gallo, PhD, who coined the term "Energy Psychology" and whose book of the same name is a sound introduction for professionals, has developed tools and techniques that have benefited many. Fred's books are also foundational texts for the field, and by systematizing these treatments, then organizing them into a simple treatment system, he has given the field a solid underpinning.

I also gratefully acknowledge Tapas Fleming, LAc, developer of the Tapas Acupressure Technique (TAT), among the easiest EP techniques to learn, yet one which harnesses similar power for shifting traumas. Her quiet wisdom, gentle compassion, and grounded teaching techniques have demystified EP and healed many lives.

I acknowledge an immense debt of gratitude to Roger Callahan, PhD, the originator of Thought Field Therapy (TFT), and the author of *Tapping the Healer Within* and other books. He articulated and popularized his methods in the 1970s and 1980s, and development of these methods led to most other subsequent EP techniques, including the publication of *The EFT Manual* by Gary Craig and Adrienne Fowlie.

I am immensely grateful to the late Dorothea Hover-Kramer, EdD, RN, and to David Gruder, PhD, cofounders of the Association for Comprehensive Energy Psychology (ACEP). Dorothea's marvelous book *Second Chance at Your Dream* applies the insights of EP to redefine aging as a period of blossoming creativity. I am also grateful to David for organizing the many steps in spiritual, psychological, and emotional healing into a unified developmental scheme in his seminal book *The New IQ.*

This field owes a great debt to Francine Shapiro, PhD, who popularized Eye Movement Desensitization and Reprocessing (EMDR), and furthered this technique by insistence on rigorous clinical studies. These paved the way for adoption of EMDR in primary care settings, which let to gradual acceptance of other EP techniques.

My great appreciation also goes to my wonderful friends Bruce Lipton, PhD, and his partner, Margaret Horton. Bruce's book *The Biology of Belief* hit various best-seller lists in 2005 when it came out, has sold over 100,000 copies, and catalyzed the idea in popular awareness that *genes are merely blueprints, and that it's the environment outside our cells that determines genetic expression.* Bruce has also advanced the idea that the cell's "brain" is its membrane, for it is the membrane, influenced again by the environment, that admits the signals that trigger the processes of life. Bruce's book created a fertile public awareness for these radical new ideas, in which books like this one, and *Soul Medicine,* can bear fruit.

I deeply appreciate the editing of John Travis, MD, coauthor of *The Wellness Workbook,* who gave me the benefit of his brilliant and perceptive mind. He went through this manuscript with his eagle eye prior to it being sent out for peer review, corrected some of the key concepts, and fine-tuned the language of the text. He challenged my hidden assumptions, as well as picked apart any imprecise science and reassembled it correctly. The final draft has benefited from his decades of experience and compendious knowledge of both conventional and alternative medicine.

I have also received encouragement from some of my heroes: Larry Dossey, MD, very kindly granted me interviews, or permission to publish his work, in several of my anthologies. Caroline Myss, PhD, did the same, and also encouraged and furthered the publication of

Soul Medicine. Barbara Marx Hubbard, one of the shining lights of our generation, first traced for me the implications of some of these ideas for human and planetary evolution. Bob Nunley, PhD, and Ann Nunley, PhD, besides being instrumental, along with Norm Shealy, in founding Holos University, also developed a technique called Inner Counselor, which incorporates the most powerful transformative techniques of transpersonal psychology.

I am also extremely grateful to the salespeople who believed in this book and represented it effectively to bookstores; with over 100,000 new titles published each year, it's hard to stand above the crowd unless you have passionate advocates in the sales cycle. I particularly appreciate Eric Kampmann, president of Midpoint Trade Distribution; also Gail Kump, the deft and articulate cheerleader who persuaded Barnes and Noble to put the first edition on the front table of all their stores the week it was released. As a result of their efforts, the first (hardcover) edition went through three printings and sold some 15,000 copies. The second (paperback) edition was even more successful, being adopted as a text by several universities. Reid Tracy and Hay House, distributors of this third edition, have been dedicated backers of EP.

Books and articles dealing with health and healing go through the process of "peer review," in which colleagues and experts read the draft and comment on the material from the perspective of their expertise. I deeply appreciate those who read all or part of this manuscript and offered their suggestions and advice. I've received dozens of suggestions over the past many years that have strengthened the book and been incorporated into this third edition.

It is impossible for me to find the quiet creative space to write books or articles in the pressured and deadline-driven publishing office where I work nine to five (or more usually five to nine—five a.m. to nine p.m.); getting away on a cruise, on a "vacation," or to a spa has been the only thing that made it possible. So besides writing part of this book while looking out the window of the library on the cruise ship *Dawn Princess,* I wrote parts at Gley Ivy Hot Springs, Harbin Hot

Springs, Tahoe State Park, and the Prince Kuhio Resort in Kauai, Hawaii. The paperback revision would never have been completed without a week in Palm Springs, California, where Deb Elkington, RN, kindly made her vacation home available to me.

I'm very grateful to the capable team at Energy Psychology Group who handle enormous amounts of detail every day so that I don't have to! This includes my dedicated assistant Deb Tribbey, editor Stephanie Marohn, training coordinator Lisa Bacon, certification coordinator Marion Allen, webmaster Will Bouschor, content manager Mitch Koester, social media editor Catherine Hughes, video editor Kaiya Kramer, and our twenty-plus certified trainers.

I appreciate the hundreds of selfless volunteers of the Veterans Stress Project (www.StressProject.org). Through their efforts, thousands of veterans and their family members have received free or low-cost energy medicine sessions. Our volunteers have been the bedrock of research conducted by the nonprofit I chair, the National Institute for Integrative Healthcare (NIIH.org), of which the Veterans Stress Project is a part. On the Stress Project website, they post a stream of videos and stories written by veterans, talking about the life-changing transformations they've experienced. I also appreciate Olli and Tim Toukolehto, who created the truly awesome online tapping coaching program called Battle Tap. This allows veterans to receive help whenever and wherever they need it, rather than relying only on office visits with a therapist or coach. I'm convinced we'll see many other online EP apps and sites in the coming years.

Preface to the Third Edition

It's now been about a decade since the publication of the first hardcover edition of *The Genie in Your Genes*. The revisions I've made to the book since then tell us a lot about how much the field of Energy Psychology has changed. Ten years ago I predicted that we'd see research showing the effect of emotions on gene expression, but I could not point to much in the way of evidence for that hypothesis. By the time I wrote the paperback edition five years later, I could list thirteen studies. Now, there are hundreds of studies that demonstrate the link between what we think, feel, and believe, and which genes are promoted or silenced. Science is gradually tracing—in detail—the precise regions on DNA strings that are affected by experiences such as psychological trauma, emotional resiliency, and spiritual epiphany.

Around the same time I wrote that paperback version, I also founded the peer-reviewed journal *Energy Psychology: Theory, Research, and Treatment* (www.EnergyPsychologyJournal.org). I'd had a difficult time getting my research published in conventional journals. I sometimes ran into entrenched skepticism, but more often I encountered honest ignorance. Reviewers had no background in energy therapies and didn't know what to make of the papers they were reviewing. The health outcomes of participants were often a giant leap better than usual in conventional therapies, and didn't fit into the conceptual framework of incremental improvement. If I told you I'd bought a new car and it got eighty-five miles to the gallon, you'd be impressed. If I told you it got four hundred miles to the gallon, you'd think I was crazy. The results of energy therapies are often so outside the box that they baffle the imagination.

The journal has since facilitated the expert peer review and publication of dozens of papers. Many of these might never have been published had they had to run the gauntlet of uninformed peer review. I appreciate the members of the editorial board. These distinguished authorities were willing to lend their names to the masthead of the first issue based only on trust. I also appreciate the invisibl work of the peer reviewers whose expertise makes the continued high standards of the journal possible.

In the coming years, I expect to see energy medicine and Energy Psychology integrated into conventional medicine. Skeptic Richard Dawkins said, "There is no such thing as alternative medicine. There is only medicine that works and medicine that doesn't." This statement is a useful reminder that separating the worlds of "conventional medicine" and "complementary and alternative medicine" or CAM can be unhelpful. Conventional medicine is assumed to be evidence-based and effective, while CAM is by definition an alternative to "real" medical care. When CAM demonstrates good patient outcomes, it should be part of conventional medical practice.

Emerging research will facilitate this process. Studies of Emotional Freedom Techniques (EFT), for example, have shown that EFT can remediate most cases of posttraumatic stress disorder (PTSD), anxiety, and depression in just a few sessions. This opens up the possibility that the prevalence of these mental health problems will be greatly reduced in the coming decades. One of my recent keynote speeches was called "A World Without PTSD?" and, though I do not believe that we can cure every mental health problem in every person, I do believe that we've entered a new era. With enough social will and belief, we can bring the same vigorous energy to bear on eliminating mental health problems that previous generations brought to bear on eradicating cholera, typhoid, and polio.

I also predict that combination therapies will trump individual therapeutic schools. Advocates of EFT, EMDR, TFT, and other therapies vigorously champion the superiority of their methods. I believe that they all use common pathways, and that those pathways are more important in producing successful outcomes than the variations between methods. Healers with a diverse toolbox have more tools to help their clients than devotees of any particular therapeutic school.

I believe that as genetic testing falls in price and complexity, individualized treatment plans will become the norm. For instance, we will be able to test whether a particular client responds best to a mixture of qigong and EFT, or yoga, ibuprofen, and EMDR. The test won't involve a blood draw, lab work, and a wait for the results. We'll use simple saliva swabs that will show color-coded results in seconds. In this way, highly personalized medicine will become possible.

I also predict a continued upswell in the recognition of the importance of spirituality in the healing process. Studies that measure biological markers show that the beliefs of participants reveal the highest level of correlation with their health outcomes. Biological measures have already shown us that emotional problems like stress aren't "all in the mind." They have powerful negative effects throughout the body. The reductionist division of human experience into body, mind, and spirit is useful for studying microscopic phenomena, but a holistic approach is essential to grasping the big picture. The old paradigm that holds psychology separate from biology is breaking down. Even our brains are shaped by the thoughts we think.

Human beings aren't just unitary individuals; they thrive only as part of a thriving biological and spiritual ecosystem. I sometimes define my life's mission as "emotional terraforming." By this I mean the work of rendering the "emosphere"—a word I coined to describe the entire emotional atmosphere of the planet—a place fit for acceptance, growth, and love. As I look back on the ten years between the first edition of this book and the current edition, I believe that the emosphere has shifted during that time. Despite the wars, conflicts, and screaming headlines, I sense an upswing in positive and empowered emotions on a global scale. We're at the tipping point.

I believe the shift will accelerate. Just the way that the institution of slavery went from being perceived as normal to being an abhorrence in just a few years, I believe that the negative emotional conditioning that enslaves so many minds will rapidly dissipate. A century ago, our ancestors learned how to eradicate many infectious diseases. We are the generation that is catalyzing a profound global transformation, sculpting a beautiful emosphere that nourishes both us and succeeding generations.

—Dawson Church

1

Epigenetic Healing

Imagination is everything. It is the key to coming attractions.

—Albert Einstein

Frail and slight, a quiet woman shuffled up from the back of the room and stood in front of me at the microphone. "My name is June," she said. "I don't believe in this energy stuff, and if you don't want to work with me, I'll sit down again."

In front of us, the large conference room was packed. Every seat was taken, and many more people stood in the back of the room. The air was hot, as the crush of bodies overwhelmed the air-conditioning system. Everyone seemed to be holding their breath. I had just concluded a lecture on the history of energy in medicine and psychology. I then asked for volunteers to demonstrate Energy Psychology methods, so that the audience could witness how they worked in real life.

I reassured June that while there were no guarantees that Energy Psychology could help her condition, I'd be happy to try. She told us that her left shoulder was frozen. I asked her to demonstrate, and she could only move her left hand a couple of inches forward and a couple of inches to the side.

I asked about any emotional issues that might underlie her physical complaint. June told us, in a monotone, that her adult son had been kidnapped while on a mission as a peace worker in a third-world country. His kidnappers held him for several months, and finally killed him. She was in touch with the U.S. State Department throughout the ordeal, and finally received a phone call from a consular official to tell her that her son's body had been found. She had developed many physical problems during her son's captivity, one of which was that her shoulder froze up. She finished by telling us, "Today is the ninth anniversary of his death."

I asked her about the emotional intensity of each step of the tragedy, asking her to rate them on a scale of zero to ten, with zero being no intensity, and ten being the maximum possible intensity. After listening to her carefully, I finally decided to work with June on the phone call from the State Department, which she said was a seven in intensity. I then performed a very fast and basic emotional energy release technique called EFT (Emotional Freedom Techniques), used by thousands of doctors and therapists worldwide, as she thought about the phone call. "Rate the intensity again," I asked, and she reported that it had gone down to zero.

"How's your shoulder doing?" I asked. She hesitantly moved it forward. It went farther and farther. She raised it up all the way, till it was perpendicular to her body. She began to swing her arm around in circles. Her eyes opened wide, and she stared at the swinging arm as though it were an alien oozing out of a spaceship.

After the lecture ended, June walked up to me in the hallway, exuberantly swinging her arm around and around. Her face was wreathed in smiles, her eyes lively, her voice sparkling. "I felt so horrible this morning I didn't want to come to the conference," she confided. "I was carpooling with two friends, and when they arrived at my house, they dragged me out of bed and made me come here. I can't believe what just happened."

"Usually, my logical mind can't believe it either," I reassured her. "Nevertheless, when you use these energy techniques, such shifts become routine." Although they seemed miraculous to my skeptical brain when I first witnessed them, I now understand that they are based on sound medical and physiological principles, and they have more to do with biology than magic.

Turning Gene Research into Therapy

From all around the world, in virtually every field of the healing arts—from psychiatrists to doctors to psychotherapists to sports physiologists to social workers—stories like this are being told, as the world of psychology and medicine begins to awaken to the potential of energy medicine and its effects on the expression of our DNA. They are the first loud reports of a revolution in treatment destined to change our entire civilization, reaching into every corner of medicine and psychology...and beyond them into the structures of society itself. In the space of one generation, we have discovered, or rediscovered, techniques that can make us happier, less stressed, and much more physically healthy—safely, quickly, and without side effects. Techniques from energy medicine and Energy Psychology can alleviate chronic diseases, shift autoimmune conditions, and eliminate psychological traumas with an efficiency and speed that conventional treatments can scarcely touch.

The implications of these techniques—for human happiness, for social conflicts, and for political change—promise a radical positive disruption in the human condition, one that goes far beyond health care. They hold the promise of affecting society as profoundly as the scientific and artistic breakthroughs of the Renaissance changed the course of civilization. And they are at the cutting edge of science, as experimental evidence stacks up to provide objective demonstration of their effectiveness.

Along with the case histories accumulating from pioneers in this new medicine and new psychology, scientists are discovering the precise pathways by which changes in human consciousness produce changes in human bodies. As we think our thoughts and feel our feelings, our bodies respond with a complex array of shifts. Each thought or feeling unleashes a particular cascade of biochemicals in our organs. Each experience triggers genetic changes in our cells.

The Dance of Genes and Neurons

These new discoveries have revolutionary implications for health and healing. Psychologist Ernest Rossi begins his authoritative text *The Psychobiology of Gene Expression* with a challenge: "Are these to remain abstract facts safely sequestered in academic textbooks, or can we take these facts into the mainstream of human affairs?"[1]

The Genie in Your Genes takes up Rossi's challenge, believing that it is essential that this exciting genetic research progress beyond laboratories and scientific conferences and find practical applications in a world in which many people suffer unnecessarily. Rossi explores "how our subjective states of mind, consciously motivated behavior, and our perception of free will can modulate gene expression to optimize health."[2] Nobel Prize–winner Eric Kandel, MD, believes that in future treatments, "Social influences will be biologically incorporated in the altered expressions of specific genes in specific nerve cells of specific areas of the brain."[3] Brain researchers Gerd Kempermann and Frederick Gage of Salk Laboratories envision a future in which the regeneration of damaged neural networks is a cornerstone of medical treatment, and doctors' prescriptions include "modulations of environmental or cognitive stimuli" and "alterations of physical activity."[4] In other words, when the doctor of the future tears a page off her prescription pad and hands it to a patient, the prescription might well be—instead of, or in addition to, a drug—a particular therapeutic belief or thought, a positive feeling, a gene-enhancing physical exercise, an act of altruism, a day of gratitude, or membership in a social club. Research is revealing that these activities, thoughts, and feelings have profound healing and regenerative effects on our bodies, and we're now figuring out how to use them therapeutically.

The Dogma of Genetic Determinism

This picture of a *genetic makeup that fluctuates by the hour and minute* is at odds with the picture ingrained in the public mind: that genes determine everything from our physical characteristics to our behavior. Even many scientists still speak from the assumption that our genes form an immutable blueprint that our cells must forever follow. In her book *The Private Life of the Brain,* British research scientist and Oxford don Susan Greenfield says, "the reductionist genetic train of thought fuels the currently highly fashionable concept of a gene for this or that."[5]

Niles Eldredge, in his book *Why We Do It,* says, "genes have been the dominant metaphor underlying explanations of all manner of human behavior, from the most basic and animalistic, like sex, up to and including such esoterica as the practice of religion, the enjoyment of music, and the codification of laws and moral strictures.... The media are besotted with genes...genes have for over half a century easily eclipsed the outside natural world as the primary driving force of evolution in the minds of many evolutionary biologists."[6]

Medical schools have had the doctrine of genetic determinism embedded in their teaching for decades. The newsletter for the students at the Health Science campus of the University of Southern California proclaims, "Research has shown that 1 in 40 Ashkenazi women has defects in two genes that cause familial breast/ovarian cancer...."[7] The *Los Angeles Times,* August 11, 2007, tells us that "Researchers have identified two mutant forms of a single gene that are responsible for 99% of all cases of a common form of glaucoma."[8] Making a single gene responsible for a disease gives journalists and scientists a simple and satisfying explanation.

Such explanations abound. On National Public Radio on October 28th, 2005, an announcer declared: "Scientists today announced they have found a gene for dyslexia. It's a gene on chromosome six called DCDC2." The *New York Times* ran a similar story the following day, under the headline, "Findings Support That [Dyslexia] Disorder Is Genetic." Other media picked up the story, and the legend of the primacy of DNA was reinforced.

There's only one problem with the legend: it's not true.

There's a second major problem with the legend: It locates the ultimate power over our health and well-being in the untouchable realm of molecular structure, rather than any place we can control, such as our lifestyle, thoughts, and emotions. In her book *The DNA Mystique,* Dorothy Nelkin states, "In a diverse array of popular sources, the gene has become a supergene, an almost supernatural entity that has the power to define identity, determine human affairs, dictate human relationships, and explain social problems. In this construct, human beings in all their complexity are seen as products of a molecular text...the secular equivalent of a soul—the immortal site of the true self and determiner of fate."[9]

In reality, genes contribute to our characteristics but do not determine them. Blair Justice, PhD, in his book *Who Gets Sick,* observes that "genes account for about 35% of longevity, while lifestyles, diet, and other environmental factors, including support systems, are the major reasons people live longer."[10] The percentage by which genetic predisposition affects various conditions varies, but it is rarely 100%. The tools of our consciousness—including our beliefs, prayers, thoughts, intentions, and faith—often correlate much more strongly with our health, longevity, and happiness than our genes do. Larry Dossey, MD, observes, "Several studies show that what one *thinks* about one's health is one of the most accurate predictors of longevity ever discovered."[11] Studies show that a committed spiritual practice and faith can add many years to our lives, regardless of our genetic mix.[12]

How did the dogma that DNA holds the blueprint for development become so firmly enshrined? In his entertaining book *Born That Way,* medical researcher William Wright gives a detailed history of the rise to supremacy of the idea that genes contain the codes that control life—that we are who we are, and we do what we do, because we were simply "born that way."[13] We often hear phrases like "She's a natural born athlete," or "He's a born loser," or "She has good genes," to explain some aspect of a person's behavior. The idea of genetic disposition has moved far beyond the laboratory to become deeply entrenched in our popular culture.

Lee Dugatkin, professor of biology at the University of Louisville, points out that after the basic rules governing the inheritance of characteristics across generations were made by Mendel, and the structure of the DNA molecule was discovered, scientists became convinced that the gene was the "means by which traits could be transmitted across generations. We see this trend continuing today in research labs throughout the world as well as in the media in reports of genes for schizophrenia, genes for homosexuality, genes for alcoholism, and so on. Genes for this, genes for that."[14] Researcher Carl Ratner, PhD, of Humboldt State University, draws the following analogy: "Genes may directly determine simple physical characteristics such as eye color. However, they do not directly determine psychological phenomena. In the latter case, genes produce a potentiating substratum rather than particular phenomena. The substratum is like a petri dish which forms a conducive environment in which bacteria can grow, however, it does not produce bacteria."[15]

Since the 1970s, researchers have been turning up findings that are at odds with the prevailing mindset. They have accumulated an increasing number of findings that behaviors aren't just transmitted genetically across generations; they may be newly developed by many individuals during a single generation. While the process of genetic evolution can take thousands of years, as genes throw off mutations

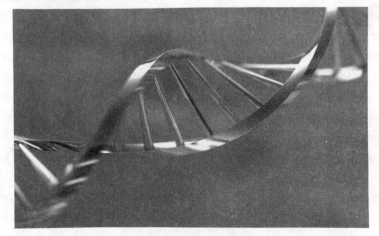

The DNA spiral has become a defining icon of our civilization

that are sometimes successful, and often not, evolution through experience and imitation can occur within minutes—and *then* be passed on to the next generation.

Edward O. Wilson, the father of sociobiology, hinted at the very end of the twenty-fifth anniversary edition of his tremendously influential book, *Sociobiology,* that, in future research, "Learning and creativeness will be defined as the alteration of specific portions of the cognitive machinery regulated by input from the emotive centers. Having cannibalized psychology, the new neurobiology will yield an enduring set of first principles for sociology.... We are compelled to drive toward total knowledge, right down to the levels of the neuron and gene."[16] The notion that the *genes in the neurons of our brain can be activated by input from our emotive centers* is a big new idea, and indicates a degree of interconnection and feedback at odds with the straight-line, cause-and-effect model of genetic causation.

As well as beings of matter, we are beings of energy. Electromagnetism pervades biology, and there is an electromagnetic component to every biological process. While biology has been largely content with chemical explanations of how and why cells work, there are many tantalizing preliminary research findings that show that electromagnetic shifts accompany virtually every biological process. The energy flowing in, around, and out of neurons and genes interacts constantly with the outside environment. Genes are how organisms *store* information, while energy is about how they *communicate* information. Researching genes without looking at the energy component of DNA is like studying a computer hard drive without plugging in the power cable. Hard drives are composed of thousands of sectors, substructures that store information.[17] You can develop impressive theories about why the storage device is constructed the way it is, and the interesting way in which the sectors are arranged, but until you plug the hard drive in and watch it functioning in the context of the energy flow that animates it, and the other components of the computer ecosystem in which it's nested, you understand only structure and not function.

Death of a Dogma

The idea that genes are the repositories of our characteristics is also known as the Central Dogma. The Central Dogma was propounded by the co-discoverer of the double helix structure of DNA, Sir Francis Crick. He first used the term in a 1953 speech, and restated it in a paper in the journal *Nature,* entitled "Central Dogma of Molecular Biology."[18] It has been so influential that data contradicting the central dogma have often been dismissed as mere anomalies, since they require much more complex interactions than genetic determinism can explain.[19]

One of many problems with the dogma, for instance, is that the number of genes in the human chromosome is insufficient to carry all the information required to create and run a human body. It isn't even a big enough number to code for the structure (let alone function) of one complex organ like the brain. It also is too small a number to account for the huge quantity of neural connections in our bodies.[20] Two eminent professors express it this way: "Remembering that the information in the human genome has to cover the development of all other bodily structures as well as the brain, this is not a fraction of the information required to structure in detail any significant brain modules, let alone for the structuring of the brain as a whole."[21]

The Human Genome Project was initially focused on cataloging all the genes of the human body. At the beginning of the 1990s, the original researchers expected to find at least 120,000 genes, because that's the minimum they projected it would take to code all the characteristics of an organism as complex as a human being. Our bodies manufacture about 100,000 proteins, the building blocks of cells. All of those 100,000 building blocks must be assembled with precise coordination in order to support life. The working hypothesis at the start of the Human Genome Project was that there would be a gene that provided the blueprint to manufacture each of those 100,000 proteins, plus another 20,000 or so *regulatory genes* whose function was to *orchestrate* the complex dance of protein assembly.

The further the project progressed, the smaller the estimates of the number of genes became. When the project finished its catalog, they had mapped the human genome as consisting of just 23,688 genes. The huge symphony orchestra of genes they had expected to find had shrunk to the size of a string quartet. The questions that this small number of genes give rise to are these: If all the information required to construct and maintain a human being—or even one big instrument, such as the brain—is not contained in the genes, where does it come from? And who is conducting the whole complex dance of assembly of multiple organ systems? The focus of research has thus shifted from cataloging the genes themselves to figuring out how they work in the context of an organism that is in "a state of *systemic cooperation* [where] every part knows what every other part is doing; every atom, molecule, cell, and tissue is able to participate in an intended action."[22]

The lack of enough information in the genes to construct and manage a body is just one of the weaknesses of the Central Dogma. Another is that genes can be activated and deactivated by the environment inside the body and outside of it. Scientists are learning more about the process that turns genes on and off, and what factors influence their activation. We may have lots of information on our hard drives, but at a given time we will be utilizing only part of it. And we may be changing the data as well, like revising an email before we send it to a friend. One of the factors that affect which genes are active is our experience, a fact completely incompatible with the doctrine of genetic determinism.

Yet our experiences themselves are just part of the picture. We take facts and experiences and then assign meaning to them. What meaning we assign, mentally, emotionally, and spiritually, is often as important to genetic activation as the facts themselves. We are discovering that our genes dance with our awareness. Thoughts and feelings turn sets of genes on and off in complex relationships. Science is discovering that while we may have a fixed set of genes in our chromosomes, which of those genes is active has a great deal to do with our subjective experiences, and how we process them.

Our emotions and behavior shape our brains as they stimulate the formation of neural pathways that either reinforce old patterns or initiate new ones. Like widening a road as traffic increases, when we think an increased flow of thoughts on a topic, or practice an increased quantity of an action, the number of neurons our bodies require to route the information increases. In just the way our muscles bulk up with increased exercise, the size of our neural bundles increases when those pathways are increasingly used. So the thoughts we think, the *quality of our consciousness,* increase the flow of information along certain neural pathways. According to Ernest Rossi, "we could say that *meaning* is continually modulated by the complex, dynamic field of messenger molecules that continually replay, reframe, and resynthesize neuronal networks in ever-changing patterns."[23] In the succinct words of another medical pioneer, "Beliefs become biology"—in our hormonal, neural, genetic, and electromagnetic systems, plus all the complex interactions between them.[24]

The Inner and Outer Environment

Memory, learning, stress, and healing are all affected by classes of genes that are turned on or off in temporal cycles that range from one second to many hours. The *environment* that activates genes includes both *the inner environment*—the emotional, biochemical, mental, energetic, and spiritual landscape of the individual—*and the outer environment.* The outer environment includes the social network and ecological systems in which the individual lives. Food, toxins, social rituals, predators, and sexual cues are examples of outer environmental influences that affect gene expression. Researchers estimate that "approximately 90% of all genes are engaged...in cooperation with signals from the environment."[25]

Our genes are being affected every day by the environment of our thoughts and feelings, as surely as they are being affected by the environment of our families, homes, parks, markets, churches, and offices. Your system may be flooded with adrenaline because a mugger is running toward you with a knife. It may also be flooded with adrenaline because of a stressful change at work. And it may be flooded with adrenaline in the absence of any concrete stimulus other than the thoughts you're having about the week ahead—a week that hasn't happened yet, and may never happen. Let's take a look at the evolutionary purpose of these physiological events, and whether they're *adaptive* (helpful to your body) or *maladaptive* (harmful to your body).

Scenario One: Ten thousand years ago, when a mugger (or a member of a hostile tribe) ran at you with a sharp blade, you quickly took action. Your blood flowed away from your digestive tract toward your muscles. Your brain became hyperactive and your reproductive drive shut down. Thousands of biochemical changes took place in all the cells of your body within a couple of seconds, enabling you to run away from the attacker, or defend yourself.

You were already one of a select group of humans who had survived the dangers of a hostile world long enough to breed. Over tens of thousands of years, those with quick responses had survived long enough to produce offspring, and those with slow responses died before they could breed. So by the time a hostile tribesman ran at you with a blade, those thousands of years of evolutionary weeding had already produced a human admirably suited to fight or flee. The changes that occurred in your body in response to a threat were *adaptive;* they were *useful* adaptations for survival.

Scenario Two: Fast-forward ten thousand years. You're in a meeting that includes all the employees of your company. The firm has just been bought by a competitor. You know that the new owner is going to consolidate the work force. They aren't going to need everybody.

The manager of your division announces that after the meeting, when you return to your desk, you'll find either a pink slip, indicating that you're terminated, or nothing at all, meaning that you've survived the purge. Those who find pink slips are instructed to clear out their desks immediately and report to personnel for a severance check.

Suddenly, there are two tribes in the room: those that will survive, and those that will not. Worse, nobody but the manager knows who's in what tribe. The stress level in the room is unbearable. Who is your enemy? Who is your ally? You have no idea. You walk back to your desk, dreading what you will see, and dreading the lineup of fired and retained employees you will witness in the next hour.

Your desk has no pink slip. Neither does that of Harry, who works across from you. Suddenly, you realize that the downsizing means you'll be thrown cheek to jowl with Harry who, though another survivor, is an incompetent liar. You look across to Helen's desk, and you see a pink slip. Helen is the most talented person in the building, someone on whom you've secretly depended for your success. Because her verbal skills are poor, the management failed to realize that she's indispensable. You realize your job has just become a lot worse, yet you will cling to it like a *Titanic* survivor gripping the last life jacket.

You've been working sixty-hour weeks for the last six months, suspecting that this Damocles' sword will eventually fall. Your body has been ready for fight or flight for all that time, not knowing what your fate will be. The employment market is tight; you know that many of the employees fired today will have to take Draconian pay cuts in menial new jobs.

Even before the current crisis, your body was in fight-or-flight mode as you climbed the corporate ladder. Today, it's on high alert. Your mouth is dry. You're so tense you could put your fist through the wall. You can't wait to get out of the office and have a few beers to unwind. Yet you know that tomorrow you'll be back at your desk— and now you'll have a huge new portion of the work that management has reassigned from the fired employees.

Scenario Three: It's Sunday evening. You've had a good weekend. You unwound by griping to your spouse on Friday night, then by playing baseball with your kids in the park on Saturday morning. You went to a movie, a comedy, with another couple on Saturday night and enjoyed a lot of laughs. You had sex with your partner after you got home. Church was good on Sunday morning, and you saw all your old friends there and had a chance to socialize.

You're sitting on the porch with a beer, and you suddenly realize you're going to have to go back into that hellhole of a job in just a few hours. Your stomach knots. Your jaw clenches. You crush the beer can. You start thinking of the injustices of the previous week, wondering how you escaped the axe. Didn't management see the glaring errors in your performance? You grind your teeth as you think of the injustice of them firing Helen, after she's kept the whole division going, in her quiet way, for years. What ingratitude! What blindness! What ineptitude! How did those morons get to be managers in the first place?

Can you escape? No chance, the money's good, the pension plan's good, and no other job has comparable medical benefits—vision and dental too, plus it covers the kids, for heaven's sake! Do you want to be pounding the pavement looking for a job like Helen will be doing tomorrow? God forbid!

Your Body Reads Your Mind

Scenario Two and Three are—in terms of what you're doing to your body—*maladaptive* responses. "Maladaptive" means that they aren't helping you; they're responses to stress that are hurtful to you. All the stress hormones are flowing, just as they were in Scenario One, but they're doing your body no practical good. No promotion will come as a result of you overloading your system with cortisol, one of the primary stress hormones. You won't feel better after being high on adrenaline and norepinephrine, two others.

What *will* happen, though, is that the circulation of these stress hormones through your system on a regular basis will compromise your immune system, weaken your organs, and age you prematurely. You're activating genes that worked perfectly well for the caveman in Scenario One, but are counterproductive to the modern person in Scenarios Two and Three. Herbert Benson, MD, president of Harvard Medical School's Mind-Body Medical Institute, says, "The stressful thoughts that lead to the secretion of stress-related norepinephrine impede our evolutionary-derived natural healing capacities. These thoughts are often only in our minds, not a reality."[26] According to another report, "Bruce McEwen, PhD, director of the neuroendocrinology lab at Rockefeller University in New York, says [such stress] wears down the brain, leading to cell atrophy and memory loss. It also raises blood pressure and blood sugar, hardening arteries and leading to heart disease."[27]

So while the fight-or-flight response may have been adaptive ten thousand years ago, with Mother Nature cheering you on, today it's often maladaptive, and Mother Nature is saying, "Stop! You're ruining your body!" The trouble is that major evolutionary changes take a long time—sometimes thousands of years—and modern humans are having difficulty making adaptations in the short space of a single lifetime. We try to change our stress-addicted patterns in various ways. But the counteracting experiences we attempt—attending a four-evening stress clinic at the local hospital, a self-improvement workshop at a personal growth center, a weekend retreat at a church camp, or sitting in a Zen monastery for a few days—are like a tissue in a hurricane when compared to the evolutionary forces hardwired into our physiology.

Biochemically speaking, your body *cannot tell the difference* between the injection of chemicals that is triggered by an *objective* threat—the tribesman running at you with a spear—and a *subjective* threat—your resentment toward management. The biochemical and genetic effects, as far as your body is concerned, are the same. Your body can't tell that one experience is a physical reality, and the other is a replay of an abstract mental idea. *Both* are creating a chemical environment around your cells that is full of signals to your genes, several classes of which activate the proteins associated with stress. A researcher observes: "Our body doesn't make a moral judgment about our feelings; it just responds accordingly."[28]

The understanding that much of our genetic activity is affected by factors outside the cell is a radical reversal of the dogma of genetic determinism, which held for half a century that who we are and what we do is governed by our genes. Research is illuminating a new biology in which *consciousness* plays a primary role.

Recent studies performed by Ronald Glaser, of the Ohio State University College of Medicine, and psychologist Janice Kiecolt-Glaser investigated the effect that stress associated with marital strife has on the healing of wounds, a significant marker of genetic activation. The researchers created small suction blisters on the skin of married test subjects, after which each couple was instructed to have a neutral discussion for half an hour. For the next three weeks, the researchers then monitored the production of three of the proteins that our bodies produce in association with wound healing.

They then instructed the same couples to discuss a topic on which they disagreed. Research staff was present during both the neutral discussion and the disagreement.

The researchers found that the expression of these healing-linked proteins was depressed in those couples who had a fight. Even those couples who had a simple discussion of a disagreement, rather than a full-fledged verbal battle, showed slower healing of their wounds. But in couples who had severe disagreements, laced with put-downs, sarcasm, and criticism, wound healing was slowed by some 40%. They also produced smaller quantities of the three proteins. "'These are minor wounds and brief, restrained encounters. Real-life marital conflict probably has a worse impact,' Kiecolt-Glaser adds. 'Such stress before surgery matters greatly,' she says, and the effect could apply to healing from any injury. In earlier studies done by Kiecolt-Glaser, hostile couples were most likely to show signs of poorer immune function after their discussions in the lab. Over the next few months, they also developed more respiratory infections than supportive spouses,"[29] and similar studies show worse blood pressure readings,[30] and increased stress hormone production[31] as, "throughout the body's entire somatic network, emotions are triggering hormonal and genetic responses."[32] The genetic effects from such environmental experiences can, in some cases, make the difference between life and death. Pharmacologist Constance Grauds, RPh, in her book *The Energy Prescription,* says, "An undisciplined mind leaks vital energy in a continuous stream of thoughts, worries, and skewed perceptions, many of which trigger disturbing emotions and degenerative chemical processes in the body."[33]

Over two thousand years ago, the Buddha declared: "We are formed and molded by our thoughts. Those whose minds are shaped by selfless thoughts give joy when they speak or act." Today's research is reinforcing what wise students of the human condition have known for millennia. Neuroscientist Candace Pert, PhD, tells us that "the molecules of our emotions share intimate connections with, and are indeed inseparable from, our physiology.... Consciously, or more frequently, unconsciously, we choose how we feel at every single moment." Practices for well-being once prescribed only by sages and priests are now being advocated by geneticists and neurobiologists.

In the tales of the Arabian Nights, when Aladdin rubbed the magic lamp, the genie appeared and granted him three wishes. In the story, once he makes his wishes, the magic vanishes. He had to think long and hard on what to choose for his three wishes.

In the real world, given the lamp of our understanding and the genie in our genes, we have an unlimited supply of wishes. Whatever wishes we put into the lamp manifest genetically. If we fill our lamps with healing words, our genes rush to fulfill our wishes—within seconds. If, like the couples in the wound study, we fill our lamps with poison, we damage the ability of our inbred genetic servants to heal us. Whereas the mechanisms driving these changes have been mysterious to the world of allopathic medicine (the conventional system of treating symptoms with concrete agents, like drugs, to produce an opposing effect), the healthy outcomes of energy therapies are beyond dispute. In the coming pages, we will look, in detail, at the precise genetic and electromagnetic mechanisms that make such healing magic not only possible, but also scientifically predictable.

Steps in Genetic Expression

The process by which a gene produces a result in the body is well mapped. Signals pass through the membrane of each cell and travel to the cell's nucleus. There, they enter the chromosome and activate a particular strand of DNA.

Around each strand of DNA is a protein "sleeve." This sleeve serves as a barrier between the information contained in the DNA strand and the rest of the intracellular environment. In order for the blueprint in the DNA to be "read," the sleeve must be unwrapped. Unless it is unwrapped, the DNA strand cannot be "read," nor can the information it contains be acted upon. Until the information is unwrapped, the blueprint in the DNA lies dormant. That blueprint is required by the cell to construct other proteins that regulate virtually every aspect of life.

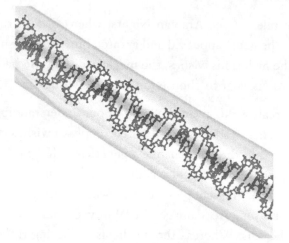

DNA blueprint in protein sheath

When a signal arrives, the protein sleeve around the DNA unwraps and, with the assistance of RNA, the DNA molecule then replicates an intermediate template molecule. The blueprint that has up to this point been concealed within the sleeve can now be acted upon. This is what scientists mean when they say that a gene *expresses*. The genetic information contained in the chromosome has gone from being a dormant blueprint into *active expression*, where it *creates other actions* within the cell by constructing, assembling, or altering products. The DNA blueprint that has up to this point been inert, concealed within the sleeve, is now revealed, providing the basis for cellular construction. Just as an architect's blueprint contains the information to build a building, the chromosomes contain the blueprints to construct aggregations of molecules. Until the architect's blueprint has been removed from its sheath, unrolled, laid flat on the builder's table, and used to guide construction, it is simply dormant potential. In the same way, the blueprints in our genes are dormant potential until the genes express and are used to guide the construction of the proteins that carry out the constructive tasks of life.

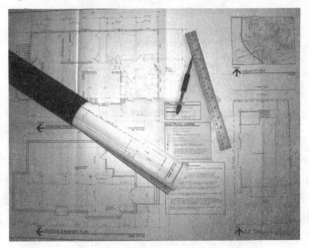

Architectural blueprint and cardboard tube

Proteins are the building blocks used by our bodies for every function they perform. Proteins control the responses of our immune systems, form the scaffolding that supports the structure of each cell, provide the enzymes that catalyze chemical reactions, and convey information between cells, among many other functions. If DNA is the blueprint, then RNA comprises the working drawings required for construction and proteins are the materials used in construction. Molecules are assembled into coherent protein structures by the instructions in our DNA. That structure determines not only our *anatomy*—the physical form of our bodies; it also drives our *physiology*—the complex dance of cellular interactions that differentiate

45

a live human being from a dead one. A corpse has anatomy, but no physiology. Proteins are used in every step of our physiology; the word "protein" itself is derived from the Greek word *protas,* meaning "of primary importance."

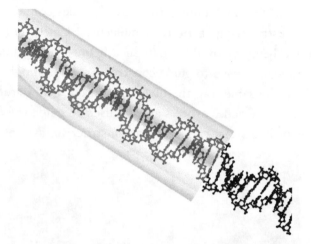

Protein sheath opens to permit gene expression

Even the simple DNA > RNA > Protein formula has recently been upset by the discovery that there are many more varieties of RNA than previously believed, and that some play a powerful role in regulating genes, rather than being simple carrier molecules. One, called XIST, has the ability to suppress an entire chromosome, the second X chromosome in females. Some single microRNAs regulate the production of hundreds of proteins, and there may be over 37,000 microRNAs, more than the number of genes.[34] So the simple molecular picture described by Sir Francis Crick turns out to be vastly more complex than initially believed.

This whole chain of events starts with a *signal.* The signal is delivered through the cell membrane to the protein sleeve, which then unwraps in order to let the information in the gene move from potential (like an unbuilt building) to expression (like a finished skyscraper). And while scientists have mapped each part of the process of gene expression and protein assembly, comparatively little attention has been paid to the signals, the source of initiation for the whole process. Ignorance of the signal required to take the blueprint out of the tube is what has allowed several generations of biologists to assume that all you needed to start construction was the blueprint, which gave rise to the doctrine of genetic determinism.

Signals from Outside the Cell

Stem cells are undifferentiated cells, "blanks" that the body can make into muscle, bone, skin, or any other type of cell. Like a piece of putty, they can be formed into whatever kind of cell the body needs. When you cut your hand and your body needs to repair the break in the skin, the trauma sends a signal to the genes associated with wound healing. These genes express, stimulating stem cells to turn themselves into healthy, fully functional skin cells. The signal results in the putty being formed into a useful shape. Such processes are occurring all over our bodies, all the time: "Healing via gene expression is documented in stem cells in the brain (including the cerebral cortex, hippocampus, and hypothalamus, muscle, skin, intestinal epithelium, bone marrow, liver, and heart."[35]

When there is interference with this signal, which in the wound healing studies comes from the emotional states of angry subjects, the stem cells don't get the message clearly. Not enough putty is turned into useful shapes, or the process of molding the putty takes a long time, because the body's energy is instead being sucked away to build the threat-response biochemicals triggered by the angry emotion. Wound healing is compromised.

Notice that these *signals do not come from the DNA;* they come from *outside* the cell. The signals tell the proteins surrounding the DNA strands to unwrap and allow healing to begin. In the prestigious journal *Science,* researcher Elizabeth Pennisi writes, "Gene expression is not determined solely by the DNA code itself but by an assortment of proteins and, sometimes, RNAs that tell the genes when and where to turn on or off. Such *epigenetic* phenomena orchestrate the many changes through which a single fertilized egg cell turns into a complex organism. And throughout life, they enable cells to respond to environmental signals conveyed by hormones, growth factors, and other regulatory molecules without having to alter the DNA itself."[36]

The word that Dr. Pennisi uses here, *epigenetics,* is new to our lexicon. The spellchecker I am using in a 2004 version of Microsoft Word does not recognize it. The issue of *Science* from which her quote is taken was a special issue in 2001 devoted to the new science of epigenetics. Epigenetics, referred to by *Science* as "the study of heritable changes in gene function that occur without a change in the DNA sequence,"[37] examines the sources that *control gene expression from outside the DNA*. It's a study of the signals that turn genes on and off. Some of those signals are chemical, others are electromagnetic. Some come from the environment inside the body, whereas others are the body's response to signals from the environment that surrounds the body.

Although studying the static structure of the hard drive gives us lots of useful information, the signals that activate different sectors of the hard drive turn that information into a running program. My hard drive contains Microsoft Word, even when it's turned off. But I have to boot up the computer (energy) and then click on the Word icon (a signal) before it becomes active. Epigenetics looks at the sources that activate gene expression or suppression, and at the energy flows that modulate the process. It traces the signals that tell the genes what to do and when to do it, and looks for the forces from outside the cell that orchestrate the whole. Epigenetics studies the environment, such as the signals that initiate stem cell differentiation and wound healing.

The activation of genes is intimately connected with healing and immune system function. In the studies of wound healing and marital conflict outlined previously, you can see a clear link between the *consciousness* of the participants in the study and the *creation of proteins* (coded by gene activation) required to promote wound healing and stem cell conversion in their bodies. The healthy mental states of functional couples signaled their bodies to turn on the expression of the genes involved in immune system health and physical wound healing. Such epigenetic signals suggest a whole new avenue for catalyzing wellness in our bodies.

Magic Precedes Science

When a revolutionary new technique or therapy is described, it can take a while for science to catch up. Funding must be obtained to conduct studies. Studies must be designed and approved to test the new technique. Then data are collected, and papers are written. Those papers are reviewed by committees of the researchers' peers, and published. The ideas are then critiqued by others, refined, and replicated. This process takes years, and often decades. Much of the medical progress in the last fifty years has resulted from studies that built upon studies, from step-by-step incremental experimentation, with each step extending the reach of our knowledge a little bit further.

This evolutionary progress over the lifetimes of the last few generations has encouraged us to think that this is the way that science progresses. Yes, it is a way—but it is *not the only way*. There are scores of important medical procedures that were discovered years, or decades, or even centuries, before the experimental confirmation arrived to demonstrate the principles behind the treatment. Larry Dossey, in his book *Healing Beyond the Body,* urges us, "Consider many therapies that are now commonplace, such as the use of aspirin, quinine, colchicine, and penicillin. For a long time we knew that they worked before we knew how.... This should alarm no one who has even a meager understanding of how medicine has progressed through the ages."[38] In *The Cosmic Clocks,* Michael Gaugelin observes, "The scientist knows that in the history of ideas magic always precedes science, that the intuition of phenomena anticipates their objective knowledge."[39]

The incremental approach to experimentation, with each study advancing the frontier of knowledge a little further, has served medicine well in areas such as surgery. But the incremental approach has broken down when it comes to many of the pressing afflictions rampant in our society, such as depression, fibromyalgia, chronic fatigue syndrome, posttraumatic stress disorder, and autoimmune diseases. Cancer rates, when adjusted for age, have barely budged in fifty years.[40] Surgical procedures to excise cancer tumors have improved, radiation has been refined, and drug cocktails have been created, but these are variations on old themes. Much of our medical system is set up to perform heroic measures on people who are very near death, slightly delaying the inevitable at enormous cost. Ralph Snyderman, eminent physician and researcher at Duke University, sums it up with these words: "Most of our nation's investment in health is wasted on an irrational, uncoordinated, and inefficient system that spends more than two-thirds of each dollar treating largely irreversible chronic diseases."[41]

Total health spending in the United States is over two trillion dollars a year; the amount spent on *all* alternative therapies is estimated at just *two-tenths of 1%* of that figure.[42] For every naturopath or licensed acupuncturist in the United States, there are seventy allopathic physicians,[43] even though the treatments of the former can work where mainstream medicine fails,[44] are believed effective by over 74% of the population,[45] and can certainly be successful in supplementing conventional therapies.[46] They also often work better than mainstream medicine for many of the predominant diseases of postindustrial cultures, such as autoimmune conditions and cancer.[47] Epigenetics gives us tools to understand why our health can be affected by so many different healing modalities, and how we can learn to create an environment that supports our own healing, whichever modality we choose.

Epigenetic Medicine

We may be comfortable with incremental exploration, yet many changes are sudden rather than incremental. The expansion of a balloon as air is injected is smooth and incremental. A balloon popping is sudden and discontinuous. Water heated in a kettle shows little change. Then, suddenly and discontinuously, it bursts into a boil. This is the kind of breakthrough of which we find ourselves on the verge. Like the first bubbles appearing in the bottom of a pan, the possibilities of epigenetic medicine, combining integrative medicine with the breakthroughs of the new psychology, are popping through the most fundamental assumptions of our current model.

We are starting, as a society, to notice the provocative research showing the effects our thoughts and emotions have on our genes. "Science goes where you imagine it,"[48] says one researcher, and leading-edge therapies are now imagining science going in the direction of some of the powerful, safe, and effective new therapies that are emerging. Hundreds of thousands of people are dying each year, and millions more are suffering, from conditions that might be alleviated by epigenetic medicine. This book is an attempt to present this new science in a user-friendly manner that connects with everyday experience, and to explore the potential it holds for creating massive health and social changes in our civilization in a very short time.

2

You: The Ultimate Epigenetic Engineer

We are in a school for gods, where—in slow motion—we learn the consequences of thought.

—Brugh Joy, MD

"Josephine Tesauro never thought she would live so long. At 92, she is straight backed, firm jawed, and vibrantly healthy, living alone in an immaculate brick ranch house high on a hill near McKeesport, a Pittsburgh suburb. She works part time in a hospital gift shop and drives her 1995 white Oldsmobile Cutlass Ciera to meetings of her four bridge groups, to church, and to the grocery store. She has outlived her husband, who died nine years ago, when he was eighty-four. She has outlived her friends, and she has outlived three of her six brothers.

"Mrs. Tesauro does, however, have a living sister, an identical twin. But she and her twin are not so identical anymore. Her sister is incontinent, she has had a hip replacement, and she has a degenerative

53

disorder that destroyed most of her vision. She also has dementia. 'She just does not comprehend,' Mrs. Tesauro says.

"Even researchers who study aging are fascinated by such stories. How could it be that two people with the same genes, growing up in the same family, living all their lives in the same place, could age so differently?

"The scientific view of what determines a life span or how a person ages has swung back and forth. First, a couple of decades ago, the emphasis was on environment, eating right, exercising, getting good medical care. Then the view switched to genes, the idea that you either inherit the right combination of genes that will let you eat fatty steaks and smoke cigars and live to be one hundred or you do not. And the notion has stuck, so that these days, many people point to an ancestor or two who lived a long life and assume they have a genetic gift for longevity.

Josephine Tesauro and her sister

"But recent studies find that genes may not be so important in determining how long someone will live and whether a person will get some diseases—except, perhaps, in some exceptionally long-lived families. That means it is generally impossible to predict how long a person will live based on how long the person's relatives lived.

"Life spans, says James W. Vaupel, who directs the Laboratory of Survival and Longevity at the Max Planck Institute for Demographic

Research in Rostock, Germany, are nothing like a trait like height, which is strongly inherited....'That's what the evidence shows. Even twins, identical twins, die at different times.' On average, he said, more than ten years apart."

This report and photos, drawn from the *New York Times* in late 2006, illustrates the dramatic difference that epigenetic factors make in health and aging. Dr. Michael Rabinoff, a psychiatrist at Kaiser Permanente hospital, says, "It is known that identical twins, despite sharing the same genes, may not manifest the same psychiatric or other illness in the same way or not at all, despite the condition being thought to be highly genetic."[1] Same genes, different outcomes. Gary Marcus, PhD, professor of psychology at New York University, says it's more accurate to think of genes as "providers of opportunity" or "sources of options" than as "purveyors of commands."[2]

Think about your own life. What makes the difference between you living like Josephine Tesauro—or like her sister? Clearly, the big health differences between them can't be the result of genes, because they both started life with the same genes. Yet the intervening years have produced very different results in old age. The epigenetic signals that make one person vibrant and the other decrepit come from outside the gene, outside the cell, and sometimes outside the body.

Cataloging the entire list of genes in the human genome is an impressive accomplishment. It's like piecing together a jigsaw puzzle of a photograph of all the members of a giant orchestra, sitting on stage, holding their instruments, ready to play. It's a static diagram of where everyone sits and what instrument they're clutching. But it tells you nothing about the choices the conductor makes for the program, about the rhythm or tone of the music, about the experience of sitting in the concert hall while a piece is being played. It tells you nothing about the swirling maelstrom of notes, what they each sound like, and how they mingle to form music. It tells you nothing about their effect on the audience. In the words of the late physicist Richard Carlson, "all the genome provides is the parts list. ...How things interact is what's more important in biology than just the things that are there. The genome tells us very little, if anything at all, about how things interact."[3] For biologists, understanding the mechanics of enormously complex self-organizing systems like the human body is a challenge of much greater magnitude than mapping the genome itself. And tracing the epigenetic influences that govern the music of the body's function is a challenge of even greater magnitude, though we see evidence of such epigenetic control every day.

To get the right answer, you have to ask the right question. Only since the concept of epigenetic control has emerged in the last decade have scientists begun to design experiments that ask these questions. As they are published, they are starting to illuminate the precise pathways by which our body takes a signal from the external environment and turns it into a set of chemical or electromagnetic instructions for our genes. One such study has gained wide attention, because it shows some of the steps required for one such interaction.

DNA Is Not Destiny

One of the first animal studies that demonstrated that an epigenetic signal can affect gene expression was done with mice. While mice and humans are very different in size, they are very similar genetically, so mice are often used as subjects in laboratory experiments. In the early 1990s, researchers discovered that a gene that had long been known to affect the fur color of mice, called the agouti gene, was related to a human gene that is expressed in cases of obesity and Type II diabetes. As well as having yellow coats, agouti mice eat ravenously, have an increased incidence of cancer and diabetes,[4] and tend to die early. When they produce offspring, the baby mice are just as prone to these conditions as their progenitors.

Randy Jirtle, PhD, a professor of radiation oncology at Duke University and winner of the inaugural Epigenetic Medicine award from the National Institute for Integrative Healthcare, discovered that he could make agouti mice produce normal, slender, healthy young. He also discovered that he could accomplish this by changing the expression of their genes—but *without making any changes to the mouse's DNA.* This neat trick was accomplished, just before conception, by feeding agouti mothers a diet rich in a chemical known as "methyl groups." These molecule clusters are able to inhibit the expression of genes, and sure enough, the methyl groups eventually worked their way through the mothers' metabolisms to attach to the agouti genes of the developing embryos.

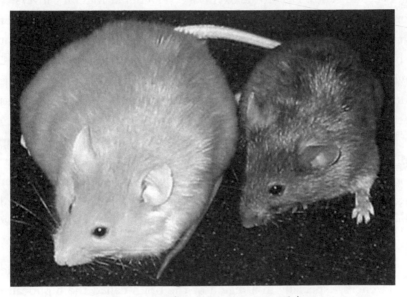

Agouti mice (gene suppression on right)

In an interview with *Discover* magazine, Jirtle said, "It was a little eerie and a little scary to see how something as subtle as a nutritional change in the pregnant mother rat could have such a dramatic impact on the gene expression of the baby. The results showed how important epigenetic changes could be."[5] The article was entitled "DNA Is Not Destiny: The new science of epigenetics rewrites the rules of disease, heredity, and identity." Such reports are starting to crop up in news reports with increasing frequency, as the importance of epigenetic influences becomes clearer. "The tip of the iceberg is genomics... The bottom of the iceberg is epigenetics," says Jirtle—and the larger scientific community is beginning to agree with him. In fact, in 2003, a Human Epigenome project was launched by a group of European scientists, and a U.S. project has now begun.[6]

Nurturing Epigenetic Change

The pathway by which epigenetic signals affect the expression of genes has many steps. Diet is the one demonstrated by the Jirtle study. A second clue comes from a series of experiments that show that *being nurtured* generates chemical changes in the brain that trigger certain genes. Dr. Moshe Szyf is a researcher at McGill University in Montreal, Canada, who studies the interactions between mother rats and their offspring. Members of his research team noticed that some rat mothers spent a lot of time licking and grooming their pups, while other mothers did not. The pups that had been groomed as infants showed marked behavioral changes as adults. They were "less fearful and better adjusted than the offspring of neglectful mothers."[7] They then acted in similar nurturing ways toward their own offspring, producing the same epigenetic behavioral results in the next generation. This by itself is an important finding (confirmed by many other experiments) because it shows that epigenetic changes, once started in one generation, can be passed to the following generations *without changes in the genes themselves.*

When researchers examined the brains of these rats, they found differences, especially in a region of the brain called the hippocampus, which is involved in our response to stress. A gene that dampens our response to stress had a greater degree of expression in the well-adjusted rats.

The brains of these rats also showed higher levels of a chemical (acetyl groups) that facilitates gene expression by binding to the protein sheath around the gene, making it easier for the gene to express. Additionally, they had higher levels of an enzyme that adds acetyl groups to the protein sheath.

The anxious, fearful rats had different brain chemistry. The same gene-suppressing substance as in the Jirtle mouse study (methyl groups) was more prevalent in their hippocampi. It bonded to the DNA and inhibited the expression of the gene involved in dampening stress.

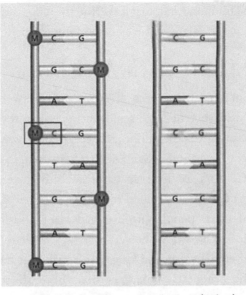

DNA strand with and without methyl group (in box) attached

To test their hypothesis that these two substances were causing epigenetic behavioral changes in the rats, Dr. Szyf and his team injected the brain cavities of fearful rats with a substance that raised the number of acetyls in the hippocampus. Sure enough, the behavior of the rats changed, and they became less fearful and better adjusted. The researchers also took the offspring of loving mothers and injected their brains with methyl groups. This produced the opposite effect; these rats became more fearful and anxious, with a heightened response to stress.

An article in *Scientific American Mind* notes depressed and anti-social behavior in mice, accompanied by methyl groups sticking to genes. It also extends this research to human beings; the brains of schizophrenic patients also show changes in methylation of genes, or acetylization of their protein sheaths.[8]

Mapping the protein pathways by which behaviors such as nurturing facilitate or suppress gene expression helps us understand the implications of our behavior and beliefs, and their role in our health and longevity. The poet William Butler Yeats said, "We taste and feel and see the truth. We do not reason ourselves into it." We intuitively feel how important childhood nurturing is. But the huge extent to which it affects adult health might come as a shocking surprise to you.

Childhood Stress Results in Adult Disease

Experiments have shown a striking link between childhood stress and later disease. One large-scale, authoritative research project known as ACE, or Adverse Childhood Experiences, was done by the Kaiser Permanente Hospital in San Diego, California, in collaboration with the U.S. Centers for Disease Control and Prevention (CDC). The researchers conducted detailed social, psychological, and medical examinations of 17,421 people enrolled in Kaiser's health plans over a five-year period. The study showed a strong inverse link between emotional well-being, health, and longevity on the one hand, and early life stress on the other. It emphasizes that there are some negative experiences that we don't just "get over," and that *time does not heal.*

The physicians at Kaiser scored patients on various measures of family functionality. Stressors included an alcoholic parent, divorced or separated parents, a parent who was depressed or who had a mental illness, and domestic violence. Over half the participants had experienced one or more of the defining childhood stressors, and where one stressor was present, there was an 80% chance that others were too, leading to a web of family dysfunctionality. A low score meant few stressors; a high score indicated several. The average age of study participants was fifty-seven, so in most cases it had been fifty years since the events occurred.

The study found that a person raised in such a family had *five times* the chance of being depressed than one raised in a functional family. Such a person was *three times* as likely to smoke. Participants who scored high on the family dysfunctionality scale were at least *thirty times more likely to attempt suicide* than those who scored low. A man with a high score was 4,600% more likely to use illegal intravenous drugs. Ailments more common in those who grew up in dysfunctional families included obesity, heart disease, lung disease, diabetes, bone fractures, hypertension, and hepatitis. The genetic links between nurturing and gene expression in children have been traced in other studies. One found that children with a gene producing an enzyme that metabolizes neurotransmitters such as serotonin and dopamine were much more likely to become violent in their teens, "but only if they were mistreated as children."[9] *Loving parenting is epigenetic therapy.* Now that we understand this, our society should be pouring every possible resource into supporting parents and nurturing children, instead of ignoring abuse till the horrible results appear in later years.

The ACE study's authors compared our society's current medical orientation to a fire crew working diligently to disperse the smoke over a burning building, while ignoring the fire below.[10] A study of rat pups might seem like an ivory tower exercise in epigenetics. It's not: The quality of childhood nurturing is creating health or disease in the real world every day.

It's the Gene Show, and You're the Director

There are certainly lifestyle factors that make a big difference in our health and longevity. Having a Body Mass Index of twenty-five or less, eating a diet rich in fruits and vegetables, daily aerobic exercise, avoiding smoking and excess alcohol—all these contribute to living to a ripe old age. These are physical behaviors we can see. Yet metaphysical things we can't see, like consciousness and intention—expressed in our beliefs, feelings, prayers, and attitudes—also play an important role in the epigenetic control of genes, by improving our emotional state and reducing our stress. The old view that our genes contain indelible instructions governing the functioning of our bodies is, in the scornful words of my teenage offspring, "*So* twentieth century."

It's taken hard science a long time to figure out that something as softly immaterial as a belief can take on a physical existence as positive or negative changes in our cells. But it turns out that these factors can affect health and longevity dramatically. Josephine Tesauro and her sister were born with an identical collection of instruments in their genes. The music they played in their first years may have been indistinguishable, but the finale of each of their life concerts is quite different.

As we hold the scale of health in our hands, with good health on one side and decrepitude on the other, we can tilt the outcome. If we can add a brick to the side of good health, we can tilt it in our favor. Let's take a look at some of the bricks we can drop on our scale. Each of these is based on sound scientific research and holds lessons we can apply from this day forward.

Beliefs and Biochemistry

A landmark study linking belief to health was reported recently by Gail Ironson, MD, PhD, a leading mind-body medicine researcher, and professor of psychology and psychiatry at the University of Miami. Dr. Ironson runs the Positive Survivors Research Center at the university, and has been awarded several grants from the National Institutes of Health. It is one of the first studies to link particular beliefs with specific changes in the immune system.[11]

Dr. Ironson measured several indicators of health in HIV patients over a four-year period. One measure was their viral load—the quantity of the HIV virus in a sample of blood. She also counted the concentration of a type of white blood cell responsible for killing invading organisms. The concentration of these "helper Tcells" (also known as CD4 cells) in the blood is one measure of the progression of AIDS. If the concentration of helper T cells drops, our bodies are less able to fend off other diseases like pneumonia. That's why the *I* and *D* in AIDS stand for Immune Deficiency; as AIDS patients lose their T cells and their immunity to disease drops, they are more susceptible to the kinds of invading organisms—opportunistic infections—that healthy immune systems easily fend off.

Studies like those conducted by Dr. Ironson are especially meaningful to physicians and biologists because they identify key *biological* markers of illness, as opposed to *subjective* measures such as the patient's level of depression, the number of doctor visits, and the dosage of medication required.

In her studies, Dr. Ironson found that there were two particularly interesting predictors of how fast HIV progressed in the bodies of her research participants. The first was their view of the nature of God. Some believed in a punishing God, while others believed in a benevolent God. She observes that, "People who view God as a judgmental God have a CD4 (helper T) cell decline more than twice the rate of those who don't see God as judgmental, and their viral load increases more than three times faster. For example, a precise statement affirmed by these patients is 'God will judge me harshly one day.' This one item is related to an increased likelihood that the patient will develop an opportunistic infection or die. These beliefs predict disease progression even more strongly than depression."

Dr. Ironson was surprised to find that many people reported a spiritual transformation subsequent to their diagnosis. This transformation was characterized by a sense of self that was profoundly changed, and resulted in different behaviors. Many kicked their habits of street drugs like cocaine and heroin, or legal ones like alcohol. Some went through such a transformation only after hitting rock bottom. Carlos, one of them, describes his experience of getting to the end of his rope:

> I was planning to finish my BA, moving to New York. I found out that my ex partner had been doing drugs and cheating with other relationships. I was very scared, and I didn't deal with it. For six months I didn't get tested. When I did find out, I had no friends in New York so I had to deal with it on my own. I turned to cocaine, my life changed dramatically; I was sort of spiraling downhill, near the lowest point in my life. It changed everything, it changed my behavior, it changed my ambition, I didn't have the same drive that I had going in after school to pursue my career. Things were so bad that any belief that I had in a higher being or in a spiritual presence was completely extinguished. I was on a course downhill. I just didn't care.[12]

After being diagnosed as HIV positive, Carlos's infection progressed rapidly into full-blown AIDS. He suffered from serious opportunistic infections, and had very low levels of T cells and high levels of viral load, despite taking HIV medication.

A common gateway to spiritual transformation was having a spiritual experience. After helping a drunk white man in distress, John, a gay African-American man with a college education, described the following experience:

> I felt like I was floating over my body, and I'll never forget this, as I was floating over my body, I looked down, it was like this shriveled up prune, nothing but a prune, like an old dried skin. And my soul, my spirit was over my body. Everything was so separated. I was just feeling like I was in different dimensions, I felt it in my body like a gush of wind blows. I remember saying to god, "God! I can't die now, because I haven't fulfilled my purpose," and, just as I said that, the spirit and the body, became one, it all collided, and I could feel this gush of wind and I was a whole person again.
>
> That was really a groundbreaking experience. Before becoming HIV-positive my faith was so fear based. I always wanted to feel I belonged somewhere, that I fit in, or that I was loved. What helped me to overcome the fear of God and the fear of change was that I realized that no one had a monopoly on God. I was able to begin to replace a lot of destructive behavior with a sort of spiritual desire. I think also what changed, my desire to get close to God, to love myself, and to really embrace unconditional love.[13]

John's story points to the second major factor Dr. Ironson noted: A participant's personal relationship with God. Her study found that patients who did not believe that God loved them lost helper T cells "three times faster than those who believed God did love them."[14] Another correlation she found was that those who felt a sense of peace also had lower levels of the body-damaging stress hormone cortisol.[15]

Dr. Ironson, in an article published in the *Journal of General Internal Medicine,* showed a fairly high number of people increase their spirituality in the year after they are first diagnosed with HIV/AIDS; 45% showed an increase in spirituality, 42% stayed the same, and 13% had a decrease in spirituality. The study showed an enormously strong association between spirituality and the progression of HIV.[16]

"I was surprised that so many people had an increase in spirituality, because being diagnosed with HIV/AIDS can be a devastating event. I could hardly believe the figures, until I saw that another article in the same issue of the journal found an increase in spirituality of 41% of newly diagnosed patients. Perhaps a life-threatening illness, not just HIV, but cancer or a heart attack, can stimulate a person to reexamine their connection to the sacred."

Dr. Ironson summarizes by saying, "If you believe God loves you, it's an enormously protective factor, even more protective than scoring low for depression, or high for optimism. A view of a benevolent God is protective, but scoring high on the *personalized* statement 'God loves me' is even stronger."[17]

This echoes another study that found that, "Patients who believed that God was punishing them, didn't love them, didn't have the power to help, or felt their church had deserted them, experience 19% to 28% greater mortality during the two-year period following hospital discharge."[18]

Unfortunately, many more Americans believe in the God of thunderbolts and retribution than believe in a benevolent God. In a study done by Baylor University's Institute for Studies in Religion, researchers found that 31% of Americans see God that way. The number of people believing in an authoritarian God goes as high as 44% of the population in the country's southern states.

Just 23% of the population believes in a Benevolent God, according to the study, while the rest fall in the middle. They believe in a Critical God (16%), Distant God (24%), or are atheists (5%).[19]

Since our view of God can have such huge effects on our health, it's worth examining our beliefs, and if our religion or spiritual orientation permits such recalibration, adjusting them to fit the most loving vision of God of which we are capable. Carlos, the young man who hit bottom in Ironson's HIV/Spirituality study,[20] says,

> You don't have to believe in any God that doesn't love you or any God that isn't here to help you. Because I had a Catholic background, during my addiction I felt like I was being judged, that I was being punished. I thought I was going to die for my sins. So when I went to this service and I heard [the minister talk about choosing a loving God, it] changed my God to one that was loving and helpful. It was revolutionary.

Shortly thereafter, Carlos went to Alcoholics Anonymous and became sober. Though you may not be in the same dire straits as Carlos was, your body will be deeply grateful if you adjust your religious faith in the direction of a loving God.

Psychology Becomes Physiology

What we believe about ourselves alters the facts. A 2007 Harvard study examined the difference between physical exertion and physical exertion plus belief. The researchers recruited eighty-four maids who cleaned rooms in hotels. The sample was divided into two groups. One group heard a brief presentation explaining that their work qualifies as good exercise. The other group did not.

Over the next thirty days, the changes in the bodies of the women who had heard the presentation were significant: "The exercise-informed women perceived themselves to be getting markedly more exercise than they had indicated before the presentation. Members of that group lost an average of two pounds, lowered their blood pressure by almost 10%, and displayed drops in body-fat percentage, body mass index, and waist-to-hip ratio."[21]

This marked physiological change occurred in just thirty days, and followed one brief session in which the researchers exposed the women to new beliefs about their level of physical activity. Imagine the effect of the background music of our own self-talk, running in a continuous loop in our heads for many hours a day, as we perform our daily routines. Making even small changes in the program can lead to significant changes in our health.

The cholera pathogen was discovered by Robert Koch in 1884 after several pandemics had raged through Asia and Europe. One of Koch's colleagues, Max von Pettendorfer, challenged his theory that the bacterium caused the disease by publicly drinking an entire vial of cholera. So strong was Pettendorfer's belief system that he did not contract the disease—though when his student Emmerich tried a similar stunt, he suffered forty-eight hours of severe diarrhea.

Prayer

Prayer is one of the most powerful forms in which intention is packaged. Prayer has been the subject of hundreds of studies, most of which showed that patients who are prayed for get better faster.

One such study was done by Thomas Oxman and his colleagues at the University of Texas Medical School. It examined the effects of social support and spiritual practice on patients undergoing heart surgery. It found that those with large amounts of both factors exhibited a mortality rate *one-seventh* of those who did not.[22] Another was done at St. Luke's Medical Center in Chicago. It examined links between church attendance and physical health. The researchers found that patients who attended church regularly and had a strong faith practice were less likely to die and had stronger overall health.[23]

These are not isolated examples. Larry Dossey, in *Prayer Is Good Medicine,* says that there are over 1,200 scientific studies demonstrating the link between prayer and intention, and health and longevity. Meta-analyses in the *Annals of Internal Medicine*[24] and the *Journal of Alternative and Complementary Medicine*[25] have compiled the results of many studies and found that prayer, distant healing, and intentionality have significant effects on healing.

Even a recent confounding study published in the *American Heart Journal* tells us more about the limits of scientists' understanding of prayer than it tells us about prayer itself. Under headlines like "Strangers' prayers didn't help heart patients heal" (*Washington Post,* March 31, 2006), stories about this large-scale study of 1,800 patients undergoing heart surgery reported that those who were prayed for had as many complications as those who did not.

A variety of explanations were advanced for why prayer had appeared to fail in this study, and some scientists opposed to prayer studies argued that it was so conclusive that further money should not be put into a consciousness-based intervention that had been so thoroughly debunked.

I was most surprised at the study's results, until I read the fine print. It turned out that, in order to "standardize" what was meant by prayer, the researchers had designed the study so that patients were prayed for only starting the day of surgery (or the evening before), and continuing for fourteen days afterward. In addition, a standard eleven-word prayer was used for every patient: "For successful surgery with a quick healthy recovery and no complications."[26]

Such sterilized prayer cannot be as successful as heartfelt, spontaneous prayer. Other studies have shown that the skill and fervor of the person praying has a marked effect on the subject of prayer. One controlled, randomized, double-blind study reported in Dossey's *Prayer Is Good Medicine* measured the ability of people to increase the growth of yeast in test tubes. Three of the people were healers (one an MD who practiced spiritual healing) and the other four were student assistants. The results showed that mental concentration and intention definitely affected the growth of the yeast. "Analysis revealed that there were fewer than two chances in a hundred that the positive results could be obtained by chance. The bulk of the positive scores was credited to the three healers. When their scores were analyzed separately, there were fewer than four chances in ten thousand that the results could be due to chance..."

In a successful study of distant healing prayer by Elizabeth Targ, MD, PhD, healers used their own unique methods. These ranged from propping the patient's photo against a statue of the Virgin Mary to Sioux peace pipe ceremonies to the "projection of qi."[27] Healers repeated their intentions for ten weeks, for at least an hour a day. In tests measuring the germination rate of prayed-for seedlings, "the more experienced practitioners produced the more powerful outcomes. These studies indicate that practice, interest, and experience make a difference in spiritual healing, which for most healers is based in prayer."[28]

The failure of the cardiac prayer study to show an improvement was due, I believe, to the scripted and structured nature of the "prayer" designed so carefully by the researchers, but which squeezed out any fervor, passionate intent, or personalization by the person doing the praying. To be powerful, intent must be deeply, personally, and sincerely engaged. The researchers in the cardiac study were not studying the effects of prayer at all; they were studying the effects of their own beliefs about what constitutes prayer.

Doing Good Does You Good

Besides helping the person prayed for, it is likely that prayer benefits the person doing the praying. Studies show that regular acts of altruism prolong our lives and improve our own happiness.[29] Prayer is good medicine for the person doing the praying as well as the receiver.

In her book *The Energy Prescription,* pharmacist Constance Grauds, RPh, describes one such study done in Michigan. It included a large sample, 2,700 men, and it studied them over a long period— ten years. It found that the men who engaged in regular volunteer activities had death rates half of those who did not. She says that, "altruistic side effects include reduced stress; improved immune system functioning; a sense of joy, peace, and well-being; and even relief from physical and emotional pain. These effects tend to last long after the helping encounter, and...increase with the frequency of altruistic behavior."[30] Another study had participants watch a movie of Mother Teresa. As they witnessed her ministering to the poor in the streets of Calcutta, India, they got more in touch with their own compassion. Their immune markers increased, even though, rather than performing an altruistic act, they were merely witnessing one.[31] Similarly, a study by the HeartMath Institute found that feelings of care and compassion increase the production of immune factors.[32] With better immune responses, those who perform altruistic acts live longer too, reducing their odds of an early death by nearly 60%.[33]

The bottom line of these and other studies is that doing good is not just morally satisfying, it also improves your overall health, affecting the production of hormones that are markers for the production of hundreds of beneficial proteins in your cells. Cultivating an attitude of compassion, and acting according to the Golden Rule, is an act of service to your own body. Jesus's words "Blessed are the merciful, for they shall obtain mercy" are literally and physically true.

Seven Minutes of Spirituality

A study that demonstrates the effect of spiritual nurturing was performed by Jean Kristeller, PhD, a psychologist at Indiana State University. She reported that when doctors spent time talking with critically ill cancer patients about their *spiritual* concerns, follow-up revealed that after three weeks, the patients reported a better quality of life and less incidence of depression. Patients who had been talked to also felt that "their physicians cared more about their health, which was in contrast to those patients in the study whose physicians did not discuss spiritual matters with them."[34]

And the length of time of the discussion that so affected patients' lives for weeks afterward? A mere *five to seven minutes!*

Meditation

The benefits of meditation are so numerous, and the subject of so many studies,[35] that it's hard to know where to start. Dr. Robert Dozor, cofounder of the Integrative Health Clinic of Santa Rosa,

California, says, "Meditation—all by itself—may offer more to the health of a modern American than all the pharmaceutical remedies put together."[36] Recently, neuroscientist Richard Davidson, PhD, of the University of Madison at Wisconsin, has published a series of experiments using PET scans and EEG recordings to study the areas of the brain that are active during meditation.

When comparing the results obtained by novice meditators against those of experienced meditators such as Tibetan Buddhist monks, it was found that the monks, "showed greater increases in gamma waves, the type involved in attention, memory, and learning, and they had more brain activity in areas linked to positive emotions like happiness. Monks who had spent the most years meditating had the greatest brain changes."[37] This means that when we meditate, we are bulking up the portions of our brains that produce happiness. Another report noted that, "In a pilot study at the University of California at San Francisco, researchers found that schoolteachers briefly trained in Buddhist techniques and who meditated less than thirty minutes a day improved their moods as much as if they had taken antidepressants."[38] Love and compassion are health skills in which we can train ourselves, and they have no negative side effects.

Epigenetic Visualizations

The use of visualizations to help patients cope with cancer was pioneered by Carl Simonton and others in the 1970s. I vividly remember an interview I did with a woman in 1989. She impressed me as someone with great strength of will and courage.

Nancy had been diagnosed with metastasized Stage IV uterine cancer in 1972. Though her condition was terminal, she had rejected conventional medical therapy entirely, reasoning, "My body created this condition, so has the power to uncreate it too!" She quit work, exercised as much as her physical energy allowed, and spent hours lying in the bath. She came up with a visualization that tiny stars were coursing through her body. Whenever the sharp edge of a star touched a cancer cell, she imagined it puncturing the cancer cell, and the cancer cell deflating like a balloon. She imagined the water washing away the remains of the dying cancer cells. She focused on what she ate, how far she could walk, her baths, and the stars.

Nancy began to feel stronger, and her walks became longer. She began to visualize what her future might look like many years from that time. She went back to see her doctor three months after the diagnosis. She did not make the appointment until she had a firm inner conviction that the cancer was completely gone. To the astonishment of her physicians, tests revealed her to be cancer-free. Curiously, many patients who use similar techniques report an inner knowing that the disease is gone, long before it is confirmed by medical tests.[39] They also use highly individualized images that work for their particular psyche.

Many years later, Nancy was still in excellent health, and she would occasionally still visualize the stars rushing through her body, carrying away whatever traces of cancer might still remain.

It's that last detail that points to the preventive possibilities in epigenetic medicine. Meta-analysis of large bodies of research indicates that many genes express differently in cancer patients than they do in people without cancer.[40]

It's possible that Nancy's ongoing "star-cleaning" visualizations, long after she was diagnosed as cancer-free, helped keep her genetic profile favorable to cancer remission. Such visualizations are also free, safe, and noninvasive. Their ongoing effectiveness could be verified with DNA screening, biomarkers, and other nonintrusive tests.

The possibilities of visualization for epigenetic healing are indicated by a recent study that examined how the expectations of seventh grade students affected their math scores. Stanford University research psychologist Carol Dweck, PhD, noticed that students had beliefs about the nature of intelligence, and it had an effect on their performance. Some students believed that intelligence is a fixed quantum, like the number of inches in your height or the number of teeth in your mouth. Others believed that intelligence can grow and develop, like a plant. She then compared the math scores of the two groups over the following two years.

She found that students who believed that intelligence can grow had increasing math scores. The math scores of those who believed that intelligence is fixed decreased.

Dweck then wondered, "If we gave students a growth mindset, if we taught them how to think about their intelligence, would that benefit their grades?" She took a group of one hundred seventh-graders who were all performing badly in math and divided them, at random, into two groups. The first group received instruction in good study skills. The second group was told our brains grow and form new neural connections when confronted with novelty and challenge. At the end of the semester, those students who had received the mini-course in neuroscience had significantly better math grades than the other group. Dweck says, "When they worked hard in school, they actually visualized how their brain was growing."[41] This visualization had concrete effects on their academic performance. Visualization can affect our health, too. What we imagine, we can create. Filling our minds with positive images of well-being can produce an epigenetic environment that reinforces the healing process.

Attitude Is Everything

"Attitude is everything with aging," says Dr. Andrew Weil, author of *Spontaneous Remission* and other books. He cites studies that show that negative perceptions about aging can shorten our lives, whereas positive beliefs prolong them: Older people with positive attitudes about aging were found to live seven and a half years longer than those with negative attitudes. He also reminds us that optimism heals: "A study of nearly one thousand older adults followed for nine years concluded that people with high levels of optimism had a 23% lower risk of death from cardiovascular disease and a 55% lower risk of death from all causes compared to their more pessimistic peers." Positive older people also have better memories and stay healthier.

Overall physical fitness is reflected in walking speed; positive elders were found to walk 9% faster than negative ones.[42]

Neurosurgeon Norman Shealy, MD, PhD, in his book *Life Beyond 100,* summarizes four personality types and links them to longevity. The first type has a lifelong pattern of hopelessness. The second group has a lifelong pattern of blame or anger. The third group bounces between hopelessness and anger. And the fourth group is self-actualized. They believe that "happiness is an inside job." Shealy bases his analysis on the work of Dr. Hans Jurgen Eysenck, who conducted a more than twenty year study of over 13,000 European subjects.

Eysenck reported that people in the fourth category tend to die of old age, and that less than 1% of people in this category die of cancer or heart disease. About 9% of people in the third group die of one of those two conditions.

In contrast, he found that 75% of people who die of heart disease, and 15% of those who die of cancer are members of the Lifelong Anger Club, group two. And group one, those with lifelong patterns of hopelessness, tend to die thirty-five years younger than those in group four; 75% of them die of cancer, and 15% of heart disease.[43] Studies of specific diseases reinforce the findings of Drs. Eysenck and Shealy. Breast cancer survivors have much shorter survival times if they have a hopeless or helpless attitude.[44,45]

While attitudes such as optimism and positivity were once regarded as accidents, research like that of Richard Davidson is demonstrating that they are also learned skills. They can be cultivated. Knowing that we are having powerful genetic effects on the production of healing proteins in our bodies provides a strong incentive to learn techniques for improving our attitudes, a therapeutic tool that can exceed the promise of most conventional therapies. As you contemplate the fork in the road between positive and negative attitudes, imagine yourself splitting into two genetically identical individuals. Both are you at the present moment. Then fast-forward twenty years. Imagine that one of the twins has taken conscious control of attitude, and the other has not. Which one would you rather be?

Why Stress Hurts

What you are thinking, feeling, and believing is changing the genetic expression and chemical composition of your body on a moment-by-moment basis. The stress hormone cortisol has the same chemical precursors as DHEA, which is associated with many health-promoting functions, as well as longevity. DHEA is the most common hormone in your body and is associated with cell repair.

Both hormones are manufactured by the adrenal glands. When the adrenals use those precursors to make cortisol, production shifts away from making DHEA. When our cortisol levels are low, the raw materials from which our bodies manufacture life-giving DHEA are freed up and production of DHEA increases. But high stress levels suck biochemical resources away from cell repair and kill brain cells.[46] Cortisol has been shown to reduce muscle mass, increase bone loss and osteoporosis, interfere with the generation of new skin cells, increase fat accumulation around the waist and hips, and reduce memory and learning abilities.[47]

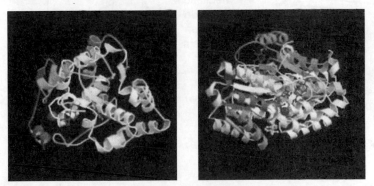

DHEA (left) and cortisol (right) are both manufactured by the adrenal gland using the same precursors

Engineering Your Cells Consciously

The body's stress response encompasses far more than shunting production away from DHEA to produce cortisol. Over 1,400 chemical reactions and over thirty hormones and neurotransmitters shift in response to stressful stimuli. So by de-stressing ourselves using attitude, belief, nurturing, self-talk, and spirituality, we are taking a role in determining which instruments in our genetic symphony predominate. This knowledge opens up a panorama for self-healing as vast as the number of moments left in your life. When you understand that *with every feeling and thought, in every instant, you are performing epigenetic engineering on your own cells,* you suddenly have a degree of leverage over your health and happiness that can make a critical difference. How you use that knowledge can determine whether your unique symphony comes to an early and discordant end, or whether you play beautiful music to a long finale.

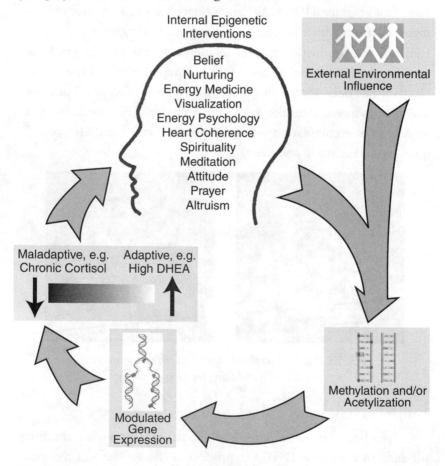

Epigenetic health cycle

When you choose beliefs, feelings, and other epigenetic influences that benefit your health, you can create a virtuous cycle of epigenetic health. In an epigenetic health cycle, you intervene consciously with positive emotions, thoughts, and prayers. Besides making you feel good psychologically, these benefit your body, modulating your gene expression toward peak health.

This peak of health differs from person to person, and there is little value in looking at your personal peak and comparing it to that of someone else, even an identical twin. For there are external influences that are beyond your control, and they can have profound epigenetic impact. Consider, for instance, two identical twins, one of which receives more nurturing than the other. Or think about twins living in different towns, one of which has severe environmental pollution while the other does not. Like the car that rams into you from behind on the freeway, there are random life situations that are beyond your control. It's not worth worrying about these.

Yet no matter how well or sick we may currently be, we still have the ability to choose our thoughts and feelings, and select those that support peak vitality. I call this the *epigenetic health cycle*.

In an epigenetic health cycle, we select positive beliefs, prayers, and visualizations that support peak health. We avoid those that do not. In this way, we consciously intervene to send epigenetic signals to our cells. These signals can reduce stress and promote the synthesis of life-enhancing hormones like DHEA, as well as thousands of other beneficial substances.

We've seen how powerful each of these little bricks can be in tipping the scale of our health. Positive self-talk, nurturing beliefs, altruism, attitude, meditation, and prayer can add brick after brick to the scale. But what if we had at our disposal a truckload of bricks to dump on the side of good health? Some of the emerging new therapies promise just this kind of decisive intervention, as we will see in the coming pages.

3

The Malleable Genome

The longest journey is the journey inward, for he who has chosen his destiny has started upon his quest for the source of his being.

—Dag Hammarskjöld, former United Nations Secretary-General

"A therapist[1] who was having her home remodeled noticed that one of the construction workers had a strange skin condition on his arms. She asked him about it, and he said, 'Oh, that's my psoriasis. Had it for years.' He turned his arms around to show her that from his wrists to his shoulders, his skin was a bubbling ocean of peeling skin with sore red tissue and fluid beneath it. She replied, 'Ooh, that must be painful. How did you get it?' 'Well I don't know,' he replied, 'I guess it started about three years ago, when my girlfriend told me she was pregnant.' The therapist asked if he might like to try a new treatment she knew. He was dubious. His doctor had told him that there was nothing to be done. The therapist replied, 'Ah, yes, what he meant was, there's nothing to be done with pills, ointments, and injections. Your mind created this, and so only your mind can take it away again.' He nodded and she showed him just a bare-bones procedure, suggesting that three times each day he do three rounds of tapping to the statement 'I want to get over my psoriasis.' Within two weeks, his skin had healed on both arms, down to a small patch the size of a coin on his elbows. In addition, he has since used the approach to overcome lower-back pain that had troubled him for years."[2]

That these kinds of shifts are possible with energy medicine and Energy Psychology is being established by a rapidly growing database of research studies and clinical case histories. What have not been at all clear up to this point are the mechanisms behind such shifts. Science is never content with knowing *what;* it rightly insists on knowing *why*. While the "what" has been accumulating in large stacks, precise experimental descriptions of the "why" have lagged behind until the right questions about epigenetic control were asked and answered.

This book could not have been written ten years ago, because there were not yet enough credible and well-designed scientific studies to support its hypotheses. Today, there are, and the number of published experiments will grow exponentially in the coming decade. With a catalog of genes in place, researchers are now focusing on how these genes work. In some cases they work singly, but most often they work in concert, both with each other and with signals from the inner and outer environments.

X-ray diffraction image of human DNA bound in protein

Very few human processes are turned on or off by a single gene. Most processes require many genes, acting together to produce a common result. The idea, fostered by the mass media, that there is a gene for this or a gene for that, is incorrect. Genes are implicated in conditions in a variety of ways. Headlines like the October 29, 2005, proclamation in the *New York Times* stating "Two More Genes Linked to Dyslexia" (in addition to a third gene announced a year earlier) oversimplify the cascade of genetic factors involved in conditions. After a subtitle that reads "Findings support that disorder is genetic," the story goes on to tell us that "people deemed simply lazy or stupid because of their severe reading problems may instead have a genetic disorder that interfered with the wiring of their brains before birth. 'I am ecstatic about this research,' said Dr. Albert Galaburda of Harvard Medical School, a leading authority on developmental disorders..."

Such "breakthroughs" create elation that is often followed by disappointment, as the complexity of the genetic interactive systems later becomes clear. For example, more sober reports have implicated some six hundred genes that express differently in patients with heart disease. Researchers have shown that hundreds of genes are implicated in certain other diseases for which the genetic profile has been mapped.

As well as *many* genes being involved in most changes of state, different genes are often involved at *different time periods* of that change of state. Not just from day to day, but from second to second, genetic cascades are turned on or off by our experience. Some genes may engage early, others may express afterward, and yet others may reach peak expression many hours later, in a complex and coordinated dance. There are several ways of profiling genes; one way they can be cataloged is to look at the *speed at which they reach peak expression* when stimulated by an environmental influence.

Some genes are activated quickly, others more slowly. Genes that activate very quickly (sometimes *within one or two seconds* of a stimulus) are called *immediate early genes* or IEGs. Their function is often to trigger the activation of other genes. In general, *early activated genes* reach their peak of expression in roughly an hour. A second class of genes, the *intermediate genes,* reach their peak of expression in about two hours. *Late genes* take longer periods to reach their peaks, up to eight hours, and their effects may last for a period of a few hours, or for a period of years. Certain classes of late activated genes, once expressed, may remain "on" for your entire lifetime. An early firing gene may have, as a primary purpose, the activation of several intermediate and late-firing genes.

Besides being identified with the speed at which they express, genes can be classified by the kinds of triggers that turn them on and off. One such class of genes is called *experience-dependent genes* or activity-dependent genes. These genes are involved in activities or experiences such as growth, healing, and learning. Another class of genes we will examine in more detail is *behavioral state–dependent genes.* These genes come into expression during periods of stress or emotional arousal, or in different states of awareness such as dreaming and dreamless sleep.

Gene Chips

How do we know which DNA molecules are expressed in, for instance, a blood sample from a cancer patient? One of the newest tools that has enabled researchers to conduct experiments that show particular genes being triggered is the DNA microarray. Such gene chips assemble thousands of different strands of DNA onto a single wafer. When exposed to a sample, they can then demonstrate which of the strands have been affected by the sample.

The characteristic of DNA that allows identification of expressed genes is simple in principle. The double helix shape of a DNA molecule looks like a spiraling zipper. During replication, the molecule becomes partially "unzipped." The two halves of the zipper separate, and each seeks another half-molecule to bond with. While it is unzipped and separated, bonds on the unzipped portion seek other interlocking half-zippers to attach to. Gene chips contain hundreds or even thousands of tiny wells, like pixels on an LCD screen. To the bottom of each of these wells, a particular unzipped strand is

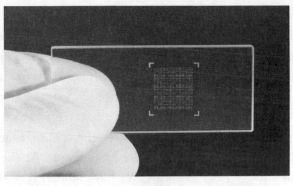

Gene chip

attached during the process of manufacturing the chip. These "sticky" half-molecules seek their counterparts. By examination of which ones are able to bond, researchers can identify exactly which DNA strands in a sample are active.

A gene chip yields results that are also somewhat like an LCD screen with thousands of pixels. Each pixel is a different color. Researchers can note which pixels change color when exposed to a sample, and are thus able to "read" the gene chip to find out which molecules have been able to bond with a counterpart in the sample. This sophisticated technology allows researchers to identify DNA states, and changes in DNA, in a variety of conditions.

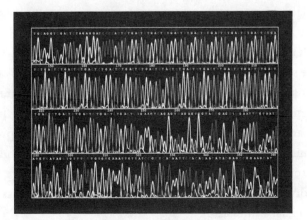

Portion of a visual map derived from a gene chip,
showing the expression of various genes[4]

Gene chips will be put to many more experimental uses in the years to come, giving us pictures of how psychospiritual states affect genes. They have already been used to study the effects of acupuncture,[5] and chapter 11 summarizes new research using gene chips to measure the epigenetic influence of meditation, relaxation, and other environmental inputs that reduce emotional stress. Future research will examine what gene changes occur before and after prayer, therapeutic touch, energy therapies, and other consciousness-based treatments. At the National Institute for Integrative Healthcare, we have an active research program to measure how emotional de-stressing and physical healing are correlated; chapter 13 contains details of these exciting studies.

Immediate Early Genes

This class of genes responds within minutes to events that happen in our lives, and to cues from our environments. They mediate between the environment and the body's neurochemical processes. They activate other genes, which in turn code for the proteins that govern our cells' ability to adapt. Early activated genes reach their peak expression in around one hour, whereas the peak is two hours for intermediate activated genes. But many immediate early genes express in much shorter periods—between *two seconds* and *two minutes.*

A class of immediate early genes regulates our body's wakefulness and sleep. They are the chronobiological or "clock genes." Researcher Marina Bentivoglio, of Stockholm's prestigious Karolinska Institute, says, "The study of immediate early genes indicates that sleep and wake, as well as synchronized and desynchronized sleep, are characterized by different genomic expressions, the level of IEGs being high during wake and low during sleep. Such fluctuation of gene expression is not ubiquitous but occurs in certain cell populations of the brain."[6] Immediate early genes can be activated both by cognitive changes in the individual, and also by cues from the outside, such as threats, food, or sexual stimulation.[7]

An example of the pathway followed in such transformations is demonstrated by an immediate early gene called *C-fos*. It is part of a class of immediate early genes that modulate our body's response to stress; this class is activated by stressful situations—whether they're interoffice rivalries, marital disagreements, or attacks by wild animals. C-fos activates brain neurons to produce a protein called *fos*. Fos then binds to the DNA molecule where it triggers the transcription of other genes. The stresses that trigger the activation of C-fos can be physical traumas. They can also be stressful social or psychological situations. In this way, *this family of immediate early genes sets up the response of the rest of the body's mechanism for dealing with stress.*

Gary Marcus, PhD, author of *The Birth of the Mind: How a Tiny Number of Genes Creates the Complexity of Human Thought,* says, "A single regulatory gene at the top of a complex network can indirectly launch a cascade of hundreds or thousands of other genes," and, "by compounding and coordinating their effects, genes can exert enormous influence on biological structure." The word he uses, "cascade," is often associated with regulatory gene expression. The firing of a regulatory gene at the top of a cascade can lead to a massive biological chain reaction. He gives examples of experiments in which "a simple regulatory gene leads directly and indirectly to the expression of approximately 2,500 other genes."[8]

An epigenetic signal from the outside environment, when it activates such a cascade, can completely change the biological characteristics of an organism. Marcus uses the example of the African butterfly. When the weather is cool, typical of the period before the dry season, which is when the butterfly has to blend with dried-up plants, it develops brown wings in the cocoon. When the weather is warm, indicating the coming rainy season, which is when it needs to blend with an explosion of brightly colored tropical foliage, its wings are colored. Same genes, completely different outcome. It's all due to regulatory genes, which are switched on or off by an outside environmental influence, in this case, temperature.

Stress from the environment can also provide epigenetic cues. Hans Selye, the German physician who coined the term "stress," originally broke it down into two poles: *distress,* or negative stress, and *eustress,* or positive stress—the kind of stress that causes an athlete to excel, drives an entrepreneur to persevere with a creative project, or inspires a painter to reach new heights of inspired creative expression. Unfortunately, human experience being what it is, the word "stress" has become associated exclusively with distress, while the word "eustress" has disappeared from the lexicon.

Immediate early genes are also critical to the functioning of our immune systems. Distress, whether sourced from within or outside us, can depress the expression of genes that enhance the functioning of our immune system. With medical students in the midst of their final exams as his subjects, researcher Ronald Glaser studied the effect of stress on one of the immune system's messenger molecules. The molecule, interleukin-2, instructs helper T cells (white blood cells that devour diseased cells and intruders) to attack. He found that during this stressful period, the students showed a significant drop in interleukin-2 production,[9] implying a corresponding drop in the transcription of the gene that regulates interleukin-2 production. In follow-up studies, Glaser also found that the stress precancerous subjects were experiencing led to reduced expression of two immediate early genes associated with immune function: c-myc and c-myb.[10]

Conversely, positive influences—eustress—can bolster the genetic component of our immune systems. Immunologist M. Castes, PhD, showed that emotionally supportive experiences of children in therapeutic support groups improved aspects of their immune system function that depend on genetic activation. The group in his experiment went through a six-month program of self-esteem workshops, guided imagery, and relaxation. When compared with a control group that had not had the same environmental stimuli, the children in the experimental group had both fewer episodes of asthma and fewer incidences of the use of anti-asthma medication. Immune factors in the blood of the experimental group increased, as did gene expression of the factors governing interleukin-2 production.[11]

Immediate early genes can also affect the developing fetus. Some of the genes activated by immediate early genes shape the form and functioning of the body. When stress proteins are present during

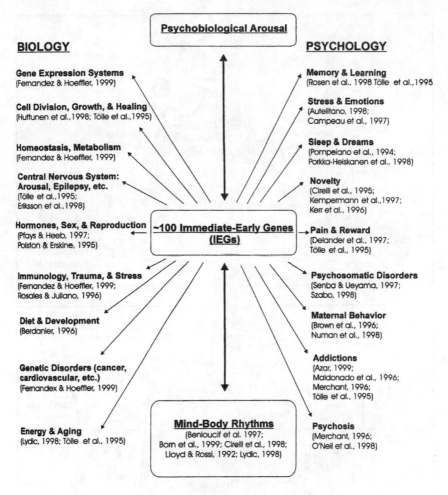

Psychobiological Arousal

BIOLOGY

Gene Expression Systems
(Fernandez & Hoeffler, 1999)

Cell Division, Growth, & Healing
(Huttunen et al.,1998; Tölle et al.,1995)

Homeostasis, Metabolism
(Fernandez & Hoeffler, 1999)

Central Nervous System:
Arousal, Epilepsy, etc.
(Tölle et al.,1995;
Eriksson et al.,1998)

Hormones, Sex, & Reproduction
(Pfays & Heeb, 1997;
Polston & Erskine, 1995)

Immunology, Trauma, & Stress
(Fernandez & Hoeffler, 1999;
Rosales & Juliano, 1996)

Diet & Development
(Berdanier, 1996)

Genetic Disorders (cancer,
cardiovascular, etc.)
(Fernandex & Hoeffler, 1999)

Energy & Aging
(Lydic, 1998; Tölle et al., 1995)

**~100 Immediate-Early Genes
(IEGs)**

PSYCHOLOGY

Memory & Learning
(Rosen et al., 1998 Tölle et al.,1995

Stress & Emotions
(Autelitano, 1998;
Campeau et al., 1997)

Sleep & Dreams
(Pompeiano et al., 1994;
Porkka-Heiskanen et al., 1998)

Novelty
(Cirelli et al., 1995;
Kempermann et al.,1997;
Kerr et al., 1996)

Pain & Reward
(Delander et al., 1997;
Tölle et al., 1995)

Psychosomatic Disorders
(Senba & Ueyama, 1997;
Szabo, 1998)

Maternal Behavior
(Brown et al., 1996;
Numan et al., 1998)

Addictions
(Azar, 1999;
Maldonado et al., 1996;
Merchant, 1996;
Tölle et al., 1995)

Mind-Body Rhythms
(Benloucif et al. 1997;
Born et al., 1999; Cirelli et al., 1998;
Lloyd & Rossi, 1992; Lydic, 1998)

Psychosis
(Merchant, 1996;
O'Neil et al., 1998)

*Immediate early genes play a vital role in regulating a great
many psychological and physiological functions*[14]

fetal development, they can shape the anatomy or rate of growth[12] of
the child. "The stress may be momentary, and the arousal of the early
genes brief. Yet the effects triggered by the activation of the genes
they act upon may produce long-term changes."[13]

Behavioral State–Related Genes

During various states of awareness, like sleeping and waking,
strong emotional arousal, distress and eustress, different patterns of
genes express. These genes are related to our behavioral state, and

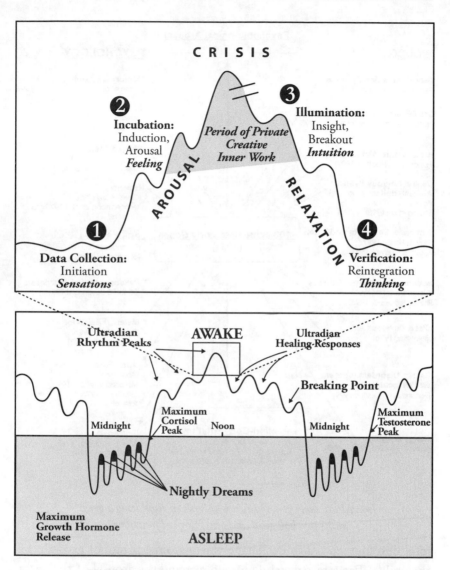

Ultradian rhythms. Gray area in top box shows peak of cycle;
gray area in bottom box shows sleep[15]

are therefore known as behavioral state–related genes. They provide a link between our thoughts and our bodies, between biology and psychology, and are an important piece of the puzzle explaining how psychological states can affect our bodies, and vice versa. They also explain how psychotherapy, prayer, worship, and social rituals can have positive effects on our physical well-being. They offer a pathway by which we can influence physical health by immersing ourselves in behavioral states that promote health, and avoiding behavioral states that can hurt us.

Therapeutic experience suggests that behavioral states are usually linked to daily (*circadian*) rhythms, or to periodic, several-times-per-day (*ultradian*) rhythms. Circadian rhythms follow the twenty-four-hour clock, subject to the modifications of circumstance. Ultradian rhythms are briefer rhythms coordinated within circadian rhythms. They last about 90 to 120 minutes, and correlate with measures of our energy level such as blood glucose, metabolic rate, hormone release, and insulin production.[16] Peak activity of the left and right hemispheres of our brains also alternates according to 90- to 120-minute ultradian rhythms,[17] and when we go to sleep, REM or dreaming periods follow a similar schedule.[18] Ninety to 120 minutes is also the average time between gene expression, and the synthesis of the proteins required by the body to convey information between cells, provide energy, create the scaffolding of cells, and accomplish many of the body's other functions. The ancient sages who developed traditional Chinese medicine several thousand years ago seem to have been aware of ultradian rhythms; they divided the therapeutic day into two-hour intervals. Acupuncture charts show a daily clock in which the body's energies fluctuate every two hours.

Rossi notes that ultradian "valleys" correspond with a need for relaxation after periods of intense creative work,[19] and recommends an ultradian rest period in the afternoon, if that is when behavioral problems recur.[20] By this late in the day, he believes that many people, after ignoring the peaks and valleys of their ultradian cycle for many hours, have "an accumulated ultradian deficit and stress syndrome expressed with these common complaints:

"'I'm exhausted by midafternoon.'

"'I get stressed, tense, and irritable toward the end of the workday.'

"'I need a drink after work.'

"'My addiction gets worse later in the day when I *have* to have something."

"'I get sleepy in the afternoon."

"'The worst time is when I have to go home after school and I'm too tired to do homework."

"'Just before dinner everybody is irritable and that's when arguments start."

"Many of these acute and chronic problems can be ameliorated by taking one or two ultradian breaks earlier in the day or taking a nap after lunch,"[21] Rossi advises, especially in cases where people might already have skipped several ultradian rest periods during which their bodies were clearly instructing them to slow down. Noticing our need for ultradian rest periods after times of intense creative output can allow us to pace our days in order to avoid behavior-dependent genetic conflicts.

Secretion of hormones such as ACTH and cortisol, which are released on the usual 90- to 120-minute ultradian cycle, peak just before wakefulness. Most researchers do not believe that these fluctuations are under our conscious control. Yet many people are able to decide, before they go to bed, exactly what time they will wake up.

Like many travelers, I set my internal alarm clock when I'm on a trip. Just before dropping off to sleep, I decide when I want to wake up each morning. When I wake up and look at the clock, I'm usually within a few minutes of my target time. Often, it's the exact minute. If I then want to sleep some more, I'll say to myself, "I'll wake up fully in twenty minutes," and usually I will. The certainty that this biological function will work reliably is so ingrained in my awareness that I long ago stopped carrying a travel alarm clock in my kit, even though when presenting a workshop, it's crucial to be on time. This experience, common to a great many travelers,[22] suggests that *intentionality conditions aspects of our behavioral state–related genetic activity long thought to be outside of our conscious control.*

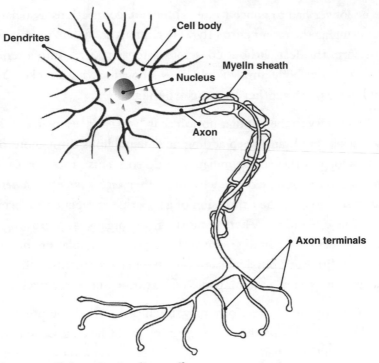

Epigenetic stimuli can affect gene expression in neurons

Experience-Dependent Genes

Experience-dependent genes are *genes that are activated by learning and novelty*. This class of genes generates the protein synthesis required to *instruct stem cells to differentiate* in order to replace injured or damaged cells in the tissues of our muscles and organs—the foundation of growth and healing. It also stimulates stem cells into forming new neurons in the brain, not just in the young, but at any age. Stimulated by novel activities and learning, these new neurons form new synaptic connections within the brain. The experiences we are having each moment are actually changing the structure of our brains.

Experiences build neuronal pathways. When you first learned the correct way to swing a tennis racket, it took great concentration to remember your instruction each time. Then, at some point, the neural synapses that coded your swing were so well developed that you no longer had to concentrate. The nerve connections associated with swinging the racket correctly were copious enough to permit you to perform this feat without conscious attention. Step onto a tennis court, and your body immediately knows how to swing a racket. You could move on to another learning experience.

Contrary to the popular notion that "you can't teach an old dog new tricks," our brains keep adding new neural links throughout our lives, as long as they are stimulated to do so.[23] This process is called *neurogenesis*. Learning experiences and other *highly attentive states of awareness* switch on the expression of genes that stimulate the formation of new neurons. Whereas most of our organs stop growing in our late teens, our brains—with the ongoing stimulation of new behavior, discovery, physical exercise, novel environments, and fresh new memories—are a teeming mass of creation our whole lives.

One of those creations may be health where before there was disease. "Many of the so-called miracles of healing via spiritual practices and therapeutic hypnosis...probably occur via this type of

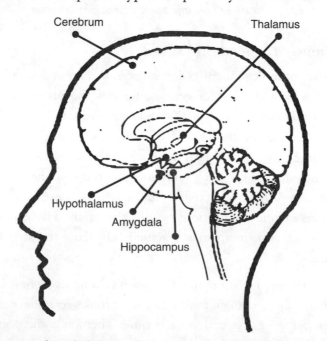

Hippocampus, hypothalamus, and amygdala are engaged during fight-or-flight

activity-dependent gene expression in stem cells throughout the brain and body."[24] Rossi declares that "fascination during novel and numinous life experiences plays a fundamental role in focusing our attention and engaging activity-dependent gene expression neurogenesis, and healing in general."[25] A healer and healee might go into a highly attentive state of awareness at the same time, such as when a rabbi is praying, a Reiki master is laying on hands, or a compassionate doctor is counseling a patient. This shared intent, with its associated electromagnetic patterns of resonant brain frequencies, might be mutually reinforcing. Healer and healee entrain to the same brain wave forms during these periods of heightened consciousness. Two resonant brains might create a feedback loop and build a stronger field, initiating a bigger epigenetic signal to spark neurogenesis and build the neural highways necessary for miraculous healing.

The process of turning short-term memories into long-term memories is key to neurogenesis. Short-term memory utilizes only *existing* pathways of molecular communication between nerve cells. Long-term memory, on the other hand, is processed by the portion of our brains known as the hippocampus. As it codes for long-term memory, the hippocampus stimulates experience-related gene expression, especially involving a gene known as zif-268, which leads to the growth of new synapses and *new neural pathways* in the brain. London cabbies, who have to navigate a crazy quilt of medieval streets each day, tend to have larger hippocampuses.[26] So do symphony violinists. Conversely, long-term stress, which keeps brain cortisol levels chronically high, has been shown to damage the hippocampus, inhibiting memory and learning.

Evolving technologies like positron emission tomography (PET) scanners and functional magnetic resonance imaging (fMRI) machines allow us to produce sophisticated images of brain activity. Researchers are now using these tools to map the changes that occur during psychospiritual experiences and changes of consciousness. As subjects think certain thoughts, practice certain behaviors, or harbor certain emotions, researchers can determine which areas of their brains are firing. Emotions such as fear and anger are associated with different patterns of brain arousal.[27] We are now also starting to be able to associate changes in the brain with changes in genetic state; as certain genes are activated, certain areas of the brain show increased activity. This genetic activation in the brain sends neurological signals throughout the body. Candace Pert, PhD, author of *Molecules of Emotion,* calls this the *psychosomatic network*. Through the psychosomatic network, thoughts and emotions are transformed into physiological effects. In the other direction of the feedback loop, physiological experiences gathered by our senses translate into mental and emotional states.

Burying Trauma in Muscles

"I am looking at and seeing the violent crash. I see my father's body across the railroad tracks. I feel the shock and horror in my mother's body and consciousness as she witnessed his death."[28]

These words were spoken by a woman receiving a head massage. Her face "contorted in agony" as she suddenly, vividly, and spontaneously recalled the death of her father when she was a child. Until the massage therapist began to work on her body, the memory had been buried, inaccessible to her conscious mind. She thought she had no memory of the event, but when the right muscle group was stimulated, the memory leapt vividly into her awareness.

For decades, massage therapists have recounted such stories of spontaneous awakening of memory when tissues are stimulated. They can scarcely fail to notice the link between body and mind; when manipulating muscle and connective tissue, emotional release of buried traumatic memories sometimes takes place. Science is now catching up and starting to describe some of the mechanics of this phenomenon. It has also become apparent to many psychotherapists that the verbal processing of trauma, *without physical release,* provides only partial relief. While buried emotional traumas can be released by bodywork, the link can work the other way, with physical symptoms disappearing once a psychospiritual shift occurs.

Stanislav Grof, MD, PhD, who coined the term "spiritual emergency" to describe a dramatic spiritual breakthrough manifesting as a psychotic episode, said that spiritual emergencies might be accompanied by involuntary twitching and other spontaneous body movements. Harvey Jackins, who founded one of the most widely used forms of peer therapy, known as Re-Evaluation Counseling or Co-Counseling, believes, on the basis of thousands of clinical observations, that genuine psychological shift is *always* accompanied by shuddering, moaning, twitching, tears, sweating, or some other physical sign of discharging emotions. A 2004 meta-analysis of thirty-seven studies of massage therapy published in *Psychological Bulletin* showed their effectiveness for the relief of anxiety and depression, with "benefits similar in magnitude to those of psychotherapy" alone.[29]

Using *psychological counseling and physical manipulation in tandem* may provide the most effective emotional release. Candace Pert asserts that the body *is* the unconscious mind. Psychotherapy that ignores the body may even cause harm. Remembering traumatic incidents without physical-emotional release can retraumatize people by igniting the same neuronal pathways as the original event and building more neural strands to reinforce pain-laden brain structures.

The link between areas of the body and traumatic emotional states is illustrated by many phenomena. One is the recent discovery that removing "worry wrinkles" may remove the underlying worry too. This effect was stumbled upon by plastic surgeons giving patients cosmetic injections of Botox. Botox, a therapeutic variant of the protein present in botulism toxin, paralyzes muscles into which it is injected. When injected into the facial muscles of patients with deeply lined skin, it paralyzes the muscles, and the skin smooths out for a few months.

What cosmetic surgeons began noticing, however, was that in some of their Botox patients who were depressed, the depression lifted after the injection. According to one report:

Kathleen Delano had suffered from depression for years. Having tried psychotherapy and antidepressant drugs in vain, she resigned herself to a life of suffering.

Then she tried Botox, the drug that a few years ago became the rage for smoothing facial wrinkles.

In 2004, her physician injected five doses of the toxin into the muscles between Delano's eyebrows.... Eight weeks later...her depression had lifted.[30]

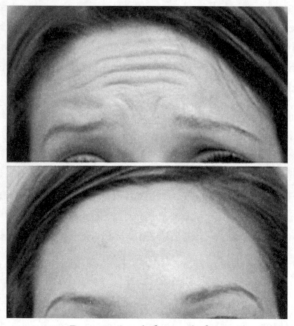

Botox patient before and after

The alteration of the physical structure seemed to catalyze an alteration of the mental state. A happier "look," even one artificially induced, produced a happier experience. Though we know that changing the mind changes the body, it also seems that the reverse is true: Changing the body changes the mind.

Evidence of the relationship between the body and emotions has recently come from an unlikely source: the science of mathematics. A mathematician from the University of Tokyo, Yoshiharu Yamamoto, PhD, hooked up accelerometers to the arms of patients diagnosed with major depression. The accelerometers measured how often subjects changed their rate of motion. He found striking differences in the activity patterns of depressed and healthy people, with depressed people moving less, and in bursts of activity unlike the normal subjects. They had more frequent long rest periods, and less frequent short rest periods. As he looked for an analogy with which to compare the charts he compiled during his study, Dr. Yamamoto observed that they looked most like the patterns of electromagnetic activity of nerve cells that have been removed from contact with other neurons and isolated in a petri dish. Isolation looked similar to him, whether the social isolation of a depressed person—or the physical isolation of an individual cell.[31]

Psychotherapists have long observed that when therapeutic breakthroughs are achieved, the body, too, often heals. During a therapy session with "Celeste," a young woman with arthritis chronicled in Ernest Rossi's *The Psychobiology of Gene Expression,* Celeste goes from very limited mobility in her hands to making a fist to being able to stretch her fingers wide. She's delighted by the changes in her body that occur during the hour-long session with Rossi. And while he acts as a therapist, he also speculates which genes are expressing:

> **Celeste:** My right hand is doing some stuff.
>
> **Rossi:** Your right hand is doing some stuff?
>
> **Celeste:** Yeah. My left one feels like lead, but my right one.... I don't know, I think it started shaking a little bit, or something.

Rossi's comments of this exchange: "Evidence of psychobiological arousal and behavioral state-related gene expression.... The therapist wonders how to engage the psychogenomic dynamics of immunological variables such as interleukin-1, 2, and 1B associated with Cox-2 that has been implicated in rheumatoid arthritis that is Celeste's presenting condition."

> **Rossi:** [Celeste's hand...surprisingly forms a fist]. Oh my goodness! Something new seems to be happening?

Celeste: Yeah!...

Rossi: Wow! Yes, something new is beginning to happen! [Celeste now extends her fingers up into the air]....

Celeste: I sure don't know what this is [laughing]....

Rossi's comments: "Illumination and activity-dependent gene expression. Celeste experiences playful activity-dependent exercise as a creative breakout of her typically restrained hand and finger movements associated with her rheumatoid arthritis. Future research will be needed to determine if...the CREB genes associated with new memory and learning, as well as the ODC and BDNF genes associated with neurogenesis and physical growth, are actually being engaged...."

At the end of the session, Celeste is stretching her arms and hands in delight at her newfound mobility. Rossi closes by hoping that "the experiential theater of demonstration therapy will be sufficiently numinous to activate zif-268 gene expression in her REM dreaming tonight,"[32] which will help cement the changes in her body.

Recent studies are allowing us to understand the role of genetics in the psychosomatic network. For instance, the hypothalamus is a structure in the brain that transforms the activity of the frontal lobes into hormonal messenger molecules. These communicate with the endocrine glands, which affect other systems, including the immune system, digestive system, and musculoskeletal system. Portions of the hypothalamus synthesize a hormone known as CRH (corticotrophin-releasing hormone), which stimulates the production of a dozen other messenger molecules that influence stress and relaxation.

The gene that initiates the production of CRH is located on chromosome 8, a chromosome so vital to our function that it has scarcely changed for millennia: "CRH synthesizing and secreting neurons are found [in] their highest densities...in the prefrontal, insular, and cingulate areas [of the brain], where they mediate cognitive and behavioral processing.... Secondary messengers within the cell convey the extracellular signals from the environment (including psychosocial cues) to the nucleus of the cell, where they initiate gene expression."[33] Our bodies have an exquisite ability to turn external cues into the signals required for optimal internal responses.

Eric Kandel, MD, who received the Nobel Prize in Medicine in 2000, says that "Changes in gene expression...alter the strength of synaptic connections and structural changes that alter the anatomical pattern of interconnections between nerve cells of the brain."[34] In one experiment, Kandel discovered that when new memories are established, the number of synaptic connections in the sensory neurons stimulated jumped to around 2,600, a *doubling* of its previous count of 1,300. *Unless the initial experience was reinforced,* however, the number of connections dropped back to 1,300 within three weeks. If we reinforce our novel experiences by repetition, we strengthen the neural net to support them; if we do not, our newfound neural circuitry quickly decays—not over years, but *in less than a month.* This means that new thoughts, actions, and habits must be continuously updated in order to take root.[35] Like a song on the radio that becomes ingrained in the cultural collective, many people must hear it many times. But if it isn't heard for a while, the memory of even a Top Forty tune begins to fade. Who today remembers "It's a Long Way to Tipperary" or "At the End of the Road"?—both top of the charts a century ago.

Insight changes the brain as well. In an article entitled "The Neuroscience of Leadership," David Rock and Jeffrey Schwartz, PhD, report on studies that use "MRI and EEG technologies to study moments of insight. One study found sudden bursts of high-frequency 40 Hz oscillations (gamma waves) in the brain appearing just prior to moments of insight. This oscillation is conducive to *creating links across many parts of the brain.*" This is the part of the brain that "is involved in perceiving and processing music, spatial, and structural relations (such as those in a building or painting), and other complex aspects of the environment. The findings suggest that at a moment of insight, a complex set of new connections is being created."[36]

Gene expression in long-term memory encoding also has an ultradian rhythm of between 90 and 120 minutes, and the number of new synaptic connections between neurons can double in as little as an hour once the experience-dependent genes are activated.[37] One of the ways in which memories are encoded is when we replay a scene in our minds. Memory is not static, and as we *combine old memories with present situations,* we stimulate neurogenesis. We used to think that memories remained unchanged over time, like taking a photograph out of an album and putting it back in again. We now know that we recombine the old material with bits of information from the current environment. Like printing out a photo on whatever printer is closest, then scanning it back in using whatever computer we're using currently, content is subtly reconstituted each time we remember.

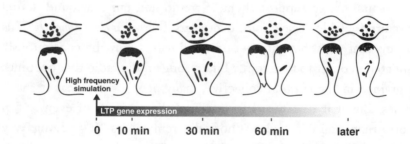

High frequency simulation

LTP gene expression

0   10 min   30 min   60 min   later

Within an hour of gene expression in response to environmental stimulation, one synaptic connection has become two[38]

If you don't *use* the new connections you develop during neurogenesis, you lose them. If you aren't using a synapse, your brain disassembles it; bodies have no tolerance for wasted capacity.[39] Kandel's work also showed that if novel learning experiences were not reinforced, the baseline of 1,300 synaptic connections could drop to 800.[40] Your brain works rather like an efficient electrician upgrading a house. It installs more electrical wiring wherever the current is flowing most strongly, to accommodate increased capacity. It gets the wire it needs by stripping out old unused circuits.

Novel experiences not only lead to the growth of new brain tissue, they are linked to psychological well-being, too. There is a link between clinical depression and "a lack of new cell growth in the brain."[41] As a consequence, the hippocampi of the brains of depressed patients shrink in time by as much as 15%, as distress and social trauma result in environmental signals that inhibit the expression of experience-dependent genes.[42] Our hippocampi are involved in the recall of memories, perhaps while we sleep; such repeated replaying is central to the process of creating durable long-term memories,[43] with a beneficial effect on neurogenesis. Hippocampi also contain stem cells, those "blank" cells that do not become specialized until stimulated by an epigenetic environmental signal, which means that an aging brain can regenerate. Neuronal stem cells are found in other areas of the brain and spinal cord as well and, far different from the old static picture of brain development, are generated by the body up till the very last moments of our lives.[44] Psychologist Martin Seligman, PhD, in his book *Authentic Happiness,* sums it up by saying "Neurons are wired to respond to novel events,"[45] and as long as we keep cultivating them in our lives, we keep stimulating neurogenesis.

Rebooting Memory for Healing

The fluctuating nature of memory, with synaptic connections being created and destroyed, means that memories may be strengthened or diffused. Psychotherapy seeks to bring painful memories back to the forefront of consciousness, and then shift them. A series of experiments studying rat brains suggests that if a painful or fear-laden memory is triggered and then processed, its impact is diminished.

Rossi, who has more than three decades of experience treating patients, summarizes these experiments as follows: "When the rat brain is infused with anisomycin (an inhibitor of protein synthesis) shortly after the reactivation of a long consolidated memory, the memory is extinguished. The same treatment of the brain with anisomycin but without reactivating the consolidated memory leaves the memory intact. This means that the gene expression and protein synthesis cycle is reactivated when important memories are recalled and replayed…. Most paradigms of psychotherapy involve a combination of the same two-step process…. (1) a reactivation of old traumatic memories, which is (2) immediately followed by some form of therapeutic intervention designed to heal the old hurt."[46] Each time we reboot an old memory, we may be unconsciously modifying it even as we think we are "just remembering." This phenomenon can help with the healing process, especially when combined with strong feelings. These allow us to cement an association between an old trauma and a new, positive meaning.

One study showed an increase in immune system function during a drumming and storytelling ritual. In this study, 111 healthy volunteers were exposed to an hour-long ritual, much like the kind of communal experience our ancient ancestors might have enjoyed around the campfire. The improvement in immune function after the drumming and storytelling ceremony was demonstrated by increased activity in helper T cells. In addition, levels of the healthy hormone DHEA increased, while the stress hormone cortisol dropped.[47]

Many traditional healing rituals, such as shamanic journeys, faith healings, passion plays, the Catholic Mass, and exorcisms, involve the same mechanism of heightened emotional arousal, followed by a release. Rossi points out that psychotherapies old and new use this approach. Sigmund Freud first had patients free-associate, then, in the second step, find an insight that reframed the meaning of the memories in a significant way. New therapies such as Eye Movement Desensitization and Reprocessing (EMDR) also reactivate painful old traumas, after which they are infused with positive images and feelings.[48] Psychotherapies such as cognitive behavioral therapy (CBT) also challenge dysfunctional ideas and traumatic incidents by presenting positive alternative cognitions. What EMDR, EFT, and Energy Psychology do, in addition, is *add a layer of physical stimulation*. Like ancient drumming or dancing ceremonies, this physical component is crucial to the rapid healings seen in these therapies.

Creating Your Own Designer Brain

Learning is demanding. Giving ourselves new challenges, like taking a college course in a subject completely beyond our existing fields of expertise, reaching out for new friendships, acquiring a new artistic ability, and learning a new sport, all stretch our consciousness. Yet this positive stress is part of the process by which we grow the capacities of our brains. Experiments with rats being taught new tasks found that those rats that were mildly stressed learned faster than those that were not.[49]

Other experiments demonstrate that *unpredictability* and *novelty* are crucial aspects of learning. The association between a stimulus and a response—a known reward for a known action—takes learning only to the first step. After that, stimuli must be unpredictable in order to maintain responses and continue engaging experience-dependent genes. If we *expect* a reinforcement for a certain response, the novelty value of that reinforcement quickly wears off and learning stops. It is the unexpected, not the known, that commands our attention.[50]

Rossi calls this the *novelty-numinosum-neurogenesis* effect, and characterizes it as a "core dynamic of psychobiology. It integrates experiences of mind (sensory-perceptual awareness of novelty with the arousal/motivational aspects of the numinosum) with biology (gene expression, protein synthesis, neurogenesis, and healing).... Activity-dependent creative experiences in the arts, cultural rituals, humanities, and sciences as well as the peak experiences of everyday life are all manifestations of the novelty-numinosum-neurogenesis effect. When reviewing awesome art or architecture, when moved by cinema, music, and dance, when enchanted by drama, fantasy, fairy-tale, myth, or poetry, we are experiencing mythopoetic transmissions of the numinosum...."[51] Every time you expose yourself to such learning experiences, you are taking an important step toward health and long-term mental acuity.

A fascinating series of experiments examined how we can fool ourselves into believing we saw or did something when, in fact, we did not—and those beliefs translate into neurochemicals. In one study, 148 young British college students were served in a bar. Everything about the bar was real: the bottles, the glasses, the napkins, the sights, and the smells.

Unbeknownst to the experimental group, there was one thing that was fake: the alcohol. Researchers had substituted the alcohol in the bottles of spirits, beer, and wine with mere tonic water. The bartenders mixed the drinks as though they were serving the real McCoy, and *the subjects became tipsy,* acting in a manner similar to the control group, who were being served the real thing. Their bodies generated the neural signals and neurochemicals resulting in intoxicated behavior *simply because the students held the belief* that they were drinking real alcohol. "'When students were told the true nature of the experiment at the completion of the study, many were amazed that they had only received plain tonic, insisting that they had felt drunk at the time,' the researcher commented, concluding that, 'It showed that even thinking you've been drinking affects your behavior.'"[52] Beliefs create behavior.

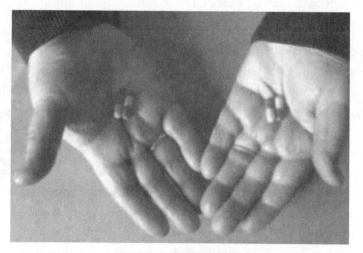

Which is the placebo?

An experiment at Yale showed that students' perceptions of a stranger could be altered by a stimulus as innocuous as handing them a cup of coffee. On the way to the lab, not knowing they were subjects in a study, students bumped into a lab assistant burdened with clipboards and books—and a cup of coffee. The laden assistant asked the student to hold the coffee for a moment. It was either a mug of steaming java or a cup of iced coffee.

When they got to the lab, students then rated a hypothetical person they read about. Those who had held the iced coffee rated the person as colder, more selfish, and less social. Students who had momentarily held the hot coffee did the reverse. In another study, students playing a game at a table with a briefcase at the other end were much more competitive than those whose table held a backpack. It seems incredible, but even such tiny cues can condition perceptions and behavior.[53] Other studies show that our bodies produce endorphins in response to a placebo. Beliefs become biochemistry.[54]

What's happening in our brains can override what's happening in our bodies. Under hypnosis, subjects can be induced to really "see" things that aren't there. They can be trained to look at common English words, and perceive them to be gibberish. In a provocative summary of this research published in the *New York Times,* Dr. Amir Raz said that the brain's internal beliefs and perceptions, "'overrode brain circuits devoted to reading and detecting conflict.' A number of other studies of brain imaging point to similar top-down brain mechanisms.... Top-down processes override sensory, or bottom-up information, said Dr. Stephen M. Kosslyn, a neuroscientist at Harvard. People think that sights, sounds, and touch from the outside world constitute reality. But the brain constructs what it perceives based on past experience, Kosslyn said." Beliefs can create reality.

Researchers have noticed that we can still read and make meaning out of words even if they are jumbled. Read the following three paragraphs quickly:

Olny srmat poelpe can raed tihs.

I cdnuolt blveiee taht I cluod aulaclty uesdnatnrd waht I was rdanieg. The phaonmneal pweor of the hmuan mnid, aoccdrnig to rscheearch at Cmabrigde Uinervtisy, maens taht it deosn't mttaer in waht oredr the ltteers in a wrod are, the olny iprmoatnt tihng is taht the frist and lsat ltteer be in the rghit pclae. The rset can be a taotl mses and you can sitll raed it wouthit a porbelm.

Tihs is bcuseae the huamn mnid deos not raed ervey lteter by istlef, but the wrod as a wlohe. Amzanig, huh? And I awlyas tghuhot slpeling was ipmorantt! Now you can tlel tehm taht it inst! Plseae aslo tlel all yuor fneirds to buy *The Ginee in Yuor Gnees* bceuase it's scuh an azaming book!

You probably found that you could scan and comprehend these words almost as fast as if they had been unscrambled. There are also many visual tricks like the one below. An object or word can seem one thing, or seem another, depending on our perceptions.

Good or evil? Reality doesn't change, though our perception may

A team at Yale came to the startling realization that "the cortical map reflects our perceptions, not the physical body," adding that, "the brain is reflecting what we are feeling, even if that's not what really happened." Anna Roe, the chief researcher, said, "We think we know what's out there in the physical world, but it's all interpreted by our brains. Everything we sense is an illusion to a degree."[55]

One possible mechanism to explain the ability of our brains to override our senses is the surprising recent discovery that the bundles of nerve cells running from our brain to our *senses outnumber the ones running in the other direction* by a factor of ten to one! For every neural bundle running from our senses to our brain, there are roughly *ten* neural bundles running from our brain to that sensory organ. So there's a lot more bandwidth for signals going *from* the brain than there is for signals going *to* it. University of Oregon neuroscientist Michael Posner, PhD, says, "The idea that perceptions can be manipulated by expectations is fundamental to the study of cognition."[56]

Since we are building these neural pathways with every thought and feeling, we have an opportunity, by taking control of the quality of our thoughts and feelings, to build a neural network focused on the transmission of positive, healing, and joyful impulses. As we consciously cultivate these mental and emotional states, which then become ingrained in our neural network, we may indeed see, in time, the beautiful world we imagine. A wise fool exclaimed: "If I hadn't believed it, I wouldn't have seen it with my own eyes."

Designing Happiness

Far from who and what we are being determined by our genes, we are rewriting the expression of our genes in every second, by our choices of what to do, say, and think. The choices we make with our consciousness are being genetically encoded in our brain structure daily, reinforcing the neural pathways that correspond to experiences we have frequently, and reducing pathways we use infrequently. But more than the "use or lose it" axiom, activity-dependent genetic expression tells us that we can "experience it and create it" as we encode new pathways in our brains deliberately.

This research reminds us that we hold many of the levers of healing in our own hands. It makes us aware that it is not doctors, hospitals, acupuncturists, homeopaths, chiropractors, energy workers, or other health professionals who determine our sickness and health. They can tilt the balance, but not nearly as much as we can.

Each of us, as individuals, creates a big chunk of our emotional and mental environment, thereby turning genes on and off in our cells. This opens up vast and exciting potential. While it may require hundreds of scientific studies to chart the links between specific environmental influences and the expression of particular genes, you don't need to wait till they're published in order to improve your own health right now. You can grab the epigenetic levers of health and start moving them immediately.

This research is also an antidote to the helplessness that many patients report when enmeshed in the medical system. When we realize that we have some conscious control over the biochemical environment in which we bathe our cells, we suddenly become acutely aware of which ingredients we are dropping into the stew. Like an expert chef, we can choose to put only tasty thoughts and feelings into our cells. We would no more put toxic thoughts into our consciousness than we would throw rat poison into our soup.

We likewise become aware of which emotions we harbor. We perceive emotions not simply as arising from experiences that happen *to us,* but as aspects of our environmental cocktail that we can *cultivate* to bring beauty and nourishment to the garden of our health. Over the last few decades, research has sought to understand the mechanisms that underlie the health effects of positive consciousness. We know that altruism, optimism, prayer, meditation, spirituality, social connectedness, gratitude, intention, and energy medicine have positive effects on health and longevity. Now we're starting to understand that our consciousness conditions our genetic expression, moment by moment. This insight allows us to *use consciousness change as a medical intervention.* For instance, studies have shown meditation to have benefits that are similar to antidepressant medications, regulating the serotonin and dopamine levels in our brains, as well as stimulating our immune systems.[57] Other research shows that we can alleviate our brain's response to chronic pain through meditation.[58] Knowing that we can unlock a hugely beneficial internal pharmacopeia of gene-altering, naturally occurring substances through consciousness, without any of the side effects of artificial drugs, gives us powerful leverage for well-being.

4

The Body Piezoelectric

I'm deeply sure that we will never be able to understand the essence of life, if we restrict ourselves to the molecular level.... A surprising subtlety of biological reactions is stipulated by the mobility of electrons and can be explained only from the position of quantum mechanics.

—Albert Szent-Györgyi, Nobel Laureate, 1968

Electricity and magnetism are at the foundation of medicine, ancient and modern. Electrical pulses from heart pacemakers regularize the heartbeats of tens of thousands of cardiac patients. Electromagnetic devices like MRIs, EEGs, and EKGs allow doctors to scan the insides of patients' bodies without resorting to risky and invasive surgery.

The effects of electrical shocks were observed by the Greeks and Romans more than two thousand years ago. In his dialog *Meno,* set down around 400 BCE, Plato described a stupefying electric fish, the torpedo fish, that lived in the Mediterranean Sea. His near-contemporary Aristotle observed that the torpedo fish would narcotize its prey. In 100 CE, the Roman writer Pliny also commented that the torpedo fish, while not sluggish itself, would induce torpor in

111

other fish, and described "how to extract the medicinal ingredient of the torpedo fish into oils and ointments used for various ailments."[1]

Piezoelectricity is one of the most fascinating forms of electricity, and one that is essential to the understanding of the mechanisms of healing. Piezoelectricity is generated by mechanical means. When pressure is applied to certain structures, they polarize into positive and negative electrical poles, and generate electricity.

Cardiac pacemaker:
A common application of an electromagnetic field in medicine

A common application of piezoelectricity is the lighter in your home barbecue, or a modern gas grill. When you turn the knob on your grill to the "light" position, you hear a clicking sound. That sound is a ceramic plate being struck by a metal pin. The ceramic material is piezoelectric; in response to mechanical stress, it produces an electric spark that ignites the gas used in the burners.

The first documented use of piezoelectricity was by the Ute Indians, who lived in what is now the American state of Colorado. They created hollow rattles made of buffalo hide, into which they inserted quartz crystals. When the rattle was shaken, the quartz crystals struck each other, creating a mechanical stress that generated a piezoelectric discharge in the form of light. The light shone through the translucent skin of the rattles. During sacred ceremonies, thousands of years ago, the rattles would be shaken, and would glow in the darkness of the Colorado night, calling the spirits into the sacred circle.

Ute quartz rattle

Marie Curie was the first woman in France to receive a doctoral degree. She and her husband, Pierre Curie, discovered the medicinal effects of radiation and coined the term "radioactivity." Together with Jacques, his brother, Pierre Curie first demonstrated the effects of piezoelectricity in 1880 by showing that many different types of crystals generate minute currents of electricity when subjected to mechanical stress. Marie's medical research leading to the development of practical X-ray machines was facilitated by her husband's development of sensitive piezoelectric measurement devices. Pierre and Marie Curie received the Nobel Prize for physics in 1903 for their work. Marie also later received a second Nobel Prize, in 1911, becoming the first person to win or share two Nobel prizes.

The First World War saw the first large-scale application of piezoelectricity, with the development of sonar. Developed to track submarines underwater, sonar devices employ the piezoelectric characteristics of quartz crystals sandwiched between two steel plates. When current is passed through the plates, the quartz crystal produces a sudden motion that results in a sharp chirp being sent out underwater. By measuring the length of time it takes for the echo of that chirp to bounce off the hull of another vessel and return to its point of origin, the sonar operator can determine the distance of the other vessel. As the distance changes over time, the sonar operator can also determine the other vessel's speed.

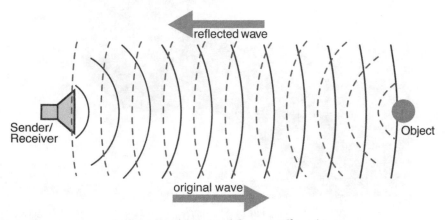

A sonar signal is emitted, bounces off an object,
and returns to the originating source

The success of sonar a century ago prompted intense interest in, and development of, piezoelectric devices. Among them were phonograph needles, microphones, and television remote controls. The piezoelectric principle is used today in thousands of advanced applications, including echo-locating units in some new cars that sense the distance between the bumper and an approaching object, and sound a proximity warning alarm.

So what are gas grills, car electronics, and Indian rattles doing in a book about the link between consciousness and your cells? The answer is simple: The human body is also a piezoelectric generator, and some of the structures in your anatomy have, as one of their primary purposes, the conduction of piezoelectricity from one part of your body to another. Energy is the currency in which all transactions in nature are given or received.

When you sign up for a massage and lie on the table having your muscles stroked, you are having a direct experience of a piezoelectric

114

effect on the human body. Any kind of mechanical stimulation of the body creates piezoelectricity. This includes not-so-pleasant sources of piezoelectric stimulation, such as banging your shin against a table while navigating a dark room. Either of these experiences creates a piezoelectric charge in the cells surrounding the point of contact, and a piezoelectric current that travels along the most conductive channel available within the body.

Many kinds of tissue in our bodies have piezoelectric properties, including bone,[2] actin, dentin, tendon, and our tracheal and intestinal linings, as well as the nucleic acids of our individual cells.[3] Tendons and ligaments are part of the connective tissue system. Sheaths of connective tissue surround every organ in our bodies, and the connective tissue system encases and joins all the other structures. Via it, information is continuously flowing through your body in the form of electromagnetic currents. Although there are many varieties of electromagnetic activity generated by our cells, as well as electromagnetic fields affecting the body from the external environment, piezoelectric induction is an important method of cellular signaling used in the body's internal environment to receive and transmit information.

Electrical Medicine in Western Science

The link between electrical currents and healing has been recognized for centuries. The term "electricity" was coined by William Gilbert in 1600 in his book *De Magnete*. A few decades later, electricity was being artificially generated, stored, and transmitted. Stephen Gray, in the early 1700s, showed that some materials were better conductors of electricity than others. Another Stephen, Stephen Hales, applied this insight to physiology, speculating that nerves might conduct electricity within the body. It was not long before adventurous researchers began to apply electricity to medicine. In 1753, Johann Schaeffer published *Electrical Medicine,* the first book on the subject. And Luigi Galvani demonstrated in 1786 that static electricity generated outside the body could be conducted through the nervous system to produce the contraction of a muscle within the body.

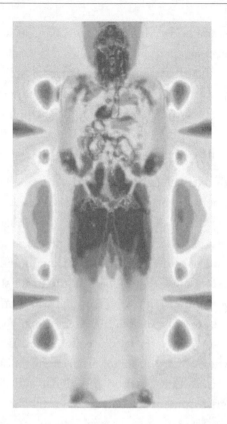

*Human field image generated by an advanced experimental MRI designed by the
Magnetic Resonance Group at the University of Nottingham, England*

In the 1830s, Carlo Mateucci demonstrated that injured tissues generate an electrical current, and in 1868, Jules Bernstein first described "bioenergy," in which positively charged ions generate electricity as they move across cell membranes. He discovered that negatively charged chloride ions cling to the inside of a cell membrane, while positively charged sodium ions cling to the outside of the membrane. When a nerve receives an impulse from an adjoining synapse, the polarization reverses momentarily. This change of polarization ripples down the axon like an electrical current, transmitting energy from one end of the neuron to the other. However, the chemical nature of this exchange led scientists toward chemical explanations for the body's signaling systems, and electromagnetic signals that occurred outside the well-understood mechanisms of the nervous system began to receive less experimental scrutiny.

One of the nineteenth century's most influential researchers, Emil Du Bois-Reymond, constructed a device to demonstrate the effect of electricity, conducted through nerves, on living tissue. A species of fish known to emit electrical impulses was wired to the nerves of a frog's leg. When the fish generated a current, the frog's leg twitched, pushing a lever, which rang a bell—history's first example of a biotechnology machine.

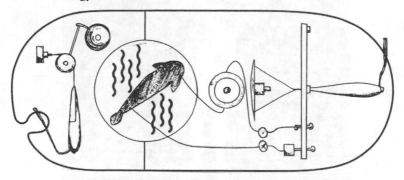

Nineteenth-century demonstration of the
conduction of electricity in the nervous system

The application of electricity to medicine accelerated in the twentieth century. In 1902, a Frenchman named Leduc reported that he could narcotize animals with a current of 35 volts AC at a frequency of 100 cycles per second. In the United States, however, the 1910 Flexner Report castigated electromagnetism in medicine as "irregular science," stunting its exploration and development. Meanwhile, in Europe, progress continued: In 1924, Willem Eindhoven, a Dutch physician, won the Nobel Prize for his discovery that the heart generated its own electromagnetic field. At that time, measurement of the heart's field required the use of the most sensitive instruments available; today scientists are able to detect electrical and magnetic fields millions of times fainter.

In 1929, Hans Berger, using progressively more sensitive galvanometers, was able to detect and describe the brain's electrical field.

The heart has by far the strongest magnetic field of any organ; it's about five thousand times stronger than that of the brain.[4] Berger's work contributed to the development of the electroencephalogram (EEG), which maps the electrical field of the brain. Later, the magnetic fields of the heart and brain were mapped by magnetocardiograms and magnetoencephalograms.

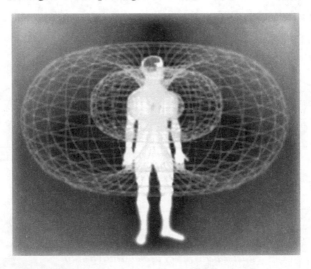

Electromagnetic field of the human heart[5]

In the 1960s, Robert Becker, MD, demonstrated improved regeneration of limbs in salamanders after stimulation by an electrical current. This work was later applied to humans, where it was shown to reduce the time it took for bone fractures to heal. In the 1970s, Nobel Laureate Albert Szent-Györgyi reminded scientists that: "Molecules do not have to touch each other to interact. Energy can flow through...the electromagnetic field."[6] He was also "impressed by the subtlety and speed of biological reactions, [and] proposed that proteins may be semiconductors."[7] This was in sharp contrast to the prevailing view, which focused research on mechanical and chemical interventions such as drugs and surgery, and sneered at the possibility that invisible energy could be affecting cells.

Electromagnetic energy is fundamental to living organisms. Certain strains of bacteria orient themselves to Earth's magnetic field. They have been shown to contain microcrystals of magnetite, a black mineral form of iron oxide. Particles of magnetite are the smallest magnets occurring in nature. Small crystals of this magnetic substance are present in the brains of certain animals that require the ability to orient to Earth's magnetic field, such as homing pigeons, bees, and migratory fish.[8] Magnetite was discovered in human brain tissue cells in 1992.[9] It occurs in linear chains of up to eighty crystals, often attached to a membrane.

Chain of magnetite crystals

Magnetite crystals in human hippocampus

Magnetite microcrystals have been linked to our ultradian and circadian rhythms. We demonstrate this effect every time we fly a great distance and experience jet lag, as our body's circadian rhythms adapt to a new diurnal pattern, and our personal electromagnetic field has to adapt to its new location on Earth's electromagnetic grid. Minute electromagnetic changes can cause the brain to produce norepinephrine, a neurotransmitter involved with the stress response.[10]

The more we look for electromagnetism in nature, the more we find it. Images from GPS satellites available on Google Earth have recently allowed researchers to determine that some large mammals like cows also have the ability to sense Earth's magnetic field. Cows orient themselves to magnetic north. At high latitudes, where the geographic pole and the magnetic pole are far apart, they orient toward the magnetic pole, not the geographic one.[11] It is possible that humans have some similar ability, which could explain improbable navigational feats, like the ability of Tahitian navigators in outrigger canoes to paddle their way across five thousand miles of trackless ocean to Hawaii. On his first voyage to Tahiti, in 1769, the British captain James Cook picked up a Tahitian guide named Tupaia. Wherever the mariners traveled subsequently, even thousands of miles away, Tupaia was able to point correctly in the direction of Tahiti, whether it was day or night, a feat that Captain Cook could repeat only after using his sextant and compass.

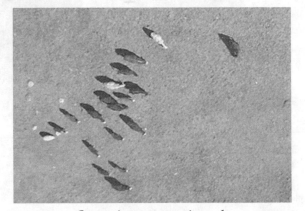

Cows orient to magnetic north,
regardless of where they are on Earth's surface

When water is exposed to magnetic fields, then examined using infrared spectroscopy, it demonstrates reduced hydrogen bonding and other minute changes in its molecular structure. In a seminal series of experiments by Bernard Grad, PhD, of McGill University, these same molecular changes were demonstrated in samples of water on which healers had performed "the laying on of hands." Grad performed scores of experiments on seed germination and plant growth over many years. He found that when seeds were watered with the water that had been held by the healer, they grew significantly faster and larger than those that received water that had not been held.[12]

He wondered if the reverse effect might not also be true. So he compared the growth of control groups of plants with the growth of plants given water that had been held by patients being treated for psychotic depression. Sure enough, plants irrigated with the unhappy water demonstrated very little germination, and significantly slower growth of those seeds that did sprout.[13] Grad later confirmed similar effects of the "laying on of hands" in the healing of cancers and wounds in laboratory animals.[14] Grad's experiments were later replicated and extended by other researchers.[15] They provide a foretaste of more recent experiments showing that the fields generated by the hands of healers exhibit the same frequencies employed by electromagnetic healing devices. Therapists practicing Qigong and other forms of energy healing have been found to emanate large electromagnetic fields from their hands.[16,17]

Ciba-Geigy, a giant multinational pharmaceutical company, patented a process to create genetic mutations in fish eggs—using only electrical fields. Using their process, "They were able to grow trout having distinctive hooked jaws that had been extinct for 150 years."[18] Both mechanical generators of electromagnetic fields, and human ones, can produce fields with epigenetic properties.

A report from the U.S. National Institutes of Health states that "bioelectromagnetics essentially underlies biochemistry, in that chemical reactions of biological importance are mediated by the electromagnetic force."[19] Electrical and magnetic signals also initiate protein folding and regulate DNA. A recent report from the Institute of Electrical and Electronics Engineers (IEEE) reviews twenty-five years of research in electromagnetism to spell out the precise cybernetic mechanisms by which cells harmonize their activities. It states that cells rely on a low-voltage electromagnetic circuit to transmit information, whereas they use a chemical circuit to transmit power.[20] The weight of evidence for the role of electromagnetism in biology is overturning the prejudices embodied in the Flexner Report, and the century of suspicion that it engendered for the role of energy in medicine. The history of medicine provides us with many such cautionary reminders of how hostile skeptics, more interested in reinforcing their prejudices than in healing, can slow the adoption of therapies with a robust base of evidence, and delay the day when their benefits are available to suffering patients.

Pulsed Electromagnetic Field Therapy

One of the most recent therapeutic uses for electromagnetism in healing is the use of pulsed electromagnetic stimulation (PEMS). PEMS machines deliver timed magnetic pulses at calibrated strengths, and have been successful at treating a wide variety of ailments. PEMS has been successfully demonstrated, in more than two thousand studies, to be useful for treating arthritis, depression, hypertension, multiple sclerosis, Alzheimer's disease, epilepsy, osteoporosis, pain, inflammation, and Parkinson's disease.[21] Magnetic fields also appear to enhance the ability of diseased or damaged cells to utilize oxygen, thus speeding their recovery. The increased oxygen absorption may be linked to another effect of PEMS stimulation, which is that patients report decreased pain almost as soon as the field is turned on.

A magnetic field affects all cells within its range. It travels through bone, beds, and plaster casts. Magnetic fields seem to work by affecting the electrical charge of cells. A normal cell has an electrical potential of about 90 millivolts. An inflamed cell has a potential of about 120 millivolts, and a cell in a state of degeneration may drop to 30 millivolts. By entraining the electrical fields of the cells within range to the magnetic pulses emitted by the PEMS machine, cells can be brought back into a healthy range. Not only are electrical changes observed in individual cells, they are observed in collections of cells, in organs, and in whole organ systems. Entraining the electromagnetic field "intrinsically interwoven into the fabric of the system" assists in the signaling process of large numbers of cells in a coordinated healing process.[22]

Diseased cells show differences beyond their electrical charge. The biological software of invasive cancers, for instance, begins to produce an increasing number of glitches; they show an increasing degree of mutation in the DNA sequence. In the words of a cancer research team at the University of Illinois, Chicago, "there is a consensus in the field that increasing genomic deregulation also appears to be paradoxically associated with increasing malignancy among the most invasive and metastatic tumor cells."[23] The genetic profile of cancer cells begins to deviate more and more from that of healthy cells along with their electrical charge.

A genetic mutation in a sequence is indicated by arrows

In certain types of brain cancer, epigenetic deviations are responsible for more tumors than DNA mutations. When the protein sheath around the DNA does not replicate properly, tumor-fighting genes are silenced. Healthy protein formation is as important as healthy gene formation, and points again to the importance of epigenetic control of the DNA replication process.[24]

One study reported on the results from sixteen medical centers using PEMS to treat depression in three hundred patients who had been unresponsive to SSRI drugs such as Prozac and Zoloft. Patients sit in a special chair for forty-five minutes per session, while magnetic pulses are directed at the parts of their brains linked to depression. Some 45% of the patients in the study experienced relief from depression using this method.[25]

Magnets have shown themselves effective in many kinds of therapy. But until the discovery of magnetite in the human brain, there were few credible explanations of why magnetic therapy "produced improvements in a wide range of medical conditions, including tendonitis, blood circulation, diabetic neuropathy, bone cysts, hypertension, optic nerve atrophy, facial paralysis, and fracture healing."[26]

Robert Beck, DSc, was the first to realize, in the 1960s, that charts of the oscillations of Earth's magnetic frequencies looked a lot like EEG readouts from human brains.[27] Earth's predominant resonant frequency (called the *Schumann resonance*) is seven to ten cycles per second (hertz), with an average reading of 7.8 hertz.[28] This frequency is also common in the EEG readings of humans and many animals.

Beck performed experiments with healers from various regions and religions, including Amazonian shamans, Hawaiian kahunas, Christian faith healers, Indian yogis, and Buddhist lamas, and showed that, at the moment of healing, their brain wave frequencies were virtually identical. Beck discovered that, "the dominant brain wave frequency of sensitives, such as shamans and healers, comes close to 7.83 Hz and may, at times, beat in phase with the Earth's signal, thereby causing harmonic resonance."[29] Before and after the healing moment, the EEG scans of healers looked typical of ordinary states of consciousness. But during the healing state, they all shifted to around 7.8 Hz.[30] It didn't seem to matter from what spiritual tradition the healer hailed. They believed in deities ranging from Kwan Yin to Jesus Christ to White Buffalo Calf Woman. Yet they all appeared to be tapping into a universal frequency of healing that is effective regardless of the belief structure of the healer.[31]

Exposure to certain frequencies can trigger positive or negative stress, and effects on our immune systems.[32] Electromagnetic pulses can alter the production of cortisol in the adrenal glands. "When people are removed from the normal 7–10 Hz background fields by placing them in specially shielded rooms, their EEGs, mood, and diurnal (day-night) neurochemistry change. The thyroid, pancreas, and adrenal glands are all affected by these EMFs."[33] Other experiments have shown that when human beings are removed from these shielded rooms, their normal circadian and ultradian rhythms can be restored by exposing them to ten-hertz fields.[34] Human physiology requires contact with Earth's field in order to regulate itself.

Human DNA has a frequency of 54 to 78 gigahertz, (GHz, or billions of cycles per second). Plant DNA has a frequency of 42 GHz, and animal DNA, 47 GHz. The frequency of human DNA is now being used by some clinical electrostimulation devices, relieving pain in cases that have been unresponsive to conventional drug therapy. These "giga-frequencies" of human DNA may be developed in medical technologies of the future.[35]

An excellent and informative survey by researcher Leane Roffey, PhD, of over 150 studies of "healing energies," some of which measured the electromagnetic energy emanating from the hands of healers, found that more than half of them demonstrate a significant effect.[36] Rossi believes that the ubiquity of healing practices across time occurs because: "Healers in many different cultures developed and utilized many different worldviews and belief systems to deal with essentially the same question: 'How can we use human consciousness, psychological experiencing, and our perception of free will to communicate with our bodies in ways that facilitate healing and well-being?'"[37] It seems that shamanic healers discovered the secret of aligning themselves with Earth's frequency millennia ago, which makes electromagnetism one of the earliest forms of healing, as well as one of the newest in forms such as PEMS machines.

Electrical Medicine in Direct Observation

In the 1950s, a German scientist named Reinhard Voll began to take careful measurements of the electrical charge at different points on the surface of the skin. He discovered that certain spots had a lower electrical charge than others. Voll's instruments revealed that these points of electrical difference corresponded with amazing fidelity to the acupuncture meridians described in ancient Oriental medicine. It seems that the ancient practitioners of Oriental medicine, which boasts a five-thousand-year-old pedigree, possessed the sensitivity to derive, *purely by observation,* a map of the energy pathways in the body similar to one demonstrated by modern scientific instrumentation.[38] Acupuncture is a practical healing application using the electromagnetic meridians these ancients discovered in the human body.

Ming dynasty meridian chart

Studies show that points on the meridians have much lower electrical resistance (averaging 10,000 ohms at the center of a point) when compared to the surrounding skin (which averages a much higher 3,000,000 ohms).[39] Among their other characteristics, acupuncture points propagate acoustic waves better than does the surrounding skin. They also emit small amounts of light and greater amounts of carbon dioxide.[40] When the points are stimulated with a low-frequency current, the body responds by producing endorphins and cortisol. When they are stimulated with a high-frequency current, the body produces serotonin and norepinephrine. When the surrounding skin receives the same current, these neurochemicals are not produced.[41] Other studies compared the stimulation of acupoints with stimulation of areas close by that were not acupoints.[42] One of these studies showed that stimulation of the correct acupoints in people under stress resulted in lowered heart rate and a reduction in anxiety and pain. Another showed that depressed patients were helped by meridian stimulation, with an amazing 64% reporting *complete remission* of their depression.[43]

This indicates that something beyond the placebo effect is at work when meridians are stimulated. Other clinical experiments bear this out,[44] as well as many accounts by amazed Western physicians. Isadore Rosenfeld, MD, writing in *Parade* magazine, recounts the following story: "In 1978, I was invited to China to witness an open heart procedure on a young woman. She remained wide awake and smiling throughout the operation even though the only anesthesia administered was an acupuncture needle placed in her ear."[45] Studies with a new generation of fMRI machines are illuminating some of the changes in the brain that result from acupuncture, especially the role of the meridians in reducing pain and producing anesthetic effects.[46]

Voll's discoveries of the electromagnetic properties of meridians led to some powerful clinical applications, in the form of a diagnostic technique called electrodermal screening or EDS. EDS or "bioresonance" machines use sensors that measure the electrical potential at different points on a patient's skin. They are common in Europe, though rare in the United States due to continued skepticism in the medical profession about the link between healing and electromagnetism.

Voll, and those who developed later applications of his technology, discovered that patients who were exposed to an allergen, toxin, or pathogen would show a change in the electrical fields of their skin. Berney Williams, PhD, of Holos University, an institution on the leading edge of energy medicine education, has done extensive research on the electrical characteristics of the meridians. He has found that the "epidermis and dermis of the skin provide channels of heightened electron conductivity, which are experimentally measured as electrical conductance at acupuncture points on the surface of epidermis. Such channels can be theoretically present within the mass of connective tissue, which...might be associated with the transport of electron-excited states through molecular protein complexes."[47]

The study of acupuncture meridians thus brings us full circle back to the semiconductive proteins first proposed by Nobelist Albert Szent-Györgyi in the 1970s.

EDS practitioners typically have a patient hold a vial of some substance to which they may be allergic. Readings from the machine show whether an allergic reaction is registered. By having patients pick up and put down dozens of vials, containing many common allergens, a profile can be developed of which substances may be triggering a harmful reaction.[48] Some machines, like the advanced Ondamed models, are capable of then sending a compensating frequency back into the body to counteract the effect of the toxin. The efficacy of Ondamed machines is now being explored by leading-edge physicians at the American Academy of Anti-Aging Medicine.

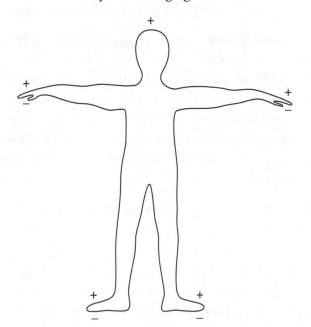

Electrical polarity of human body[49]

Spotting Disruption Before It Becomes Disease

An interesting characteristic of EDS devices, and several allied technologies, is that they can detect *future* predispositions to certain diseases *before* they become manifest through physical symptoms. This predictive capability of energy readings was first noticed by Yale University psychiatrist Harold Saxton Burr, who began studying the electromagnetic fields around animals and plants in the 1930s. He found, for instance, that the electromagnetic field of an adult salamander is present in baby salamanders, and may even be detected in salamander eggs.[50] Even though the egg is round, the outline of an adult salamander can be seen in the field. When a salamander limb is detached, the electromagnetic signature of the limb remains intact. This led him to other experiments in which he found fields around many other organisms. He also postulated, based on twenty years of experiments, that *disruptions show up in the electromagnetic field a long time before they manifest as concrete pathologies.*[51]

Our bodies give us many signals of diseases to come, long before they manifest. A 2004 study looked at levels of c-reactive protein in angry people. C-reactive protein is a stress-related protein; its levels rise dramatically in the body in response to inflammation, and it is considered a marker for future heart disease. The subjects in this particular study were all physically healthy adults who *did not show any symptoms* of heart disease. They were measured for levels of anger and depression using widely accepted standardized tests. The researchers then compared the level of anger in the subjects, and the level of stress protein in their body. They found that the angrier subjects had elevated levels of stress protein in their systems, and were at higher risk for heart disease, even though no symptoms had yet shown up.[52]

If our system is flooded with stress hormones such as adrenaline and cortisol for a few minutes, in response, for instance, to a near collision with another car on the freeway, the incident quickly ends as a biochemical event. However, if we hold onto resentments and emotionally painful thoughts for extended periods of time, the very biochemicals that are meant to save us during an emergency become toxins.

Long-term exposure to cortisol and other stress hormones has a host of bad effects. It suppresses immune response, reduces bone formation, decreases muscle mass, reduces skin elasticity, and damages cells in the brain responsible for memory and learning. If, on the other hand, we quickly release our stress and return to a biochemical baseline, we restore normal cellular operation. And that's vital to our longevity as well as our health. The same precursor hormones are used by the adrenal cortex to make both cortisol and DHEA. Just as cortisol has negative effects long term, DHEA has positive effects. It has "protective and regenerative effects on many of the body's systems, and is believed to counter many of the effects of aging."[53]

Harold Saxton Burr not only suggested that diseases show up in the patient's energy system before manifesting as symptoms, he also believed that physical diseases could be treated by restoring balance to the energy system. In a series of studies published between 1941 and 1947, he measured the electrical charge on women's uteruses. He found that a cancerous or precancerous uterus had a different electrical charge than a healthy one. [54] A more recent experiment also measured the electrical charge of the uteruses of a group of women. The researchers found that the uteruses of women with uterine cancer had a negative charge, while those without cancer had a positive charge. The negative charge in many tumors is assisting in the diagnosis and treatment of breast cancer and other diseases.[55] Conduction is also different in healthy organs and unhealthy ones. When a current is passed through a healthy organ in one direction, the electrical resistance exhibited by the organ is measured. The electrodes are then reversed, and in a healthy organ, the resistance is the same. In an unhealthy organ, however, the resistance changes.[56]

Besides their value in diagnosis, electrical fields have great value in treatment as well. A meta-analysis of fifteen studies of the effect of electrical stimulation on the healing of chronic wounds found that, taken as a group, the wounds of the subjects exposed to electrical stimulation healed 144% faster than those that were not.[57] Indeed, one audacious series of experiments by French doctor Jacques Benveniste demonstrated the effects of electromagnetic fields in a novel way. Increased secretion of histamine increases heart rate. Rather than administering histamine itself, Benveniste simply exposed a beating heart to the *electrical frequency* of the histamine molecule, and by doing so speeded up the rate of contraction.

Next, the electrical signature of a second hormone that *decreases* heart rate was applied to the same heart. It increased the flow of blood in the coronary arteries, just as the organic compound would have done.[58] The electromagnetic signatures of the compounds were having the same effect as the compounds themselves. At one point, to silence his many critics, Benveniste recorded the signals on a computer floppy disk in Paris, and mailed the disk to colleagues at Northwestern University in Chicago. After unwrapping the package and performing the experiments, the American researchers found that the effects of the signatures on the disk were "identical to effects produced on the heart by the actual substances themselves."[59] Other experiments have measured the electromagnetic signal of DNA molecules in a vacuum. The DNA matter is then removed. However, the vacuum still retains the imprint of the DNA's vibrational signature.[60]

DNA Regeneration as Favorite Movie

A team of Russian scientists led by Peter Gariev of Moscow's Quantum Genetics Institute claims to have furthered Benveniste's work. They scan healthy tissues with a laser, and record the wave patterns of the photons (light waves) emanating from the cells. They then convert this information to a wide band wave signal which they refer to as a "DNA movie." This wave signal is then beamed at an organism, either close by, or at a distance. It activates similar programs in the organism's stem cells, and induces them to differentiate and develop into the same kind of cell as the healthy tissue from which the signals were created.

Gariev and colleagues tested their DNA movie theory in a series of three experiments with rats. They administered to the rats a lethal dose of a toxin called alloxan, which destroys the pancreas. The pancreas is an endocrine gland with several vital functions, a primary one being the production of insulin.

In the control group, which did not receive the healing signals, all the rats died of diabetes within four days. The experimental group of rats, after their pancreases had been compromised by alloxan, were exposed to the wave frequencies of healthy pancreatic tissue from newborn rats of the same species. The waves stimulated the stem cells of the sick rats, who proceeded to regenerate their pancreatic tissue.

The experiment was first performed in Moscow, after which it was replicated in Toronto and then in Nizhni Novgorod. In the three experiments, 90% of the rats had their pancreases restored.[61] Advances in the development of high-fidelity acoustic and optical receivers and transmitters open up exciting new possibilities for cell regeneration, without the unpleasant side effects of physically cutting and splicing tissues.

Ultrafast Cellular Communication Through Coherent Light

Living tissues emit light. Biologists scoffed at this phenomenon when it was first discovered, and skeptics still hotly contest it. The Russian embryologist Alexander Gurwitsch first reported photon emissions from living tissues in the 1920s. The principal biophoton researcher in the last half-century, Fritz-Albert Popp, discovered a wide spectrum of photon emissions from living cells. His work was cut short, however, when he was unceremoniously ejected from his university appointment at the University of Marburg in Germany in the late 1970s, his lab shuttered, and his equipment seized. Orthodox biologists at the time regarded the possibility that cells emit light as preposterous and unworthy of research.

Popp went on to found the International Institute of Biophysics in Neuss, Germany, in 1996, which is now the largest of some forty scientific groups working on biophotons. Biophoton emissions have now been discovered in many different animals and plants, and many different cell types, using an instrument called a photomultiplier, which allows detection of these very low-level light emissions. Biophotons have now been observed emanating from liver, heart, nerve, lung, skin, and muscle cells.

Virtually all organisms studied thus far emit biophotons, at rates ranging from a few photons per cell per day to hundreds of photons per organism per second. Distressed and diseased cells emit significantly more photons than healthy cells in close proximity. Researchers have measured the emission of biophotons from cancer cells at four times the rate of healthy cells, making photon detection a potentially useful source of information about the disease.[62]

Guenter Albrecht-Buehler, a biophysicist at Northwestern University Medical School in Chicago, exposed connective tissue cells to light that mimicked the wavelengths of biophotons. The cells moved toward the light. In another experiment, he blocked light from reaching developing cells, and found that they grew in random directions, instead of the regular arrays at forty-five-degree angles in which they otherwise arranged themselves.[63] Reiner Vogel, a biophysicist at the University of Freiburg in Germany, says, "The emission may give a very sensitive indication of the conditions within a cell and on the functioning of the cellular defense mechanism."[64] Biophotons might allow us both to read these cellular conditions and to influence tissues with new signals.

Despite such experimental evidence, die-hard skeptics insist that biophotons are simply random background noise from photomultipliers. Even if they allow their existence, they claim that they are random emissions and that organisms cannot be using them for intercellular communication. Their efforts to discredit Popp and his work have been effective; their point of view still pervades the Wikipedia entries for his work and for many of the other approaches described in this book. This has unfortunately impeded the development of medical devices to make use of the discovery that diseased cells have different biophotonic signatures, which could be of great benefit for the noninvasive early detection of cancer.

The careful experiments of Popp, Albrecht-Buehler, and others indicate that coherent biophotonic signals are exchanged between cells and their environments, and that these might also be a method of intercellular communication at the speed of light. This kind of communications system could send messages simultaneously throughout the body, including to those cells not connected via the neural network, and at a speed many orders of magnitude faster that neural signaling.

The Resonant Melody of Creation

Another dent to the notion that electrochemical signaling through neurons is the only or primary signaling mechanism used by the body came from a group of physicists at Denmark's Copenhagen University. They pointed out an embarrassing fact: "The physical laws of thermodynamics tell us that electrical impulses must produce heat as they travel along the nerve, but experiments find that *no such heat is produced,"* by neural bundles, according to Thomas Heimburg, an associate professor at the university. Instead, Heimburg and his colleague Andrew Jackson propose sound as the mechanism. Other researchers have described single waves called *soliton waves* as a method of signaling. Soliton waves are different from other sound waves in that they have only one peak and valley, instead of a series of them. This allows them to propagate without spreading out, or losing signal strength. Heimburg and Jackson note that nerve membranes, which are made of lipids and proteins, can change from a solid to a liquid state, and that these states can impede or facilitate the travel of soliton waves.[65] It is becoming evident that the body has multiple specialized energetic channels of communication, rather than the slow electrochemical signaling of neurons being the end of the story.

The Physical Channels of Meridians

If we really have energy flowing in acupuncture meridians through our bodies, should we not expect to find some kind of anatomical structure to carry the energy? The acupuncturist's diagram of energy meridians does not correspond to any structure described in conventional anatomy textbooks. Scientists have understandably scoffed at the notion of energy flows, since when a cadaver is dissected, no acupuncture meridians are found.

However, very careful microdissection is now showing that tiny, threadlike anatomical structures are indeed present. They were first discovered running inside blood vessels, and are called *Bonghan ducts*.

Bonghan ducts are minute tubular structures. They were discovered in 1963 by a North Korean scientist, Bonghan Kim, who stained and traced them throughout the body, and concluded that they were the physical channels of the meridian system. Kim's research remained obscure for decades, and was not made public by the North Korean government until recently. Only in the twenty-first century have advanced tissue-staining methods become available to trace these tiny, threadlike structures more precisely and analyze their anatomy. Recently developed methods such as injecting fluorescent nanoparticles into the lymphatic systems of rats have revealed intriguing details of these channels.[66]

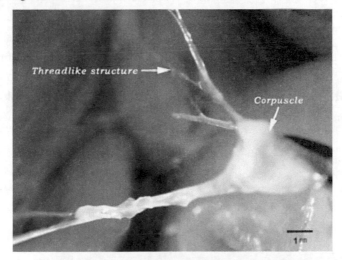

Stereomicroscope image of the threadlike Bonghan ducts branching at a corpuscle on the surface of the liver [67]

Bonghan ducts are so small that they are not visible using light microscopes. They are also often surrounded by fibrin strands, and are thus easy to mistake for the surrounding tissue. Besides being present in blood vessels, Bonghan ducts are also found in lymph vessels and other places. They often contain tiny subducts, and when they divide into these smaller channels, a node is found at the junction. Staining tissues before examining them under electron microscopes has shown that Bonghan ducts contain a large amount of DNA, unlike the surrounding tissue. DNA granules appear to flow through the ducts, raising the possibility that they might be involved in the healing and cell regeneration process. These DNA granules also differentiate Bonghan ducts from the surrounding microtissues.

So what do Bonghan ducts, acupuncture, DNA, and biophotons have in common? Professor Kwang-Sup Soh heads the Biomedical Physics Laboratory at Seoul National University, South Korea. He obtained his doctorate in high energy physics at Brown University in Providence, Rhode Island, in 1973. For the past decade, his institute has been investigating the physical mechanisms of acupuncture and the meridians.

Professor Soh's big insight is that they are all interconnected, and he currently has three teams of exceedingly bright graduate and postdoctoral students working on these research questions. One team studies biophotons, another Bonghan ducts and acupuncture meridians, and a third studies biological magnetic fields. However, they all cooperate on papers as an interdisciplinary team of biologists, pharmacologists, physicists, and physiologists. The result has been an

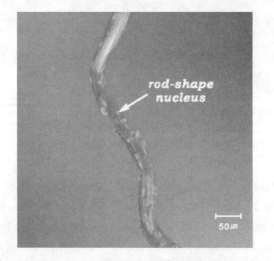

Confocal laser scanning microscope image of Bonghan duct, stained to show the rod-shaped nuclei of DNA granules[68]

outpouring of hard research data linking these fields of study. They study such phenomena as the emission of biophotons from the hands, the propagation of light along the meridians, the similarities between the luminescence emanating from cancer tissues and plant leaves, the effect on the biophotons emanating from mouse brains of changes in magnetic fields, and other advanced phenomena.

One of these studies found Bonghan ducts running on the surface of organs, not just inside blood vessels as previously believed. They form a web on the surfaces of organs. Other studies compare the emission of biophotons from the right and left hands. Professor Soh has also argued that the mass of DNA that does not code for proteins might be a store of biophotons in the protein exciplexes mentioned earlier in this chapter by Professor Berney Williams, and a coherent radiator of light signals.[69]

The possibility that DNA, biophotons, and Bonghan ducts might all be involved with healing opens up intriguing channels of inquiry. Whereas Western research has focused primarily on the nervous system, there are many provocative studies that indicate that the body has multiple signaling systems, some much faster than neural signal transmission. If healing signals do indeed travel through this system, we then have a physical model of how acupuncture, acupressure, EDS machines, and other meridian-based therapies work.

Besides its mechanical characteristics, acupuncture is also an electrical treatment. A little-known fact about acupuncture needling is that it creates an electrical charge. It does so in three ways: The first is that acupuncture needles are stainless steel, with a handle made of a second, different metal. Two dissimilar metals, in the presence of an electrolyte solution like saltwater, generate an electrical current. When placed in a salt solution, such as in human tissue, the two metals generate a small electrical current electrolytically.

Second, after a few seconds in the body, the tip of the needle is warmer than the handle by as much as twenty-five degrees Fahrenheit. The differing thermal gradients stimulate a transfer of electrons from one to the other. The tip of the needle becomes positive relative to the handle. However, if the handle is heated or the needle is twirled, as acupuncturists often do, the tip becomes negative relative to the handle.

Third, the insertion of the needle as it punctures the skin also creates a piezoelectric charge at the point of contact. When the acupuncture points on the energy meridians are stimulated, they may send piezoelectric currents through the meridians. Acupuncture points may, in fact, be portals of enhanced sensitivity through which entire meridians can be stimulated. In hundreds of clinical studies, acupuncture has been proven effective for a wide variety of ailments, from reducing the chest pain of heart patients who have been unresponsive to drugs[70] to the restoration of fertility in men[71] to the control of chronic tension headaches.[72] Many Western practitioners now also hook up their acupuncture needles to devices that produce a controlled electrical current. A current of one cycle per second (1 Hz) passed through acupuncture needles has been shown to raise the level of a patient's beta-endorphins, molecules produced in the hypothalamus that aid in pain relief.[73] A recent survey of studies using state-of-the-art fMRI, PET, SPECT, and EEG scans show brain centers such as the amygdala and hippocampus being stimulated by acupuncture, while sham points are not. Acupuncture appears to affect a wide network of brain regions, including those involved with the processing of emotions and thoughts, involuntary action, and pain.[74]

Interestingly, the same effect can be obtained without acupuncture needles.[75] The massage technique of Shiatsu or acupressure stimulates acupuncture points with the practitioner's fingers, using pressure or tapping. Several Energy Psychology techniques have the doctor or patient tap on certain points with their fingertips, and with correct application are able to produce dramatic and immediate improvements in the patient's emotional state. Acupuncture points conduct electricity even when needles aren't used.[76]

Energy Medicine's Ancient Roots

Although electromagnetic healing devices may be the newest application of energy in healing, the principles on which they are founded go back thousands of years. The ancient system of acupuncture arose out of the study of *chi* or *qi* (literally "breath," a metaphor for "life energy" or what a modern scientist might describe as electromagnetic energy fields). Ancient Chinese medical practices, collected before the first century BCE in a text attributed to the Yellow Emperor, described the cultivation of this life energy, or *qi*. It was thought to be enhanced by various physical postures, movements, and the conscious use of breath. The goal of these exercises was to achieve "a trance-like state of relaxation, wherein the *qi* can be regulated and directed by the mind to correct imbalances in the body."[77]

The principles of acupuncture may predate the Yellow Emperor by thousands of years. The summer of 1991 was one of the warmest in recent European history. During a hike in the Alps, two German tourists, Helmut and Erika Simon, came across what they first thought was the body of a hiker who had succumbed to the glacial ice, as had been the fate of several hikers in the previous few years. The Austrian authorities pulled the body loose from the ice, and only when it had been taken to Innsbruck for examination was it realized that this was no ordinary corpse. It turned out to be the mummified remains of an ancient man marvelously preserved in the ice. Radiocarbon dating showed the body to be from the period around 3300 BCE.

The study of the body, which researchers christened Otzi, has yielded many fascinating clues about the customs, dress, diet, and beliefs of the period. With him were found his copper axe, bow and arrows, and dagger. The remains of his hide coat, grass cloak, leggings, shoes, and loincloth were with the body. Human blood from four different people was discovered on his weapons. A deep cut on his right hand led archeologists to conclude that he might have been in a mortal fight for survival, fleeing high into the Alps before expiring. Later examination revealed that an arrowhead had penetrated a major artery, and would have led to death in minutes.

Otzi was forty-six years old at the time of his death, and among his physical afflictions were intestinal parasites and arthritis. He also had some fifty-seven tattoos on his skin. Some were dark blue dots.

Others were + signs and short parallel lines. Infrared photography also revealed long tattooed lines. But the location of some of the tattoos is fascinating. They correspond with the meridian lines used in acupuncture to treat stomach complaints and arthritis, the very complaints from which Otzi is known to have suffered. The tattoos were either exactly on or within a quarter-inch of traditional acupuncture points and meridians.

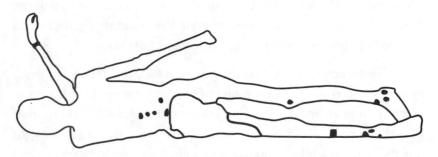

Position of some of Otzi's tattoos

It is thus possible that knowledge of the meridians predates the Yellow Emperor's classic text by thousands of years, and was known in prehistoric Europe, China, and probably India. Ancient sages and shamans developed knowledge of the flow of *qi* without any of the sophisticated technological measuring tools we use today. The Indian sage Susruta, writing around 1000 BCE, described prosthetic surgery to replace limbs, cesarean sections, and cosmetic surgery of the nose. He was apparently an expert meditator. He is said to have been able to become so still during his meditations, so tuned to his body's signals, that he was able to chart the course of the blood flowing through his arteries, and draw an anatomically accurate rendition of their locations! He wrote a book called *Susruta Samhita,* one of the core texts of Ayurvedic medicine.

Human awareness of these energy channels along which *qi* flows is ancient indeed, and methods to enhance the flow may have been part of the knowledge base of prehistoric shamans from many cultures. Of the exercises designed to enhance *qi,* T'ai Chi is one of the most widely practiced in China and the West. It emphasizes large, gentle, slow-motion movements, as opposed to the abrupt offensive movements of other martial arts. The Yang family's style of T'ai Chi, which is the most widely practiced, gained popularity in 1850 when the style's founder, Yang Luchan, was retained by the Chinese Emperor to instruct the Imperial Guard in the art.

Yang Luchan's grandson
Yang Cheng-fu demonstrating the Single Whip position

Adherents practice T'ai Chi by the thousands in parks and public spaces all over China in the mornings. Many believe that it boosts health and increases longevity, a view bolstered by a 2004 review of scientific studies of the subject in the *Archives of Internal Medicine*[78] and a 2007 study showing that it improves the immune system.[79] Clinical psychologist Michael Mayer, a modern Western Qigong master, says that "States of consciousness are expressed in postures, and just as an actor practices 'stances' to enhance the expression of feeling, so does

141

a Qigong practitioner practice his or her stance to maximize power, healing, and the expression of intention."[80]

Exercise is not associated with sacred awareness for most of us. How many times have you seen someone lifting weights while praying, or doing push-ups with reverent mindfulness? Yet in many traditional cultures, exercise and the divine are linked. Constance Grauds, in *The Energy Prescription,* says that "shamans (and yogis and Qigong Taoists) know spirit energy as the power of life itself, and view 'exercise' as a form of active communion with that power.... Sustainable exercise—exercise done with somatic awareness—may be the most powerful discipline for conducting spirit energy. It literally saturates our body with regenerating life force, from our muscles and bones to our very cells. And it takes our fitness and health to a whole new level."[81]

Mapping the flow of *qi* in the body for therapeutic purposes was a primary concern of ancient Oriental doctors. They developed an elaborate diagnostic and prescriptive system, without the benefit of any of the tools we take for granted in the West today. It is a remarkable testament to their powers of observation that so many discoveries on the leading edge of modern scientific medicine are utilizing the same energy pathways they considered so important thousands of years ago. Whether activated by an exercise regimen like T'ai Chi, an electromechanical stimulation method like acupuncture, a biofeedback or EDS machine, Energy Psychology, or your belief system, the point of therapy is to restore full function and balance to the body's electromagnetic energy system.

Frequencies of Healing

The uses for electricity in medicine continue to expand. There are some 100,000 EDS machines in use worldwide, utilizing the electrical potential of acupuncture points for diagnosis and treatment.[82] According to the U.S. Department of Veterans Affairs, some 300,000 patients have permanently installed pacemakers.[83] By way of contrast, in 1959, the Elema 135 was the first pacemaker to be offered for sale. Total number of units sold that year? Two.[84]

There are tens of thousands of EEG, EKG, and other electromagnetic devices in use; the industry is now estimated to generate about seventeen billion dollars a year for the sale of its devices.[85] Transcutanous Electrical Nerve Stimulation (TENS) machines—some oscillating at the same frequency as human DNA—employ minute electric currents to relieve pain and increase electrical energy flow in the meridians. Devices using nano-currents that act at the level of a single cell are in development. We are calling in spirits that the ancient Ute, dancing around their ceremonial fires, illuminating the Colorado prairie with flashes from their quartz rattles, could never have dreamed of.

In our book *Soul Medicine,* pioneering neurosurgeon Norm Shealy and I devote several chapters to the history and clinical applications of electricity and magnetism in healing.[86] In summary, the picture that is emerging of the mechanisms of healing utilized by these techniques is this: Electricity is generated by either the manual piezoelectric stimulation of certain points (acupuncture, acupressure, energy tapping), by distant electromagnetic fields, by quantum fields (nonlocal healing), or by an electrical device such as a pacemaker or a TENS unit. Any of these can produce a beneficial change in the body's electrical field and promote wellness. Dr. Shealy state-of-the-art SheliTENS uses the same frequencies as human DNA,[87] and he has collected many medical histories documenting the healing of a variety of conditions using electrical stimulation, including hard-to-treat autoimmune diseases.

Yet the fact that electromagnetic energy is all-pervasive in life does not answer many important questions. It does not tell us how this force travels, where it goes, or what it does. The answers to these questions lead to some exciting and very new discoveries in an entirely different field of human physiology, discoveries that have the potential to shake up medicine as dramatically as the overthrow of the dogma of genetic determinism.

5

The Connective Semiconducting Crystal

Man is equally incapable of seeing the nothingness from which he emerges and the infinity in which he is engulfed.

—Blaise Pascal, 1623–1662

Connective tissue has not been perceived by the research establishment as a glamorous research target. You don't read breathless reports in the *Washington Post* of research published in the *American Connective Tissue Review*. While you might read a story about research published in the *American Heart Journal* or *Neurobiology*, connective tissue has failed to generate the same level of excitement as other organs. This might be about to change dramatically!

You can think of connective tissue as being a system of bags that contains—and gives structure to—each of your organs, coupled with a system of wires that holds all the bags together. The wires wind through the joints of the skeleton, which supports the structure of wires and bags. Your organs are encased in sheaths of connective tissue called the fascia. The fascia surrounding muscles, called the *myofascia,* terminates in ligaments and tendons attached to the bone.

Connective Tissue System and Collagen

The tendons are composed of twisted collections of collagen bundles, each composed of collagen fibers. Collagen fibers are composed of collagen fibrils, assemblies of molecules secreted outside of specialized connective tissue cells, called fibroblasts. Taken as a whole, the connective tissue system is the largest organ of the body.

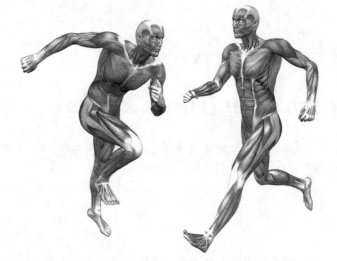

Below the skin and superficial fascia are the ligaments (white areas)

Yet the simplicity and ubiquity of the connective tissue system masks an important characteristic: Connective tissue fibers are arranged in highly regular arrays. There is a name for a *highly regular parallel array of molecules,* whether it's in liquid or solid form: It's called a *crystal.* The collagenous molecules in which all your organs are encased function as a system of liquid crystals. Crystals—highly ordered arrays of molecules—are found in several different kinds of tissue, including:

- The DNA in genes
- The photosensitive rod and cone cells at the back of the eye
- The myelin sheath of nerve cells

- The collagen molecules that make up connective tissue
- Muscle tissue's densely packed molecules of actin and myosin
- The phospholipids of cell membranes

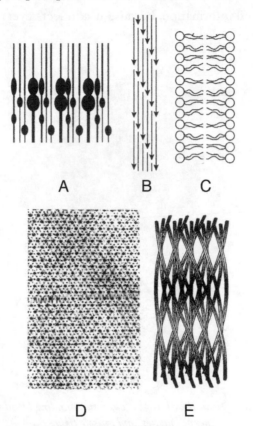

Tissues with highly regular arrays of molecules include (A) rod and cone cells in the eye; (B) collagen molecules in connective tissue; (C) phospholipids in a cell membrane; (D) cross-section of muscle tissue showing actin and myosin molecules; and (E) DNA molecules in a chromosome[1]

This crystalline structure of the collagen molecules that make up your connective tissue has a remarkable property: It is a *semiconductor.* Semiconductors are not only able to conduct *energy,* in the way the wiring system in your house conducts electricity very quickly from one point to another. They are also able to conduct *information;* think of your high-speed Internet connection. Besides many other properties, semiconductors are also able to *store* energy, *amplify* signals, *filter* information, and move information in one direction but not in another.[2] In other words, the connective tissue system can also *process* information, like the semiconductor chips in your computer. Your connective tissue system is well suited for the task of conveying both energy and information, because it connects every part of your body to every other part.

A connective tissue sheath (light color) surrounding blood vessels, nerve bundles, and muscle tissue

Think of the communication possibilities of this structure: *Every organ of your body is encased in the body's largest organ, which functions as a liquid crystal semiconductor* in the form of the connective tissue system. Another property of connective tissue is that it is a piezoelectric substance, which when compressed, generates electricity. "The piezoelectric constant of a dry tendon, for example, is nearly the same as that for a quartz crystal"[3]—the same kind of crystal the Ute Indians used to create light in their sacred rattles.

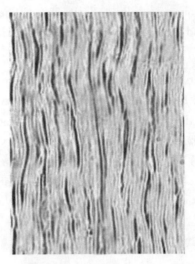

Magnified connective tissue

Semiconduction in Connective Tissues

You can see why it's time for us to start getting excited about the connective tissue system! The importance of its conductive property is hard to overstate, for it explains one of the enduring mysteries of acupuncture: how stimulating one acupuncture meridian point, for instance in the ear, can have an effect on another point, for instance in the spleen. Mae Wan Ho, a researcher who has published several papers on the crystalline nature of connective tissue, says, "Liquid crystallinity gives organisms their characteristic flexibility, exquisite sensitivity, and responsiveness, thus optimizing the rapid, noiseless intercommunication that enables the organism to function as a coherent, coordinated whole."[4]

Intercommunication also explains how tapping one part of the body, which creates a piezoelectric signal, then creates an effect in a distant part of the body, or in the entire body. Electrical signals can be carried throughout the body by the connective tissue. James Oschman, PhD, whose fascinating book *Energy Medicine in Therapeutics and Human Performance* assembles a great diversity of research from many disciplines into an understandable whole, says, "Signals generated by the piezoelectric effect...are essential biological communications that 'inform' neighboring cells and tissues.... The fully 'integrated' body may be a body that is entirely free of restrictions to the flow of signals."[5]

Cell biologists studying collagen reductively would miss these unique properties. Broken down into individual collagen molecules, connective tissue does not have the same characteristics; it takes assembly into a *parallel array structure* to produce its ability to conduct and store energy. The electrical properties of the connective tissue also explain how cells can communicate much faster than the speed of neural transmission.

Speaking into Cells

Each cell also has a skeletal structure. The shape of the cell is partially determined by a system of cylindrical protein "beams" called *microtubules*. Microtubules are the girders of our cells. They are rigid protein structures—the rebar that give cells their shape.

Microtubule bundles in the limb of a simple organism

The unglamorous role of being merely a member of the "supporting" cast has resulted in less attention being paid to microtubules by researchers, who have had much more glamorous cell structures—such as the mitochondria (the energy generators), the genes (repository of blueprints), and the cell membrane (letting signals in and out)—to occupy their attention. Being a piece of rebar in a building is unlikely to attract as much attention as being the facade, the power plant, the lobby, or the elevators.

We think rebars and we automatically assume rigidity. Microtubules do indeed provide cells with the property of rigidity. One of the overlooked properties of microtubules, however, is their transience.

Microtubules are transient in the sense that they are rebuilt often—in some cells, several times an hour. Far from being structures that are created during the division of a cell and which remain firmly in place throughout that cell's life, microtubules are rebuilt often, and quickly. In the June 2004 issue of *Science and Consciousness Review*, John McCrone writes this about the microtubules of the brain: "Do you know the half-life of a microtubule, the protein filaments that form the internal scaffolding of a cell? Just ten minutes. That's an average of ten minutes between assembly and destruction.

"Now the brain is supposed to be some sort of computer. It is an intricate network of some 1,000 trillion synaptic connections, each of these synapses having been lovingly crafted by experience to have a particular shape, a particular neurochemistry. It is of course the information represented at these junctions that makes us who we are. But how the heck do these synapses retain a stable identity when the chemistry of cells is almost on the boil, with large molecules falling apart nearly as soon as they are made?

"The issue of molecular turnover is starting to hit home in neuroscience, especially now that the latest research techniques such as fluorescent tagging are revealing a far more frantic pace of activity than ever suspected. For instance, the actin filaments in dendrites can need replacing within 40 seconds...[and]...the entire post-synaptic density (PSD)—the protein packed zone that powers synaptic activity—is replaced, molecule for molecule, almost by the hour."[6]

The conclusion of this research is that the entire brain is being recycled about once every other month, opening up an enormous field of enquiry into how neurological change interacts with changes in energy systems.

The very skeleton of each cell is being revised several times each hour, as though a building's architecture was metamorphosing each day! Far from the role of the passive supporters to which microtubules have sometimes been assigned, it turns out that they are active daily shapers of the very physical dimensions of a cell's structure. Cutting-edge scientists are left wondering not so much how we can change, but how we can endure.

Yet this is only the beginning of our reevaluation of a microtubule's role. For it turns out that their reformulation of the structure of the cell is not random. Microtubules appear to be *attuned to the energy field in which the cell exists.* Not just mere girders, microtubules may, in fact, also be antennas, receiving signals from the environment and carrying out their complex restructuring in response to these signals.[7] The cytoskeletons of cells are also piezoelectric conductors; "electric fields change their shape, and mechanical stimuli their electrical condition."[8] The role of the hollow core at the center of a microtubule is unknown, though some researchers have speculated that "superconductivity and electromagnetic focusing take place in the cores."[9] Cell biologist Bruce Lipton points out that "Conventional medicine works with the iron filings, whereas a deeper form of healing would attempt to influence the magnetic field. Most doctors don't see the field, so they're trying to figure out the relationship between the filings without even trying to incorporate the energy field in which they exist."[10] Microtubules may be a key resonator with that energy field, and some researchers have suggested that they may play a key role in receiving information required to structure cells from the "orchestra conductor" of consciousness.[11]

Anchoring Cells to the Connective System

An important class of protein sugars, called the *integrins,* conveys information between the environment outside the cell and the inside of the cell. They anchor the cytoskeleton and other internal elements of the cell's structure—even the nucleus—to the connective tissue outside of the cell. So there is a feedback loop, of information going into the cell, and information emanating from the cell and being conveyed into the connective tissue matrix.

The implications of this connectivity are staggering. It turns out that the internal structures of cells are also influenced, through the connective tissue, with the energy environment we are creating with our thoughts and feelings. It is not just DNA that is being affected by our internally produced environment; it is not just our collagenous tissues; it is the very microtubular structure of our individual cells. *Our bodies are more plastic than we once thought, and this flexibility carries with it the possibility of rapid, miraculous healing.*

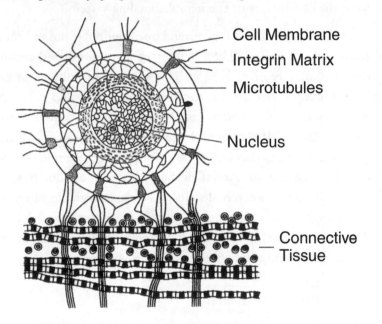

Cell Membrane

Integrin Matrix

Microtubules

Nucleus

Connective Tissue

Tissue microstructures showing connections from inside the cell (nucleus) to the environment (connective tissue)[12]

The chemical signaling mechanisms of the nervous system communicate at a speed of between ten and one hundred meters per second, depending on the diameter of the axon. This is much too slow to explain many human processes. The neural signaling mechanisms described in most medical textbooks today are inadequate to explain, for instance, how a batter can hit a baseball. At a speed of fifty meters per second, there is simply not enough time for the visual image of the ball leaving the pitcher's arm to travel from the batter's eye, through the optical nerve, to the visual cortex, then to the centers of the brain that govern volition, then to those that generate muscle movement in the upper body, then down to the muscles themselves, instructing them to swing. There is only about two-fifths of one second between the ball leaving the pitcher's hand and the completion of the batter's swing.[13] Neural signaling cannot do the job of conveying such a rapid response. Baseball catcher Tim McCarver rightly exclaimed, "The mind's a great thing as long as you don't have to use it."[14] This is just one of many functions in higher animals that cannot be explained in terms of the capabilities of the neural signaling system.

Each cell is going through around one hundred thousand chemical processes per second. These processes are coordinated among a body—a community of cells—that is composed of trillions of cells. Such coordination borders on the miraculous. How do these cells know how and when to create exactly the same reactions at exactly the same instances? In *The Field,* Lynne McTaggart asks: "If all these genes are working together like some unimaginably big orchestra, who or what is the conductor? And if all these processes are due to simple chemical collision between molecules, how can it work anywhere near rapidly enough to account for the coherent behaviors that live beings exhibit every minute of their lives?"[15] Neural signaling cannot even begin to grapple with a cybernetic task of this magnitude.

Rapid Cellular Signaling

If, on the contrary, we assume electromagnetic signals passing through a liquid crystal semiconductor encasing all the organs, with the microtubules in individual cells resonating in sympathy, many such processes suddenly make sense. Oschman sees the connective tissue system as a living network that corresponds to the operating system of a computer, enabling all the parts to work together smoothly.

Joie Jones, PhD, and his research associates have tested the results of stimulation of the vision-related meridian points in the foot, using an fMRI machine. They discovered that when these points are stimulated, neural circuits in the brain's occipital lobes are activated almost immediately, at a rate far faster than neural conduction can explain.[16] In the real world, our bodies function with an integration of stimulus and response at a speed much faster than that of neural signaling. A group of researchers led by Andrew Ahn, MD, of Harvard Medical School looked at the possibility that "segments of acupuncture meridians that are associated with loose connective tissue planes (between muscles or between muscle and bone)" had greater electrical conductivity than non-meridian points, and demonstrated this to be the case in a series of experiments published in 2005.[17] Signals travel through these electromagnetic conduction pathways in the meridians at a pace many orders of magnitude higher than the signals traveling through the neural net.[18] Using a process called electro-conformational coupling, they can then influence protein folding.[19]

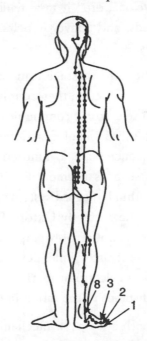

Stimulation of the acupuncture meridians in the foot associated with vision (8, 3, 2, 1) affects the visual cortex in the brain far faster than speed of neural transmission can explain[20]

Just like my brain sending a signal to my body, I can send a signal to another trusted and functional vehicle, my car, when I want to unlock it and drive home. I can do this in one of two ways. One of them takes a long time; the other occurs instantaneously. Attached to my key ring is a car key. I can insert it in the car door lock and turn it, then open the door, reach inside to the other doors, and pull up on the door locks to unlock them, too. Then I can insert the key in the ignition, turn it, and start the car. The process takes me about six seconds, and is accomplished by a physical-mechanical signaling system.

I can also use the other element attached to my key ring, the automatic door opener and engine starter. One click and, presto, the doors are unlocked and the engine starts. It takes a nanosecond to start the process, which is accomplished via an electromagnetic signaling system.

Another example of a physical signaling mechanism is a letter. I can seal it in an envelope, drop it in a mailbox, and a mechanical system of trucks, hands, and conveyor belts will deliver it to the addressee in a few days.

Or I can send the same message using an electronically based system. I can write the same letter, then simply hit the "send" key on my e-mail program. The electronic communication reaches the recipient almost instantaneously. Psychologist David Feinstein, PhD, says, "Electromagnetic frequencies are a hundred times more efficient than chemical signals such as hormones and neurotransmitters in relaying information within biological systems, a calculation based on research conducted in the 1970s by Oxford University biophysicist C. W. F. McClare.[21] This is not terribly surprising when you consider that many of the body's regulatory chemicals travel less than a centimeter in a second while an electromagnetic wave could have traveled three-quarters of the distance to the moon in that time!"[22]

Your body has both systems: a mechanical-chemical signaling system, based on the movement of charged ions across cell membranes and the diffusion of hormones and neurotransmitters; and an electromagnetic signaling system. Both the mechanical and the electromagnetic system can activate cells and genes to accomplish the intent of the user. Yet current medical research focuses almost exclusively on the former, and gives an inexplicably small amount

of attention to the latter. And conventional medical treatment protocols practically ignore the much faster and more efficient energy
signaling system.

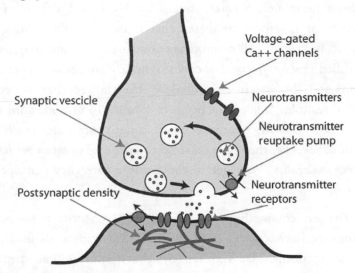

Conventional biomechanical/chemical signaling option

Biomechanical option (key) vs. electromagnetic option (button)[23]

A field of electromagnetic radiation as the cause of the structure of the body and its cells was first postulated by Russian scientist
Alexander Gurwitsch as early as the 1920s,[24] in the same decade
that the energy field of the heart was being mapped by Willem
Einthoven and the EEG was being developed by Hans Berger. Also

in the 1920s, researcher Elmer Lund at the University of Texas found that he could reorganize the cellular structure of small animals by applying an electric current strong enough to override the creature's electromagnetic field.[25] Later studies by Herbert Fröhlich of the University of Liverpool predicted that liquid crystalline phospholipids just below the cell membrane, vibrating at certain frequencies (now called *Fröhlich frequencies*) could "synchronize activities between proteins and the system as a whole."[26] He showed that at certain energy thresholds "molecules begin to vibrate in unison, until they reach a high level of coherence. The moment molecules reach this state of coherence, they take on *certain qualities of quantum mechanics, including nonlocality.* They get to the point where they can operate in tandem."[27]

The semiconductive properties of the connective tissue acting in resonance have a speed and power that far transcends other signaling mechanisms. Mae Wan Ho says that the crystalline structure of tissues and organs results in harmonic resonance of the entire structure: "When the coherence builds to a certain level...the organism behaves as a single crystal....A threshold is reached where all the atoms oscillate together in phase and send out a giant light track that is a million times stronger than that emitted by individual atoms."[28] This quantum coherence means that signals are passed back and forth, in a continuous feedback loop, from cells to brain to tissues, in virtually the same instant.

Communication is a two-way street. Not only does the environment of our thoughts and feelings communicate itself throughout the body via our liquid crystal semiconductor system, but changes in the state of our semiconductor system communicate themselves instantly to our consciousness. Our brains are receiving information from all over our bodies rapidly and continuously, and using this information to shape our choices, both conscious and unconscious. Physiology and consciousness are in an ongoing and inseparable feedback loop, rather than being two separate processes. Oschman calls this the *living matrix,* and summarizes by saying, "The connective tissue and cytoskeletons together form a structural, functional, and energetic continuum extending into every nook and cranny of the body, even into the cell nucleus and genetic material. All forms of energy are rapidly generated, conducted, interpreted, and converted from one to another in sophisticated ways within the living matrix. No part of the organism is separate from this matrix."[29] The resonant nature of the living matrix also suggests that it is possible that *our connective tissue system may be a quantum resonator,* conducting signals from the quantum field of the universe into the body, and from the body to the field.

The signals from our brains are communicated constantly via the matrix of energy conduction within our bodies. Every thought you think is echoing through your connective tissue communication system, turning genes on and off, producing either stress responses or healing responses. This understanding opens up a vast new panorama of potential self-healing.

6

Belief Therapy

If I told patients to raise their blood levels of immune globulins or killer T cells, no one would know how. But if I can teach them to love themselves and others fully, the same change happens automatically. The truth is: Love heals.
—Bernie Siegel, MD, *Love, Medicine & Miracles*

One morning at the start of a busy workday, a part-time employee walked into my office. Her name was Anabelle. Tall, slender, well dressed and poised, with commanding blue eyes and a sharp intelligence, Anabelle was a force to be reckoned with. Except for that morning...

The moment I opened the office door, Anabelle appeared to be in such obvious distress that it was clear she was falling to pieces emotionally. Instead of going to a desk, I took her elbow and guided her to a chair in the waiting room, where, without much prompting, she poured out her sad story.

Her stepfather, Jack, had abused her, verbally and physically, from the age of around seven. She ran away from home at the age of fifteen and rarely visited her parents after that. The last time Jack had hit her was on one of those visits. At that time, she was twenty-one years old. She never went back to the house; it had now been more than fifteen years since the last incident.

In the previous day's mail, she had received an embossed formal invitation to a family reunion. It had been sent to her by her mother, who was still married to Jack, and who was arranging the get-together. Anabelle knew that Jack would be there.

"How could my mother send me this invitation, knowing I'd have to see him again?" she wailed. That slip of paper summarized the whole nightmare of abuse for Anabelle, plus what she saw as her mother's condoning Jack's behavior.

I asked her if I could perform an energy intervention with her that might make her feel better. She nodded wordlessly. I then asked her to remember the moment she had opened the envelope and read the invitation, and feel where in her body the sensation of distress was most concentrated.

She responded, "My tummy," and pointed at her solar plexus. I then asked her to rate her distress, as she thought again about the scene, on a scale of one to ten, with one being calm and ten being as upset as she could possibly be. "I'm a *ten!*" she said through tight lips, with flushed cheeks, her voice rising emphatically.

I did a quick round of EFT tapping with her. The entire process took less than two minutes. "Now think back on the moment you opened the envelope," I asked her. "Remember the scene. Feel your tummy. Then tell me how upset you feel, on a scale of one to ten."

"Zero." She shrugged, and looked at me with calm puzzlement. Then she added, "It was just a scrap of paper, after all." Her belief about the meaning of that scrap of paper, and the emotional charge that accompanied it, had make a 180-degree turn.

The link between gene expression, especially the fight-or-flight emotional responses that Anabelle had been caught up in, and belief is a fertile field for research. Bruce Lipton, PhD, a former professor at Stanford University School of Medicine, is an expert on DNA. His best-selling book *The Biology of Belief* has been hailed by Joseph Chilton Pearce as "the definitive summary of the New Biology and all it implies. It synthesizes an encyclopedia of new information into a brilliant yet simple package." His early research on muscular dystrophy, studies employing cloned human stem cells, focused on the molecular mechanisms controlling cell behavior.

Protean Protein Beliefs

In 1982, Lipton began examining the principles of quantum physics and how they might be integrated into his understanding of the cell's information processing systems. He produced breakthrough studies on the cell membrane, which revealed that this outer layer of the cell was an organic homologue of a computer chip, the cell's equivalent of a brain. His research at Stanford University School of Medicine, between 1987 and 1992, revealed that *the environment, operating though the membrane,* controlled the behavior and physiology of the cell, turning genes on and off,[1,2] work that was subsequently replicated by other researchers.[3] Lipton has pioneered the application of the principles of quantum physics—especially the notion that *the quantum universe is a set of probabilities, which are susceptible to the thoughts of the observer*—to the field of cellular biology. Whereas traditional cell biology focuses on physical molecules, Lipton focuses on the electro-magnetic pathways through which energy in the form of our beliefs can affect our biology, including our genome.[4] In a truly elegant process, "a tiny field, far too weak to power any cellular activity, triggers a change at the regulatory level, which then leads to a substantial physiological response."[5]

Our beliefs—true or false, positive or negative, creative or destructive—do not simply exist in our minds; they interact with the infinite probabilities of a quantum universe, and they affect the cells of our bodies, contributing to the expression of various genetic potentials. There are protein molecules on either side of the cell membrane. The proteins on the external surfaces of the cell are receptive to external forces, including the biochemical changes in the body produced by different kinds of thought and emotion. These external receptors, in turn, affect the internal proteins, altering their molecular angles. The two sets of receptors function like latticework that can expand or contract. The degree of expansion determines the size and shape of the molecules—so-called "effector proteins"—that can pass through the lattice. Together the "receptor-effector complex" acts as a molecular switch, accepting signals from the cell's environment that trigger the unwrapping of the protein sleeve around DNA.

Two individuals may have an identical genetic sequence for a particular characteristic encoded in their cells. The beliefs of the one individual provide the signals that unwrap the protein covering and allow gene expression; the beliefs of the other individual do not. The process is complex; there are hundreds of thousands of such switches in a cell membrane, and which genes are expressed is a function of the configuration of many of them at a given moment. Attempts to correlate a particular belief with the expression of a particular gene are foiled by this complexity. Yet the general principle that our beliefs are affecting the expression of our genes holds true.

Electromagnetic Signaling

An intriguing series of experiments on the effect on DNA of intention and emotion was performed by researchers at the Institute of HeartMath in Boulder Creek, California, led by Rollin McCraty, PhD. The HeartMath experiments show that *measurable molecular changes in the DNA molecule can result from human desires, intentions, and emotions.*

In a series of papers published over the last decade,[6] McCraty and his colleagues look at various aspects of heart function and of DNA modulation under different conditions. They illuminate the relationship of *energetic* to *chemical* transmission mechanisms: "The current scientific conception is that all biological communication occurs at a chemical/molecular level through the action of neurochemicals fitting into specialized receptor sites, much like keys open certain locks. However, in the final analysis, the message is actually transmitted to the interior of the cell by a weak electrical signal. This signal, in turn, can act to either stimulate or suppress enzyme systems. It is now evident that the cell membrane is more than a protective barrier; it also serves as a powerful signal amplifier.

"From these and related findings, a new paradigm of energetic communication occurring within the body at the atomic and quantum levels has emerged—one which is compatible with numerous observed phenomena that could not be adequately explained within the framework of the older chemical/molecular model. 'Fight or flight' reactions to life-threatening situations...are too immediate and manifold to be consistent with the key-lock model of communication. However, they are comprehensible within the framework of quantum physics and an internal and external electromagnetic or energetic signaling system, which may also explain...the energetic communication links between cells, people, and the environment.

"Several of the brain's electrical rhythms, such as the alpha and beta rhythm, are naturally synchronized to the rhythm of the heart and this heart-brain synchronization significantly increases when an individual is in a physiologically coherent mode. This synchronization is likely to be mediated at least in part by electromagnetic field interactions. This is important as synchronization between the heart and brain is likely involved in the processes that give rise to intuition, creativity, and optimal performance."[7]

DNA Change and Intention

An ingenious HeartMath experiment used human placental DNA to determine whether the molecule's double helix coils became more tightly wound or less tightly wound, a characteristic that can be measured by the molecule's absorption of ultraviolet light.

Individuals trained in HeartMath techniques generated feelings of love and appreciation while holding a specific intention to either wind or unwind the DNA in the experimental sample. In some cases, there was a change of 25% in the conformation of the DNA, indicating a large effect. Similar effects occurred whether the intention was to wind the helixes tighter or to unwind them.

When these participants had no intention of changing the DNA, yet generated the same feelings, the DNA changed no more than it did with the control group, which was composed of local residents and students. When trained participants held the intention of changing the DNA but did not move into the emotional state of love and goodwill characterized by heart coherence, the DNA likewise remained unchanged. Heart coherence is a state in which the variability of the heartbeat is highly regular. Positive emotions produce heart coherence, while negative emotions produce large fluctuations in heart rate variability. A high degree of heart coherence is associated with a high degree of efficiency in the functioning of the circulatory and nervous systems.

Anger EEG readout of Heart Rate Variability[9]

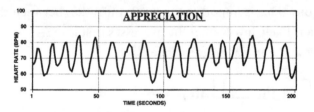

Appreciation EEG readout of Heart Rate Variability[8]

In order to determine just how specific and local the effect might be, in one experiment with a highly trained volunteer, three separate vials of DNA were prepared. The volunteer was asked to wind the DNA spirals tighter in two of the samples but not in the third. Those were exactly the results measured under later UV analysis in the laboratory; changes showed up only in the two samples to which the volunteer had directed his intention. This suggests that the effects are not simply an "amorphous energy field," but are highly correlated with the intender's intentions.

The researchers speculated that the effects might be due to the proximity of the samples to the participants' hearts, since the heart generates a strong electromagnetic field. They therefore performed similar experiments at a distance of half a mile from the DNA samples. The effects were the same. Five nonlocal trials showed the same effect, all to statistically significant levels.

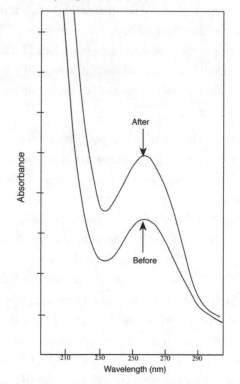

Ultraviolet absorption in DNA before and after being exposed to human intention[9]

These studies demonstrate that the DNA molecule can be altered through intentionality. The better participants were at generating a state of heart coherence, the better they were at affecting DNA with their intentions. Control group participants who were untrained and unskilled at heart coherence were unable to produce an effect despite the strength of their intentions. Both intention and heart coherence were required in order to alter the DNA molecules. The researchers suggested that, "an energetic connection exists between structures in the quantum vacuum and corresponding structures on the physical plane, and that this connection can be influenced by human intentionality." I recommend you take a deep breath, and read the prior sentence again! The implications for healing and transformation are revolutionary.

The researchers also speculated that the positive emotions affecting DNA might play a role in phenomena such as spontaneous remissions, the health and longevity rewards of faith, and the positive effects of prayer. A researcher with Johns Hopkins University observed that "intention, expectation, culture, and meaning are central to placebo-effect phenomena and are substantive determinants of health."[10]

The effects of faith, and the possibility of the direct transmission of energy from healer to healee, have long been understood by human beings. In an ancient apocryphal Chinese story, a student asks a Qigong master, "I understand that the doctors of old didn't have to use acupuncture and herbs." The master replies, "In the old days, energy was transmitted directly. The acupuncture and herbs we use today are a step below the direct transmission of energy." Near the start of the *Yellow Emperor's Classic of Internal Medicine,* the Yellow Emperor says, "I have heard that in early ancient times, there were the Enlightened People who could…breathe in the essence of *qi*, meditate, and their spirit and body would become whole." The direct transmission of healing also has its place in the Christian tradition. During a busy day of ministry, thronged with crowds, Jesus was aware of direct transmission to a single individual:

> And a woman was there who had been subject to bleeding for twelve years, but no one could heal her. She came up behind him and touched the edge of his cloak, and immediately her bleeding stopped. "Who touched me?" Jesus asked. When they all denied it, Peter said, "Master, the people are crowding and pressing against you." But Jesus said, "Someone touched me; I

know that power has gone out from me." Then the woman, seeing that she could not go unnoticed, came trembling and fell at his feet. In the presence of all the people, she told why she had touched him and how she had been instantly healed. Then he said to her, "Daughter, your faith has healed you. Go in peace."

King Charles II laying on hands

The woman who touched the hem of his garment evidently believed in direct transmission of healing grace, and apparently the Master did too, because he felt it flow from him. England's King Edward the Confessor touched many subjects who reported healing, and Charles II is reported to have bestowed "The King's Touch" on around four thousand people each year. Touching is an essential part of human nurturing from birth onward and results in the brain releasing a cascade of neurotransmitters, as well as in gene expression.

Touch and belief are part of religious traditions

The Dispensary in Your Brain

Each of us holds the keys to a pharmacy containing a dazzling array of healing compounds: *our own brain.* We are capable of secreting the chemicals that enhance our immune function, make us feel pleasure, and insulate us from pain. For instance, endorphins, the body's natural painkillers, have effects similar to powerful pharmaceutical preparations such as morphine; the word "endorphin" is itself an abbreviation of "endogenous (internally generated) morphine." Consciousness, acting through the body, can generate the molecules required for healing. Our brains are themselves generating drugs similar to those that our doctor are prescribing for us.

Immediate early genes, those that activate in time frames as short as two seconds, are among the genes that stimulate the fight-or flight-response referenced by the HeartMath experimenters. Some of the changes they produce—increased blood circulation to the muscles, enhanced blood clotting, and pupil dilation—are effected by means of proteins. The flight-or-fight stimulus is particularly interesting because modern humans—we who face few violent perils from the external environment—are capable of turning on these stress responses purely through the quality of our thinking. We can also turn on healing proteins, as researchers studying couple interactions, heart disease, and wound healing have documented.

The Fight-or-Flight Response

When you trigger the fight-or-flight response in your body, it's the equivalent of a head of state declaring war. When war is declared, every industrial resource of a nation is suddenly shifted to the production of munitions. Troops are mobilized, and young people are drafted. The communications and transportation systems of the country are put under military control. Borders are sealed, and security is tightened everywhere. Every one of the country's systems is put on a war footing.

The forebrain, with its big frontal lobes capable of language and abstract thought, is a recent biological innovation. Humans have had the symbolic brain for perhaps two hundred thousand years, the blink of an eye in evolutionary terms. Reptiles, for instance, manage to survive just fine without this complicated piece of machinery. Much older is your body's survival intelligence, which has been around for almost four billion years. A species needs a very good threat-response system to survive for long enough to develop a thinking machine like the frontal lobes.

When you're in danger, though, the body has no use for the frontal lobes. Instead, it relies on your ancient reptilian instincts to keep you alive. The fight-or-flight response hijacks all the body's systems, just like a country going to war. Your muscles tense for action and blood flows to your outer limbs. To get the blood, it diverts blood from your digestive, reproductive, and cognitive systems. Your skin blanches to prevent blood loss. Your pupils dilate. Your blood sugar rises, along with your blood pressure and heart rate, so that you have plenty of spare energy.

This mobilization comes at a price. Your immune system is depressed, as are your digestive and reproductive capacities. As much as 80% of the blood in your frontal lobes drains out to feed the muscles, which is why sages tell you not to make any decisions while you're upset.

When the crisis has passed, everything goes back to normal—if you're a dog or a cat. If you're a human being, you might use your magnificent forebrain to replay the drama over and over again in your subjective reality, triggering the fight-or-flight response in your body thousands of times after the objective need for war has disappeared.

When you *believe* you're under siege, your body has no way of telling that it's just your neurotic mind thinking abstract thoughts. Its old survival systems click into place. That's why the married couples that fight, as well as anxious and depressed patients, have a reduction in their immune function. Their cortisol rises, and the function of the

Thalamus: Routes information from the eyes and ears to other parts of the brain for processing.

Sensory Cortex: Separates threats from false alarms. Was that loud noise a gunshot or just a car backfiring?

Hippocampus: Helps evaluate threats by placing them in context of previous experiences. A frightening noise heard in a place you consider safe is less likely to scare you.

Prefrontal Cortex: Reins in the amygdala if an initial threat is deemed insignificant.

Amygdala: The brain's rapid response system. Sends the body into high alert if triggered.

What fight-or-flight looks like in your brain

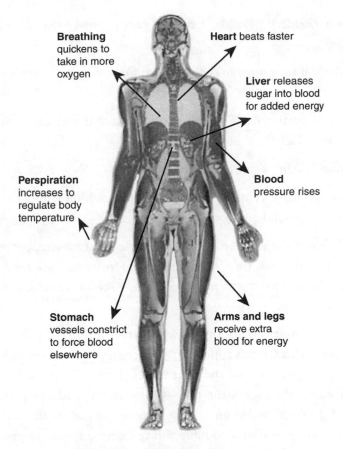

Breathing
quickens to
take in more
oxygen

Heart beats faster

Liver releases
sugar into blood
for added energy

Perspiration
increases to
regulate body
temperature

Blood
pressure rises

Stomach
vessels constrict
to force blood
elsewhere

Arms and legs
receive extra
blood for energy

What fight-or-flight looks like in your body

parasympathetic nervous system, which is responsible for relaxation and regeneration, is suppressed in favor of the sympathetic nervous system, which is the system used in fight-or-flight.

You don't need a woolly mammoth or a Mack truck charging at you to have a fight-or-flight response. A smaller version of the response is demonstrated by the behavior of my eldest son when he was five years old:

Son: "Daddy, want more canny."

Me: "Son, I'll give you some more candy tomorrow, you've already had candy today."

Son (loudly): "Daddy, neeeeed canny now!" (Escalation of response)

Me: "I'll save some in the cupboard for you to have after dinner tomorrow."

Son (assertively): "I'm going to hit sister if you don't gimme canny now!" (Fight)

Me: "Hitting sister isn't okay."

Son (pouting, crossing arms, walking away, hiding under table): "I'm not your friend anymore." (Flight)

Consider the married couple who have an argument, get angry and frustrated, and then withdraw into frustrated silence. The argument represents fight, and silence or sarcastic rejection represents flight.

Think about the meeting at work when Jim says, "I don't feel comfortable with Cindy's approach." The energy in the room changes instantly, and you can feel the hairs on the back of your neck stand on end. Suddenly, there's the prey (Cindy, flight) and the predator (Jim, fight) caught up in an energy dynamic as old as the stalking *Tyrannosaurus rex,* and with no more ability than a dinosaur to produce creative, constructive solutions.

When you start to look for it, you'll see people using mini versions of the fight-or-flight response all the time. It's so basic to the way animals operate that it's present at birth as the Moro reflex, which manifests as a startle response at about nine weeks of age, as the production of adrenaline in the newborn's bloodstream rises in response to a stimulus.

It's essential that we understand this aspect of our biological programming, because it can sabotage the very best intentions of our conscious mind if we don't. Beliefs have profound biological effects throughout every single system of the body, just like the country going to war. If you fail to understand them, you can harbor an ongoing stream of negative thoughts and emotions that make war on your own body.

Believing Good Things

Just as belief can trigger degeneration in our bodies, it can also trigger healing. Research has not yet cataloged all the proteins our bodies produce, but the estimate that scientists use most often is one hundred thousand proteins. Proteins can be assembled in many different combinations, and these combinations are also the subjects of study. The number of known sequences is at least four million, and rising, according to a team of researchers working on a database of human proteins called the Proteonome.[11] A few of them are household words: insulin, hemoglobin, glutamine, serotonin. They work synergistically with all the other systems in your body.

One of the most intriguing ways in which we activate naturally occurring healing proteins in our bodies is the placebo response. In order for new medications to be proven effective in scientific studies, they are required to demonstrate efficacy that is significantly greater than an inert pill, a placebo. A placebo is thought to be effective because the patient believes it is effective. The placebo effect has been recognized for centuries; Michel de Montaigne, a French philosopher, exclaimed in 1572 that "there are men on whom *the mere sight* of medicine is operative!" One of the remarkable things about many medications is that their effects are only slightly better than those obtained from a placebo. Some drugs and surgical procedures have results that are no better than a placebo.

A powerful demonstration of the placebo effect comes from Baylor University Medical Center in Texas. The results were published in the *New England Journal of Medicine* in 2002.[12] Bruce Mosely, MD, an orthopedic surgeon at Baylor University, wanted to find out which of two surgical procedures produced the best cure rate for osteoarthritic knees. Many of his patients had degeneration or damage to the cartilage in their knees, and there were two possible surgical procedures that might help.

The first was debridement. In this procedure, incisions are made on both sides of the kneecap and the strands of cartilage are scraped off the surfaces of the knee joint. The second common surgery is called lavage. High-pressure water is injected through the knee joint, flushing out all the old material in the joint.

To control for the placebo effect, Dr. Mosely instituted a third group. This group received neither debridement nor lavage. The patients were prepared for surgery, anesthetized, and wheeled into the operating room. There, the staff made the same skin incisions they would have made were they performing a genuine surgery. After shuffling around for the same length of time it took to perform actual surgery, the wounds were sewn up, and the patients released for post-surgical recovery. Absolutely no surgery was done to their knees.

Postoperative results were compared for all three groups during various stages of the recovery process. The results were astounding. Patients that had received the "pretend" surgery did as well as those that had received debridement or lavage. In *Soul Medicine,* I sum up the results this way: "In television interviews, some of the patients who had received the placebo operation swore it must have been real, because their knees were so dramatically improved. Some reported the cessation of pain or a vastly increased range of motion. Some who were barely able to walk before surgery were now able to run. Not only had the patient group receiving the placebo experienced recovery rates similar to those who had actually received arthroscopic surgery, at certain points in the recovery process their reported results were better. Dr. Mosely, the researchers, and his staff were astounded." Doctors in the United States perform some 985,000 arthroscopic knee surgeries each year, each one costing an averge of seven thousand dollars.[13] The total cost is nearly seven billion dollars per year.

It's not just the internal pharmacopeia required to cure osteoarthritis that is engaged by the placebo effect. Our bodies are capable of synthesizing many different substances, with radically different chemical structures, within our organs. The four adjoining illustrations of a beta blocker, histamine, growth hormone, and neuropetide represent just four of the millions of compounds your body is capable of synthesizing in response to the placebo effect. The molecules could not look more different, as you can see from their unique shapes. Yet each of these *very different substances* can be synthesized by your body in response to *the same stimulus,* popping a placebo (or fake surgery) to reinforce a belief—a miracle of biological engineering. This ability of our bodies to generate healing factors through belief offers a remarkable therapeutic tool that can be used in conjunction with any therapy, conventional or alternative.

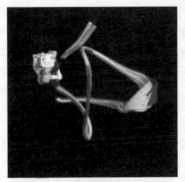

Beta Blocker

Histamine

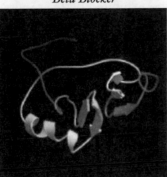

Growth Hormone

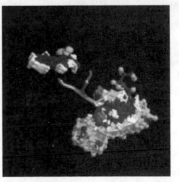

Neuropeptide

Placebos cure patients in about 35% of cases. A drug has to do significantly better for it to be worth taking. Few drugs are up to the challenge. A recent trial of St. John's wort, an herb, found that 24% of depressed patients got better taking it. Zoloft did marginally better, producing improvement in 25% of the patients. But the star of the study was the placebo, which produced improvement in 32% of those taking it.[14] In 2006, the U.S. federal government released the results of two large-scale studies of SSRI drugs. They found that the tests "failed to show that the drugs were safer or more effective than a placebo."[15]

Irving Kristol, PhD, a psychologist at the University of Connecticut who analyzed the results of drug studies for depression, found that about *three-quarters of the entire effect* of antidepressants such as Prozac and Zoloft is due to the placebo effect. Three-quarters of the improvement was due to the patient's belief system. The remainder may or may not have been due to the drug; it was hard to tell because the drug produces *physical sensations* that may alert study participants to the fact that they're taking a real drug, not the placebo—thus *increasing* the healing factor of the patient's belief system.

Kristol later published a second study, a meta-analysis of forty-seven studies of antidepressants from the U.S. Food and Drug Administration (FDA) database. He found that "an average of 80% of the effect of the drugs was due to the placebo effect. This ranged from a low of 69% (Paxil) to a high of 89% (Prozac). In four of the trials that Kristol studied, the placebo exhibited better results than the drug. The mean difference between the placebos and the drugs was a 'clinically insignificant' difference..."[16]

These results are not atypical; Prozac had to go through *ten* clinical trials in order to accomplish *four* trials with a marginally better cure rate than a placebo.[17] Two trials is what the FDA requires for proof of efficacy; currently, drug companies can conduct many trials before they can produce two that show that their drug is marginally more effective than a placebo.

The many studies that fail to show that the drug is helpful are called "file drawer studies," because they're quietly filed in dusty corners and never submitted to the FDA or medical journals—though Kristol was able to obtain them to include in his meta-analysis. The result, according to one respected medical journalist, is: "Millions of people taking *drugs that may carry a greater risk than the underlying condition.* The treatment, in fact, may make them sick or even kill them."[18]

Drug companies may go to lengths to hide the side effects of their products and to discourage negative news from reaching consumers. This is a random sampling of hundreds of published reports of malfeasance:

- An internal company memo advised staffers at GlaxoSmith-Kline to withhold information that Paxil (US)/Seroxat (UK) has no beneficial effect on adolescents. Both countries have now banned it for pediatric use because of risk of suicide. Glaxo's Study 329 found these drugs no more effective than placebo. But when published, the psychiatrists who authored the company-funded study concluded that the drug was, "generally well tolerated and effective for major depression in adolescents."[19]

- A Duke University study found that patients with heart disease who take commonly prescribed antidepressants are at increased risk for a particularly nasty side effect: death. To be precise, they had a 55% greater risk of death.[20]

- In half of patients who receive the best possible care (not available to the general public), antidepressants fail to cure the symptoms of major depression.[21]

- The net benefits of antidepressant drugs over placebo are not considered large enough to be of clinical significance, according to Britain's National Institute for Health and Clinical Excellence (NICE).[22]

- "Stimulants like Ritalin lead a small number of children to suffer hallucinations that usually feature insects, snakes, or worms, according to federal drug officials..."[23]

- From the *Washington Post,* under the headline "Comparison of Schizophrenia Drugs Often Favors Firm Funding Study": "When psychiatrist John Davis analyzed every publicly available trial funded by the pharmaceutical industry pitting five new antipsychotic drugs against one another, nine in ten showed that the best drug was the one made by the company funding the study."[24] What a surprise!

- Medical journals often don't disclose the financial ties between authors writing recommendations and the drug companies funding them. One article in *JAMA,* the *Journal of the American Medical Association,* "must surely have pleased all makers of antidepressant drugs. It warned pregnant women that if they stopped taking antidepressant medication they would increase their risk of falling back into depression. Hidden from view was the fact that most of the thirteen authors had been paid as consultants or lecturers by the makers of antidepressants. Their financial ties were not disclosed to *JAMA* on the preposterous grounds that the authors did not deem them relevant."[25]

- A report in *Pain Physician* journal on national drug control policy concludes: "Opioids are used extensively despite a lack of evidence of their effectiveness in improving pain or functional status with potential side effects of hyperalgesia, negative hormonal and immune effects, addiction and abuse."[26]

- A survey of nearly three thousand severely depressed Medicaid beneficiaries from all fifty states published in the *Archives of General Psychiatry* concluded, "In these high-risk patients, antidepressant drug treatment does not seem to be related to suicide attempts and death in adults but might be related in children and adolescents." Note that ambiguous word "might." In fact, the fine print of the statistics, indecipherable to a lay reader and many doctors, indicates that adolescents on these medications have *sixteen times the rate of death,* and 50% more suicide attempts. Might?[27]

To keep the party going in the face of such depressing news, drug companies drug psychiatrists with money; psychiatrists as a profession receive more drug company largesse than any other medical specialization.[28]

Whereas placebos have no side effects, the same cannot be said for prescription drugs. According to *JAMA,* some 250,000 people die each year from the negative effects of drugs, unnecessary surgeries, infections they pick up in hospitals, and other iatrogenic (doctor-caused) illnesses, making iatrogenic illness the third largest cause of death in the United States, just behind cancer and heart disease.[29] According to a meticulous analysis of data from a spectrum of U.S. government agencies, when all other factors are included, the number rises to 783,966, *making doctors, hospitals, and drugs the leading cause of death in America.* Each year, this costs society an estimated $282 billion. About *twice* the number of Americans die *due to infections acquired in hospitals* each year as the number who die in traffic accidents. Additionally, more than *twice* as many Americans die each year from *the negative effects of prescription drugs* as those who died in the Vietnam war. According to a recent report, an estimated 1,730,000 preventable drug-related injuries occur annually in America along with as many as seven thousand deaths.[30] Exotic drugs are not the only culprits; common acetaminophen, the active ingredient in Tylenol, is the leading cause of death in the United States, due to acute liver failure.[31]

All this tragedy does not come cheap. The costs are truly staggering. The United States spends about three times as much as Great Britain per person on health care, and twice as much as Canada.[32] Both those countries have universal health care—every single person is covered. The United States spends almost twice as much as Germany and France, and more than twice as much as Japan.[33] These are all comparable postindustrial societies and economies. Yet in the United States:

- Infant mortality rates are higher and life expectancy lower than every single one of the countries previously mentioned.[34]

- Americans get substandard medical care more than half the time, leading to "thousands of needless deaths each year."[35]

- Americans are both stressed and depressed; according to one study, "About one in five Americans now suffers from a diagnosable mental disorder."[36]

- A study entitled "Trial Lawyers, Inc.," estimates that the total costs of health-care litigation, direct and indirect, "(including suits against doctors, drug firms, HMOs, nursing homes and so on) could be as much as $200 billion—a Hurricane Katrina every year."[37]

- Health care is one of the most heavily regulated industries. The cost of regulation is reckoned to outweigh benefits by a massive $169 billion per year.[38]

The neurochemicals secreted by your brain, by way of contrast, are free. You do not have to drop a silver dollar in your ear to persuade your brain to start producing endorphins. Neither do your natural biochemicals come packaged with a scary list of side effects. Your body's natural secretions are often the same substances found in prescription drugs, but in doses that will not harm you, in forms that are readily assimilated by the targeted organs and systems, and without the side effects of prescription medications. One of the ways in which you can prescribe them for yourself is through the quality of your consciousness.

Some of the studies of meditation, prayer, spiritual practice, and social goodwill and other intangibles show effects that benefit every single system in the body. Lacking the drama of "a new gene discovered for X condition," they are rarely publicized in the mainstream media. For instance, some studies of spiritual practices and sociable behavior show that they produce a sevenfold reduction in mortality.[39] No drug comes close.

One study, at the University of Wisconsin at Madison, recruited thirty-six Vietnam veterans with coronary artery disease, who were also plagued with traumatic emotional issues. Half the vets received training in how to forgive themselves and others—a consciousness-based medical intervention—and the other half did not. Those that had received the training and practiced the forgiveness techniques showed a significant rise in the blood flow to their heart muscles.[40]

Meditation does not just make subjects calmer; it has beneficial effects on many different measures of their health. A recent study of mindfulness meditation by researchers at the University of Wisconsin at Madison showed that it produces significant rises in a variety of antibodies and blood cells—all associated with increased immune function. This new research shows that, in addition to the other benefits of meditation, it measurably improves the body's ability to resist disease and the effects of stress.[41]

Meditation has been shown to lower blood pressure and improve resting heart rate; reduce the incidence of strokes, heart disease, and cancer; diminish chronic pain; reduce anxiety and depression; and ameliorate many other diseases.[42] If meditation were a drug, it would be considered medical malpractice for a physician to fail to prescribe it. The results of studies of prayer are equally impressive.[43] A single brief period of appreciation and heart coherence in the morning positively affects our immune systems all day long[44] and sets us up with a healthier and more peaceful emotional baseline.

Despite the enormous benefits, such consciousness-based therapies are not paid for by the grotesque amount of money spent on the medical system. Patients wishing to attend a yoga class, join a gym, get a massage, visit an alternative healer, or otherwise nurture their wellness must pay for it themselves. Integrative physician Robert Dozor, MD observes, "To health insurance companies, integrative healing practices appear to be simply another expense."[45] Dean Ornish, MD, ponders, "How did we get to a point in medicine where interventions such as radioactive stents, coronary angioplasty, and bypass surgery are considered conventional, whereas eating vegetables, walking, meditating, and participating in support groups are considered radical?"[46]

Such consciousness-based interventions are safe and noninvasive, and are a good place to begin, no matter what other treatments you elect. At the very least, they can supplement the arsenal of allopathic medicine; in the many cases of "miraculous" cures, they make medical treatment unnecessary.

New Experimental Questions

To get the right answers, you have to ask the right questions. To the scientists of a generation ago, the idea that DNA might be user-programmable was unthinkable. Genes were taken to determine the characteristics of organisms, and that was that. Researchers didn't look for energies that might change DNA expression or combinations of proteins generated by thought, because they were embedded in an orthodoxy that held genes to contain the DNA sequencing around which physical, mental, and emotional development occurs.

It is taking a bold new generation to ask new experimental questions. We're just starting to find out what happens to genes when the environment changes, how DNA responds to psychospiritual experiences, how our emotions affect our health, why energy medicine works, and how we can stimulate the body's internal pharmacy to write prescriptions for healing. The results challenge medical orthodoxy. As the questions become bolder, the answers will become more surprising, and full of good news about the way we can use our consciousness to improve our happiness and health.

7

Entangled Strings

Only in the last moment in history has the delusion arisen that people can flourish apart from the rest of the living world.

—E. O. Wilson

"I n the early 1990s I was in Toronto, Canada. I went to see my doctor because I felt tired and listless. He sent me to have an electrocardiogram. Later that day, when he got the results back, he told me that my heart was at serious risk. He told me to stay calm, not exert myself, keep nitroglycerine pills with me at all times, and to not go outside alone.

"The doctors administered several tests over the course of the following three days, and I failed them all because my arteries were severely clogged. They included an angiogram, another electrocardiogram, and a treadmill stress test. When I started the bicycle test, the clinic staff didn't even let me finish. They stopped me partway. They were afraid I was going to die on the spot, my arteries were so clogged. As a high-risk patient, I was given an immediate appointment for heart bypass surgery.

"The day before the surgery, I woke up feeling much better. I went to the hospital and I was given an angiogram. This involved shooting dye into my arteries through an injection in my thigh. The surgeons wanted to discover the exact location of the blockages prior to the operation. I was prepared for surgery. My chest was shaved, and the doctors were about to mark my skin where they planned to make the incision. When the new angiograms came back from the lab, the doctor in charge looked at them. He became very upset. He said he had wasted his time. There were no blockages visible at all. He said he wished his own arteries looked as clear. He could not explain why all the other tests had shown such severe problems.

"I later discovered that my friend Lorin Smith [a Pomo Indian medicine man] in California, upon hearing of my heart trouble, had assembled a group of his students for a healing ceremony the day before the second angiogram. He covered one man with bay leaves and told him that his name was Richard Geggie. For the next hour, Lorin led the group in songs, prayers, and movement. The next day, I was healed.

"I have seen Lorin facilitate other amazing healings. Sometimes he works in a trance, invoking his grandfather, Tom Smith, who was a very famous healer. When he emerges from trance, he's unable to remember what he has said."

This story was told by former cardiac patient Richard Geggie for the book *The Heart of Healing*. Some fifteen years later, Geggie is still in excellent health.[1] It is by no means an isolated example of distant healing; there are impressive databases dedicated to cataloging studies of the phenomenon.[2]

Two careful studies of terminally ill AIDS patients by Elizabeth Targ, MD, PhD, showed similar results. The patients in her experimental groups were offered remote healing by forty religious and spiritual healers. Some were evangelical Christians, some were traditional Catholics, some were Buddhists, some were independent faith healers. One was a Jewish kabbalist, another was a Lakota Sioux shaman, and another was a Chinese Qigong master. After going through elaborate precautions to ensure that no one in the study could know which patients were being prayed for, the healers were sent an envelope containing a patient's photo, name, and helper T-cell count.

Six months later, the researchers found that those who had received remote healing showed improved mood, significantly fewer doctor visits, fewer hospitalizations, fewer days in hospital, improved helper T-cell counts, fewer new AIDS-defining illnesses, and significantly lower quantities of the HIV virus in their systems.[3]

The results of this study of healing at a distance are not unusual. Researchers have conducted several meta-analyses of distant healing research: Most studies found results far in excess of what might be explained by chance.[4,5,6]

Electromagnetic signaling explains many healing phenomena that cannot be explained by other medical models. The semiconductive properties of connective tissue explain others. However, healing at a distance, or nonlocal healing, cannot be explained by either mechanism. How is it possible for healing to occur when the person receiving the healing is too far away from the person offering the healing to be affected by the healer's electromagnetic fields? Quantum physics and string theory offer us some intriguing insights as to how this might occur.

Subatomic Alchemy

In 1907, a pioneering physicist, Ernest Rutherford of the University of Manchester, discovered that the atom could be subdivided into a nucleus of protons and neutrons, surrounded by an orbit of electrons. He showed that virtually the entire volume of an atom was empty space, rather than the solid substance conceived of in Newtonian physics, and that most of the atom's mass was concentrated in the nucleus. He also demonstrated that electrons were bound to the nucleus by electromagnetic fields. So enamored was he of his profession that he declared: "In science there is only physics; all the rest is stamp collecting." For the ensuing century, medicine returned the compliment by ignoring the discoveries and implications of quantum theory for healing.

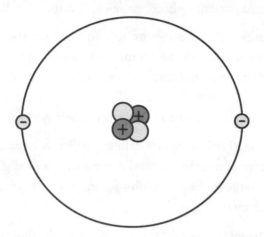

Atomic model circa 1907:
Particles of a helium atom—two electrons orbiting
a nucleus of protons and neutrons

By the start of the twenty-first century, physicists had cataloged dozens of subatomic particles—among them baryons, pentaquarks, mesons, leptons, axions, neutrinos, muons, and bosons. Many particles have characteristics that challenge our perception of linear time and orderly space, by manifesting into existence, then disappearing again only to repeat the cycle. We have observed matter vanishing into energy, then winking back in somewhere else as a different type of particle.

Even more unsettling, rather than fixed realities, these energies exist in the form of an infinite set of possibilities, a "possibility wave," out of which probabilities emerge. Quantum physics can calculate a range of "possible events for electrons and the possibility of these possible events, but cannot predict the unique actual event that a particular measurement will precipitate."[7]

Theoretically, any of the swarm of infinite possibilities present in the possibility wave can become reality. But only one does. The swarm is then said to have "collapsed" into a particular reality. One of the factors that determine the direction in which the swarm of possibilities collapses is the *act of observation*. In a quantum universe, phenomena and space and time are affected by the observer. All possibilities exist in the quantum field; the act of observation collapses them into probability.

"In the realm of possibility," says quantum physicist Amit Goswami, PhD, "the electron is not separate from us, from consciousness. It is a possibility of consciousness itself, a material possibility. When consciousness collapses the possibility wave by choosing one of the electron's possible facets, that facet becomes actuality."[8] So the scientific mind, rather than impartially witnessing objective phenomena, is itself influencing which of the infinite sea of potentials winks into existence as a phenomenon. Goswami continues, "The agency that transforms possibility into actuality is consciousness. It is a fact that whenever we observe an object, we see a unique actuality, not the entire spectrum of possibilities. Thus, conscious observation is sufficient condition for the collapse of the possibility wave."[9]

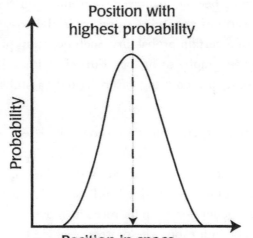

Distribution of quantum probability[10]

This is called the "observer effect." Though first observed in physics, it holds true in other disciplines. Douglas Yeaman and Noel McInnis remind us in the book *Einstein's Business* that, "A major scientific precedent for managing our outcomes was set by quantum physicists who, when seeking to determine whether light consists of particles or waves, discovered that light invariably behaves in compliance with their experimental expectations. Light always and only behaves like waves in experiments designed to detect waves, yet just as consistently shows up as particles in experiments designed to detect particles. In both cases, experimental outcomes conform to the experimenters' expectations." Physicist Werner Heisenberg said, "What we observe is not nature itself, but nature exposed to our method of questioning." In *The Intention Experiment,* her book about a large international experiment under way to gauge the effect of human intention on physical matter, Lynne McTaggart says that the observer effect implies that "living consciousness is somehow central to this process of transforming the unconstructed quantum world into something resembling everyday reality," and that "reality is not fixed, but fluid, and hence possibly open to influence."[11]

A gifted faith healer might be considered, in quantum terms, to be an observer who routinely collapses space-time possibilities into the probability of healing. A prayer is an intention that might also collapse the swarm of possibilities present in the possibility wave in the direction of a certain probability. Such quantum phenomena are not limited by geography or history. Einstein said, "The distinction between the past, present, and future is only a stubbornly persistent illusion."

Hundreds of experiments have shown the effect of an observer on material reality. A particularly charming and visual demonstration of the effect of intent was conducted by Rene Peoc'h, MD. He used a self-propelled robot he called a "Tychoscope," which contained a random number generator. He monitored its movements on a plotter. When it was put in a room, the plotter tracking the robot's movements found that it indeed moved around the room in an entirely arbitrary way (A), at random angles and for random lengths of travel.

He then introduced a cage of chicks at one end of the room. The chicks had been trained to relate to the Tychoscope as though it were the mother hen. In the presence of the chicks' intention, the robot's movements were no longer random; it approached the cage of chicks two and a half times more often than it would approach an empty cage (B).[12]

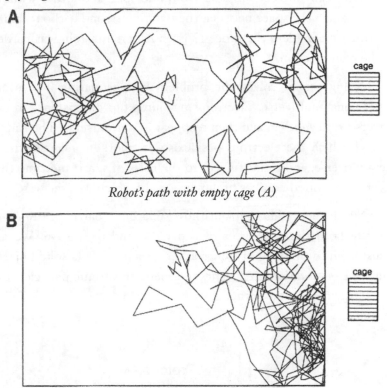

Robot's path with empty cage (A)

Robot's path with chicks (B)

Another possible explanation for distant healing comes from string theory. String theory explains phenomena such as electron tunneling. "Tunneling" is a misleading term, as it implies that electrons travel through a tunnel. In fact, they don't. Electrons in a field have been observed to jump from one orbit to another orbit without traveling through the intervening space, and without any time having elapsed. They disappear in one orbit and simultaneously reappear in another orbit. Physicist Niels Bohr was the first to describe such a "quantum leap."[13] One researcher describes tunneling this way: "Suppose that you fire a particle such as a proton or an electron at some kind of wall that it doesn't have enough energy to penetrate.... Occasionally, the particle will appear to tunnel straight through what would otherwise be an impassable obstacle, just by happening to jump from one part of its probability wave to another."[14]

How can an electron jump from one spot to another without going through the space between the two points, and without taking any time to complete the process? Even Albert Einstein was baffled by the phenomenon.[15]

String theory solves the problem by postulating an eleven-dimensional multiverse. Electrons may jump out of existence in our universe, into another, and then reappear in our universe. The tunnel through which the electrons pass exists in another universe within the multiverse, and is not subject to the rules of space and time that govern the limited number of dimensions of which we are aware.

String theory also explains how subatomic particles can demonstrate both the properties of a particle and of a wave. We are accustomed to thinking of things as either a particle (a solid object), or a wave (a vibration). Yet light, and many subatomic particles, can effortlessly manifest as either a wave or a particle.

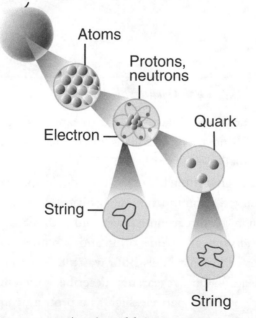

Atomic model circa 2009:
Vibrating at different frequencies, strings create matter[16]

According to string theory, everything in the universe is made up of tiny vibrating strings. These strings are identical. The reason that one manifests as a heavy particle, like a proton, and another as a particle without mass, like light, is that they vibrate at different frequencies. According to Einstein's famous equation $E=mc^2$, the more *energy* something has, the more *mass* it has. So a heavy particle is a string vibrating at a high frequency, whereas a light particle ("light" in both senses of the word) is a string vibrating at a lower frequency. Strings are also very small; if the image of an atom illustrated at the start of this section was magnified to the size of our solar system, a string would be the size of a tree.

The eleventh dimension is the dimension that may contain within it, in the words of one BBC reporter, "any number of parallel universes. Physicists say that this dimension may be only a millimeter away from us yet we have no awareness of its existence."[17] This is because the other universes are vibrating *out of phase* with ours, at a frequency that we cannot perceive.

There is vastly more mass in our universe than we can perceive. This "missing mass"—some 96% of the total—is thought to consist of "dark energy" and "dark matter," terms which, according to *Scientific American,* "serve mainly as expressions of our ignorance, much as the marking of early maps with 'Terra Incognita.'"[18] This dark matter and dark energy may be manifestations of the parallel universes.

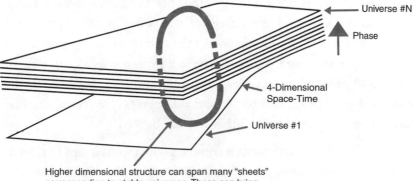

Higher dimensional structure can span many "sheets" corresponding to stable universes. These can bring knowledge or energy from other dimensions.

Model of a multidimensional universe[19]

The alternate universes postulated by string theory are like pieces of paper stacked one on top of the other. Each vibrates at a slightly different rate, so we cannot perceive them. As the vibrational rate of a string changes, it may jump out of phase in our universe, into phase in another, and then back into phase in ours. As the string resonates at a particular frequency, it produces subatomic particles. Each resonance is associated with a particular particle. As the vibrational frequency of the string changes, it expresses as different subatomic particles. Like the tunneling electron, these particles can flash into existence in our universe, then flash into another universe, and then flash back into ours. In this way, signals can pass between dimensions.

Discomfort and Novelty in Research

When looking for explanations of how the world works, we are historically much more comfortable with solid objects (particles)—such as the ion transfer theory of classical neurology, or the use of drugs and chemotherapy to treat disease. We are less comfortable with intangible phenomena (waves)—such as electromagnetic signaling, or the effects of consciousness and energy healing on disease. String theory rattles our cage, stretches our minds, and reminds us that healing can occur in dimensions that are outside of our known universe, let alone our comfort zone.

Physicist Michio Kaku, one of the originators of string theory, compares us to a fish, swimming with other fishes in a shallow pond. This fish has explored every facet of the two-dimensional universe that it inhabits. Then someone yanks the fish from the pond and lifts it high above the pond. Suddenly, the fish experiences a third dimension, "up," of which it was previously unaware. It comes back to the pond and tries to explain the remarkable perspective from which it has just seen the world. The other fish are baffled.[20]

That state of bafflement is common when we attempt to stretch our space-time-delimited minds around the complexities of quantum physics and string theory. Yet they may explain phenomena such as distant healing, which we know occur, but which current medical models, bound as they are to the pond in which we swim, cannot explain or comprehend, even with the aid of electromagnetism and rapid connective tissue signaling.

Intentions can have measurable physical effects on matter down to the subatomic level. Dean Radin, PhD, senior scientist at the Institute of Noetic Sciences in Petaluma, California, designed an ingenious experiment to determine this. He placed a low-intensity laser beam inside a shielded room, which blocks out all electromagnetic radiation. Research subjects were asked to intuitively perceive the laser light, and either block it or let it flow freely for thirty seconds. He found perturbations in the laser corresponding to "blocking" sessions, and no perturbations when the intention was free flowing.[21]

Another research group, at Princeton's PEAR lab, looked at the effect of intention on random number generators. Such generators produce, by definition, random series of numbers, and should continue doing so under all conditions, since they are not hooked up to any other device and are usually shielded from electromagnetic radiation and other sources of interference with the machine's function. When analyzing a large number of trials, however, the Princeton researchers found that intention could produce anomalies in the series of random numbers, resulting in "spikes" of non-randomness.[22] The implication of this research is that your intentions are affecting the matter around you to some degree, be it ever so slight. And since you may be busy intending this or that outcome for more than thirty seconds per day, your cumulative intentions might indeed push your destiny in one direction or another.

A fascinating example of consciousness seeing something that could not be perceived with the physical senses comes from accounts of NDEs, or "near-death experiences." NDEs involve people who die physically and are then revived. They often report floating above the operating table or hospital, traveling down a tunnel of light in which they encounter loved ones who died earlier, and then finally returning to their bodies. Of particular interest are accounts by patients who are blind. Vicky Noratuk, blind at birth, accurately saw her body, including being able to describe her wedding ring, during an NDE in which she "saw" for the first time in her life.[23] It seems that consciousness has means of perception even when our senses fail us.

Whereas electromagnetic fields are a mechanism of biological signaling implicated in healing, they cannot explain healing at a distance. Radin performed an ingenious experiment to illustrate this phenomenon, by placing the receivers of healing in a shielded room, designed specifically to block out all electromagnetic radiation. Even the cables running into the room to monitor the equipment are fiber optic instead of metal wires.

The healees were cancer patients, and the healers were their spouses or close friends. The healthy person sent healing intention to the cancer patient in the Faraday cage in ten-second bursts. These periods were selected at random by a computer. The researchers measured the skin conductance of those receiving healing. During the healing bursts, the skin conductance of the healees increased, indicating activation of the autonomic nervous system.[24] This and similar studies indicate that we have to look beyond local effects like electromagnetism to explain distant healing, and find quantum answers.

While you may be sick in this dimension, you may be the model of health in another dimension of the multiverse. Your intention in this dimension, acting in a quantum field, may collapse the swarm of probabilities in such a way as to influence health. Such ideas stretch the boundaries of our imagination, yet they hark back to shamanic journeys, or aboriginal walkabouts in the dreamtime, into which our ancestors traveled to find cures. Jean Houston, PhD, suspects that healers can identify with archetypes that "have the capacity to bring larger patterns of possibility, evolutionary cadences, and a wider spectrum of reality into conscious knowledge and experience." She speculates that instantaneous healing may be a consequence of the healer "dissolving his or her local self and being filled with an archetypal or sacred image. Archetypal space-time may also contain the optimal template of a person's health and well-being. The job of the healer is to call that template back into consciousness so that it can work upon a malfunctioning body or mind."[25]

An Entangled Universe

Another characteristic of quantum theory is entanglement—the idea that relationship is the defining characteristic of everything in space and time. The concept of entanglement arose from the observation by physicists that certain particles still appear to move in a connected fashion, without any time lag, even after they are separated by large amounts of space.[26] In his book *Entangled Minds,* Radin quotes Erwin Schrödinger, one of the early proponents of quantum theory, and the originator of the name "entanglement," as saying: "I would not call [entanglement] *one* but rather *the* characteristic trait of quantum mechanics." Not only does atomic matter become entangled, whole systems may become entangled, too. Radin quotes a March 2004 review of the research into entanglement by *New Scientist* magazine. It concludes that: "Physicists now believe that entanglement between particles exists everywhere, all the time, and have recently found shocking evidence that it affects the wider, 'macroscopic' world that we inhabit."[27]

Given the pervasive nature of the entanglement of atomic particles, it is unlikely that evolution has ignored this basic characteristic of matter in setting up human systems. Having realized that some form of epigenetic control is required to produce the complex orchestration of living systems, entanglement is a good place to look for the mechanisms of cybernetic control. According to a researcher at the Vienna University of Technology, "Entanglement could coordinate biochemical reactions in different parts of a cell, or in different parts of an organ. It could allow correlated firings of distant neurons. And... it could coordinate the behavior of members of a species, because it is independent of distance and requires no physical link."[28] British physicist David Bohm observed that entanglement applies "even more to consciousness, with its constant flow of evanescent thoughts, feelings, urges, desires, and impulses. All of these flow into and out of each other."[29] Thus entanglement offers a tantalizing glimpse into how distant intention and intercessory prayer might operate to produce healing even at great distances.

Dr. Robin Kelly, a British physician, has accumulated much of the research on the properties of microtubules (the tiny cylindrical protein girders in our cells described in chapter 5) in his fascinating book *The Human Antenna*.[30] Since they are resonant structures, he asks, with what signal are they resonating? He speculates that they receive signals from the quantum field and play a role in the communication between one cell and another, and between all cells and the quantum field. Brain cells contain very high concentrations of microtubules.

Kelly describes the insights in the early 1990s of British physicist Sir Roger Penrose and American anesthetist Stuart Hameroff into the purpose of the microtubules. Sir Roger speculated that microtubules might be sophisticated computers, processing information gleaned from the quantum world. They hypothesized that these tiny hollow spirals might function as antennae, linking the time- and space-bound cells of our bodies to the infinite and timeless world of quantum space. Kelly suspects that microtubules may be the physical structures through which intention and consciousness can be transmitted across great distances.

The first experimental evidence of "telepathy" between one strand of DNA and another comes from a 2008 article in the *Journal of Physical Chemistry*. In it, researchers reported that DNA strands that had no contact with each other, or with proteins that could facilitate their communication, were able to recognize similarities with other DNA strands from a distance, and then congregate together. Identical strands were twice as likely to associate with each other as with strands with different molecular sequences. The researchers had no explanation for the mechanism by which such a phenomenon might occur, even though they were able to observe its existence.[31]

The Mirror in Your Brain

One of the most exciting new areas of brain research is the field of mirror neurons. Mirror neurons are neurons that fire in our brains when we witness an act done by another that requires the same group of neurons. When the neurons in the other person's brain fire and that person performs the action, the neurons in our brains fire in sympathy. When another person puts on a hat, for instance, the neurons in our brains that govern that action fire when we witness their action, just as the other person's neurons do when they perform it. This whole process happens without going through the normal sensory-cognitive cycle that conventional brain models would suggest: visual images passing from the optic nerve (as our eyes witness the other person performing the action), then to the visual cortex, then to the parts of the brain that govern decision-making, and eventually being translated into signals sent via the nervous system.

The first researchers to describe the phenomenon were a team of Italian scientists at the University of Parma led by Giacomo Rizzolatti. They were studying the brain patterns of macaque monkeys, in particular the pre-motor cortex, which plans and initiates movements, which then travel to the muscles via the nerves.

The researchers identified which brain cells became active when a monkey picked up a nut. However, one of the researchers inadvertently picked up his own nut while a monkey was still attached to the brain scanner. Much to the surprise of the scientists, the same area of the brain became active in the monkey while observing the researcher's action. This initial discovery, in 1995, led the team to find many other groups of neurons that mirror the actions of others.[32] Researchers at many sites are now investigating the properties of mirror neurons.

An early clinical application was the study of autism. Researchers at the University of San Diego, led by Vilayanur Ramachandran, suspected that autistic children might not be picking up the same cues from the actions of others. When they compared a group of autistic children with a control group, they discovered that, indeed, the autistic group did not register mirror neuron activity.[33]

Albert Einstein and other scientists first proposed, in 1935, that nonlocal action was a requirement of quantum mechanics (the Einstein-Podolsky-Rosen paradox[34]), but it was not verified experimentally until much later. To find out if quantum entanglement also occurs between human beings, Dean Radin designed and conducted an innovative study. He had two people meditate, sitting side by side, in an electromagnetically shielded room, working on the hypothesis that group meditation might induce entanglement. After a time, one of the subjects was moved to a second shielded room about fifteen yards away, and hooked up to an EEG machine. Then a light was shone, at irregular intervals, into the eyes of the meditator in the first room, who was also hooked up to an EEG.

The EEG recordings were later compared. The periods in which the brain of the person into whose eyes the light was shone recorded changes in the EEG pattern were noted and compared to the EEG readouts from the person who had been moved to the second Faraday cage, as well as to the readouts for the control group. The researchers found that at the precise moment when the light was shone into one meditator's eye, the brain of the other meditator responded, while the brains of the control group demonstrated no such effect. They concluded that a human brain is capable of establishing nonlocal relationships with other brains, even when sensory communication, electromagnetic signals, and other cues have been ruled out.[35] Such links between the consciousness of one person and another require quantum signaling.

Up to this point researchers have assumed that mirror neurons fire when an action is visually observed. It would be intriguing to test whether mirror neurons fire simultaneously in the observer and the observed. Such linkages might be routine in an entangled universe in which distant particles change orbits simultaneously.

Though the possibilities for healing opened up by such quantum signaling might be immense, the medical mainstream has little time for them. Orthodoxies die hard. One of the world's top medical journals, the *Lancet*, laid out the current medical position in 2005: "Nothing in our contemporary scientific views of the universe or consciousness can account for how the 'healing intentions' or prayers of distant intercessors could possibly influence the [physiology] of patients even nearby let alone at a great distance."[36] Such bastions of conventional medicine have somehow overlooked the discovery of electricity, magnetism, quantum fields, epigenetics, and several thousand scientific studies. The great German physicist Max Planck observed, "Science advances one funeral at a time," as older dogmatists die off and new people enter the profession.

These quantum entanglements may bind human beings together in surprising ways. They may explain phenomena such as synchronistic events. Marie-Louise von Franz wrote:

> Darwin had developed his theory in a lengthy essay, and in 1844 was busy expanding this into a major treatise when he received a manuscript from a young biologist unknown to him. The man was A. R. Wallace, whose manuscript was a shorter but otherwise parallel exposition of Darwin's theory. At the time, Wallace was in the Molucca Islands of the Malay Archipelago. He knew of Darwin as a naturalist, but had not the slightest idea of the kind of theoretical work on which Darwin was at the time engaged. In each case, a creative scientist had independently arrived at a hypothesis that was to change the entire development of biological science. Backed up later by documentary evidence, each had initially conceived of the hypothesis in an intuitive "flash."[37]

The number of joint Nobel prizes, often awarded to researchers who have had no contact with each other, testifies that entanglement did not start or end in the nineteenth century. Near the beginning of the twentieth century, a British mathematician and physicist, Sir James Jeans, presciently observed: "When we view our selves in space and time, our consciousnesses are obviously the separate individuals of a particle-picture, but when we pass beyond space and time, they may perhaps form ingredients of a single continuous stream of life. As it is with light and electricity, so it may be with life: the phenomena may be individuals carrying on separate existences in space and time, while in the deeper reality beyond space and time we may all be members of one body."[38]

8

Scanning the Future

Research is the highest form of adoration.
—Pierre Teilhard de Chardin[1]

"One evening, Albert Einstein's son-in-law, Dmitri Marianoff, sat with him in a house in Berlin, Germany, after all the other members of the family had gone to bed. Into the pregnant stillness, Marianoff asked a question that had long intrigued him:

"'How is it, Albert, that you arrived at your theory?'

"'In a vision,' he answered.

"He said that one night he had gone to bed with a discouragement of such black depths that no argument would pierce it. 'When one's thought falls into despair, nothing serves him any longer, not his hours of work, not his past successes—nothing. All reassurance is gone. It is finished, I told myself, it is useless. There are no results. I must give it up.'

"Then this happened. With infinite precision the universe, with its underlying unity of size, structure, distance, time, space, slowly fell piece by piece, like a monolithic picture puzzle, into place in Albert Einstein's mind. Suddenly clear, like a giant die that made an indelible impress, a huge map of the universe outlined itself in one clarified vision.

"And that is when peace came, and that is when conviction came, and with these things came an almighty calm that nothing could ever shake again..."[2]

The creative flowering of consciousness is as mysterious as Einstein's vision. After he had that insight, it then took him another four years to work out his seminal equations showing the link between energy and matter. But the first impulse was a gift from the universe, seeding a mind open to receiving a new way of seeing the cosmos.

Experiments that measure the interaction of our consciousness with matter hold many surprises. They show us that many of the linear, cause-and-effect relationships that underpin our perception are inventions of our brains, and not the way the world actually works.

Interactive Fields

Researchers at the Institute of HeartMath have done a series of experiments on the effects of consciousness on cells. These experiments are done with rigorous protocols and are intended to replicate earlier research.[3] They extended the work of Dean Radin, PhD. Radin and some of his colleagues measured the galvanic skin response (electrodermal activity) of subjects exposed to the mental influences of others.[4] In a follow-up study, which replicated the results of earlier studies done by them and others, the researchers set up sixteen sessions. In each session, there were seven people acting as mental influencers, and ten acting as remote targets of influence. Influencers were instructed to either calm or activate a remote person's electrodermal activity.

The investigators found that, to a statistically significant degree, when the influencers attempted to calm the subjects, the subjects exhibited a lower level of electrodermal activity. When the influencers attempted to excite the subjects, the subjects showed a higher level of electrodermal activity. Building on Radin's research, the experimenters at HeartMath went further. As well as galvanic skin response, they also used an electroencephalogram (EEG) in order to measure changes in the cerebral cortex, and an electrocardiogram (EKG) to measure the acceleration or deceleration of a subject's heartbeat.

Rather than a remote influencer attempting to influence their experiences, the HeartMath subjects stared at a blank white computer monitor screen. After a period of a few seconds, an image came up on the screen. One set of images was designed to calm the subjects, such as nature scenes and smiling people, and the other set of images was designed to produce emotional arousal, such as autopsies or sexual scenes. The images were generated at random by the computer just before the instant of projection from amongst forty-five images stored on the hard drive.

The researchers wanted to find out precisely where and when emotional arousal occurred in the body, heart, and brain. They also presented the images to the subjects under two sets of experimental conditions. One was a baseline condition of normal physiological function. The second was a state of heightened heart coherence, in which their hearts were beating at an unusually even rate.

They discovered that the heart responded to the images. This was not surprising. What was surprising was that it responded *first*, before any mental activity had shown up on the EEG. It appears that the heart may perceive before the brain, rather than vice versa. But the truly astonishing finding of these experiments was that both heart and brain responded *before* the image had flashed onto the screen, before the random image generator in the computer had generated any image at all. Heart and then brain responded to the type of image *about to be* flashed on the screen, several moments before the computer made its random choice and presented it to the subject. The subject's body then responded appropriately to the emotional stimulus of the image, even though in the objective real world, that stimulus had not yet been presented to either heart or brain. In the words of the amazed researchers: "This study presents compelling evidence that the body's perceptual apparatus is continuously scanning the future."[5]

Canadian researchers, in a series of experiments published as early as 1949, noted an associated phenomenon. The subjects were epileptics undergoing brain surgery, and electrodes were placed directly on the cerebral cortex. The subjects were told, at intervals, to move their fingers. Cortical scans showed that some of the subjects recorded an increase in activity just before the instruction, "Get ready to move your fingers," was given by the researchers. Another research team replicated these results in 2000.[6] In a Newtonian universe that knows only linear time, such a phenomenon is scientifically impossible. Only a quantum universe of fields that interact continuously through time and space can explain such phenomena.

Another example of the power of prayer across time comes from a study published in the *British Medical Journal* in 2001. In Israel, Professor Leonard Leibovici took a stack of hospital case histories and divided it into two random piles. The patients in these cases had all been admitted for blood poisoning. Names in one stack were prayed for, while the others were not.

On later analysis, the group prayed for was found to have a reduced rate of fevers, shorter hospital stays, and a lower mortality rate. This kind of finding is typical of prayer studies and would not have surprised most researchers—except that the patients Leibovici prayed for *had been discharged from hospital ten years earlier.* The healing power of consciousness and intention appears to be independent of time as well as space.[7] Prayer seems to work retroactively as well as across great distances. Perhaps the whimsical injunction is true: "It's never too late to have a happy childhood!"

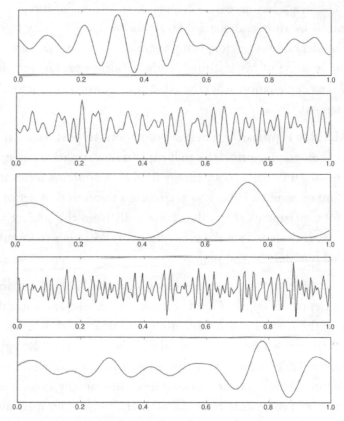

One-second EEG readout of common brain waves.
From top: alpha, beta, delta, gamma, theta

Nonlocal Perception

A second study by the HeartMath researchers examined where and when in the body, heart, and brain intuitive information outside the range of conscious awareness is processed. They found that the primary areas of the brain involved are the frontal cortex, temporal, occipital, and parietal areas, and that these are all influenced by the heart. They concluded, "Our data suggest that the heart and brain, together, are involved in receiving, processing, and decoding intuitive information. On the basis of these results and those of other research, it would thus appear that intuitive perception is a system-wide process in which both the heart and brain (and possibly other bodily systems) play a critical role."[8]

"The heart has access to realms of quantum information not constrained by time and space," HeartMath's Dr. McCraty told me during a telephone interview, many years after I first met him while working on some of his institute's early publications. He continued, "There is no explanation other than that consciousness is nonlocal and non-temporal."

McCraty is preparing a new set of papers, to postulate a theory based on holographic principles that explain how intuitive perception allows us to gain access to an energy field that contains information about "future" events. He is also preparing a rigorous new set of protocols for experiments that will use live cells from the subject's own body to see if there is a similar prior effect in those cells to intentions generated remotely by the subject.

John Arden, PhD, chief psychologist at the Kaiser Permanente Medical Center in Vallejo, California, presents a long and careful discussion of theoretical physics, subatomic particles, and their implications for the study of consciousness in his book *Science, Theology, and Consciousness*. He concludes that "nonlocality is a phenomenon operative in nature. This discovery necessitates a fundamental reevaluation of causality and the nature of nonlocal interaction."[9] Our mechanistic notions of cause and effect in time and space operate on a very limited range of the spectrum of what is possible. Though we see ordinary examples of distributed nonlocal consciousness every day, such as schools of fish that turn in tandem, or flocks of birds that bank and swoop in perfect coordination, our collective medical brain still has trouble with the idea that things far apart in space and time can affect each other, and medical treatment is prescribed as though only what is here and now has meaning.

The Half-Second Delay

Benjamin Libet, PhD, conducted a provocative set of experiments in which he noted the precise instant at which brain activity indicated awareness of a sensation on the skin. He measured when the skin became aware of the sensation and when the brain did. This led to the discovery of the "half-second delay." Libet's experiments measured the difference in time between our performance of a muscular action, such as reaching our arm out to grasp an object, and our conscious mind stating, "I decide to grasp that object."

Libet discovered that our consciousness projects itself backward in time, to believe that it became conscious of a stimulus about half a second before it actually did so. *The brain is convinced that it became aware of an action before it occurred,* though in reality it became aware of the action a half-second later. In *The User Illusion: Cutting Consciousness Down to Size,* Danish science writer Tor Norretranders says, "The show starts before we decide it should! An act is initiated before we decide to perform it!"[10] He goes on to say, "Man is not primarily conscious. Man is primarily nonconscious. The idea of a conscious 'I' as housekeeper of everything that comes in and goes out of one is an illusion; perhaps a useful one, but still an illusion."[11]

In evolutionary terms, the conscious mind is a recently developed luxury, while the subconscious, that which scans the environment for threats and opportunities, is a necessity. Many creatures from lizards on down get along quite nicely without the former. A species can't live long enough to develop a conscious mind unless its threat-assessment machinery works spectacularly well. Your conscious mind is only able to process approximately fifty bits of information a second, whereas your unconscious mind processes approximately eleven million bits per second.[12] So the conscious mind, says Brad Blanton, PhD, in his book *Radical Honesty,* is constantly making rationalizations to explain actions that the subconscious already performed.[13] They sound reasonable, but they're stories invented after the fact. Physicist Roger Penrose suggests that "we may actually be going badly wrong when we apply the usual physical rules for time when we consider consciousness!"[14] While our bright conscious minds cling to the comforting illusion that they're in charge, in reality they're part of a picture much bigger than we can ever comprehend.

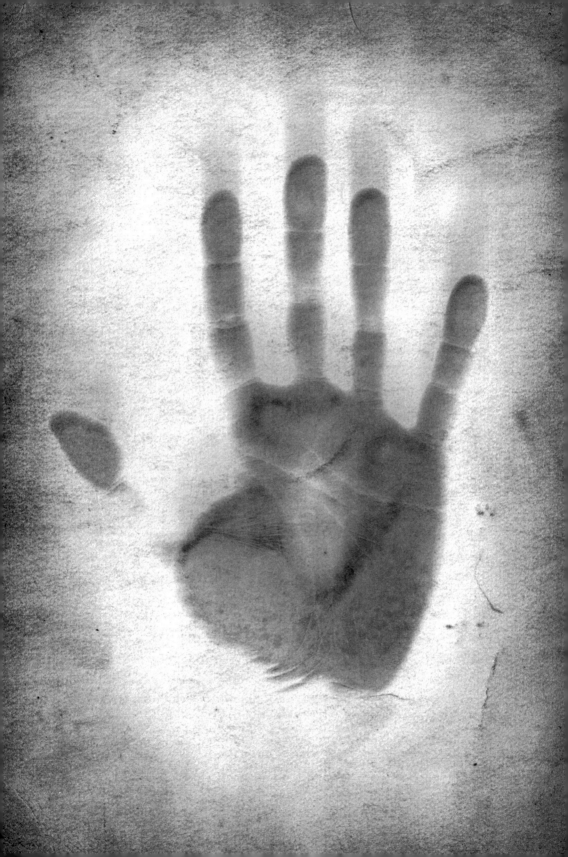

9

Writing "Miracles!" on Every Prescription Pad

But couldn't everyone's life become a work of art? Why should the lamp or the house be an art object, but not your life?

—Michel Foucault

"I rv was just fifty-four years old. He had been a cop, and then had worked as a private investigator for about twenty-five years. He liked to go sailing in Sheepshead Bay, and did woodworking in his garage. When the heart attack hit, it felt like someone had slugged him in the chest with a four-by-four beam. He says he remembers just dropping like a leaf in the wind.

"His wife and son held his hand at the bedside. The Columbia Presbyterian heart surgeon pursed his lips and looked down. 'He's been in a coma for five days in spite of everything we've done. He's on the transplant list, but I don't think he'll make it long enough for us to find him a new heart.' They cried and kissed him, and said goodbye.

"It was five months later when Irv walked into my office. He was still a bit shaky, way overweight, and he looked pale. But he sat down, smiled, and said, 'I shouldn't be here, Doc.'

"'How come?' I asked. He looked down at his hands. 'Well, because I died five months ago...'

"Or so it seemed to him. A heroic last-option quadruple bypass surgery saved his life—but just barely.

"Irv had pretty bad diabetes for about fifteen years. That set him up for his severe heart attack, and a lot of other problems. It also left him with numb and painfully burning feet and hands. I couldn't do much about his diabetes; that was a job for another doctor, but as a pain doc I sure could help him with the burning damage to his nerves.

"I adjusted his nerve medications, put him on a couple of new things, a couple of supplements, and then we just sat and talked for about twenty minutes. This was a man who had gone through a huge life crisis, and was actually still in crisis, still very wobbly. His struggle was something palpable in the room, like the shadow of death, still there. He talked about his family, his job, what had been important to him, his past sense of meaning and religious practice, and the future. Then he started to cry.

"We talked for a while, then I looked down at my prescription pad and I began to write. As a Scottish Episcopalian who was not particularly religious, I had never written such a thing before in my career. I handed it to him and he looked down at the script. The prescription read 'Long conversations with your rabbi, twice a week.' He left the office with an odd smile on his face.

"Over the subsequent six months, Irv got more involved with his synagogue. He took the opportunity to allow his terrifying brush with death to work a deep magic on his sense of himself and his day-to-day life. He finally found himself much less concerned with the small things. He still had significant symptoms, but the residual burning in his feet and hands did not bother him as much. He spent more time with his son. He complained much less and got out of the house much more.

"He came back to me and told me he had started a program, through his temple, to provide services for older people in the community. His years as a private investigator had given him the ability to find many resources for his clients, and to protect them from fraud. He said that this was what he was meant to do, and that he could not have found it without going through his illness. He allowed the pain and suffering to become his greatest teacher. As he talked to me about his new calling, his face was bright and his hands were steady. The shadow of death was gone from the room."[1]

Prescription: Belief

Imagine the healing arts of the future reformulated around the idea of thoughts, driven by the power of feelings, as shapers of our reality. When a cardiac patient visits a doctor, *the first prescription the doctor might offer might not be a drug but a precisely formulated sequence of thoughts and feelings* designed to affect the genetic predisposition of people at risk for heart disease.

James Dillard, MD, who told his patient Irv's story in *The Heart of Healing,* is a specialist in pain medicine, and director of the Pain Medicine Clinic at Beth Israel Medical Center in New York City. He wrote a compendious book on the subject that combines alternative and allopathic approaches, called *The Chronic Pain Solution,*[2] and also wrote *Alternative Medicine for Dummies.*[3] He has been featured in *Newsweek* and *People* magazines, and has appeared on *Oprah*, NPR, and the *Today Show*.

Dillard's inspired impulse to employ his prescription pad to write down the name, not of a drug, but of a spiritual exercise, may have done far more for Irv than any pharmaceutical. It engaged the customized pharmacopeia of Irv's own immune system, a resource uniquely targeted to solve Irv's body's particular problems. Doctors are realizing that there are miraculous healing effects that occur as a result of changes in consciousness such as belief, intention, spiritual practice, and prayer. The medical profession is taking increasing note of how effective prayer is as a medical intervention; prayer is even becoming pervasive in the medical community.

A large-scale study was performed by the Jewish Theological Seminary in December 2004. It surveyed 1,087 physicians. Among the doctors were practitioners of many faiths: Catholics, Protestants, Jews (broken out into groups of Orthodox, Conservative, Reform, and culturally identified but not religiously observant Jews), Muslims, Hindus, and Buddhists.

Doctors Often See Miracles

According to the results of the survey, two-thirds of doctors now believe that prayer is important in medicine. Miracles occur today, according to three-quarters of the group. Among physicians in every religious group in the study, except for less religiously observant Jews, more than 50% of participants believe that miracles occur today. Certain groups of doctors (among them Christians of all denominations and Orthodox Jews) believed to a very high degree (80% or more) that miracles happen today.

Two-thirds said that they encouraged their patients to pray, either because they believed it was psychologically beneficial to the patient or because they believed that God might answer those prayers, or both. Half of them said that they encouraged their patients to have other people pray for them. Half of them said that they prayed for their patients as a whole, and nearly 60% said that they prayed for individual patients. An average of 55% of the physicians reported seeing miraculous recoveries in patients, and a third or more of physicians (of every religious group) said they had seen miraculous recoveries—even when the percentage of doctors in that group who prayed for patients was well below one-third.[4] Between 50% and 80% of physicians—even those of weak religious faith—believe that miracles can happen today. There's good reason for their conviction; a recent meta-analysis of prayer studies found that "prayer offered on behalf of others yields positive results."[5] And to the surprise of researchers who believed that college students become increasingly secularized as they progress through school, a large-scale survey found the opposite. Though church attendance diminished, with college students being less likely to attend church than high school students, their spiritual focus, and concern for the intangible aspects of human existence, increased at the same time.[6]

Unlike linear medicine, miracles, prayer, and spirituality all embrace the idea of sudden and dramatic improvement in health. Miraculous cures are hard to study, since they cannot be predicted using the methods by which clinical trials are run. In their book *Catastrophe Theory*, Alexander Woodcock and Monte Davis note, "The mathematics underlying three hundred years of science, though powerful and successful, have encouraged a one-sided view of change. These mathematical principles are ideally suited to analyze—because they were created to analyze—smooth, continuous quantitative change: the smoothly curving paths of planets around the sun, the continuously varying pressure of a gas as it is heated and cooled, the quantitative increase of a hormone level in the bloodstream. But there is another kind of change, too, change that is less suited to mathematical analysis: the abrupt bursting of a bubble, the discontinuous transition from ice at its melting point to water at its freezing point, the qualitative shift in our minds when we 'get' a pun or a play on words."[7] Randomized clinical trails cannot study discontinuous and exceptional phenomena like miracles. We have to rely on the accounts of doctors who've seen them, and patients who've experienced them.

Discontinuity and Transformation

A serious attempt to collect stories of sudden, discontinuous personal change has been made by psychiatry professor William Miller, PhD, at the University of New Mexico, author of some twenty-five books and many articles, and clinical psychologist Janet C'de Baca, PhD. After a newspaper article about their research in rapid personal shifts, they received hundreds of phone calls from people who had undergone rapid personal changes, including miraculous healings. They coined the term "quantum change" to describe this phenomenon, a term which, unlike the word "miracles," frees this type of experience from identification solely with religious observance (though the majority of quantum changes do indeed occur in the context of religious experiences). They describe many of these cases in their book *Quantum Change*.[8]

The authors tell us, "A decade later, we have a reasonably good description of the phenomenon and full confidence that sudden, profound, and enduring positive changes can and do occur in the lives of real people. Lives are transformed utterly and permanently, as utter darkness suddenly gives way to a joyful dawn that had not even been imagined. It happens." In the book, they also look for the commonalities associated with all such quantum healings. Although they grapple to explain how and why it happens, they eventually offer five different perspectives that may explain why quantum change occurs. But there is no doubt that it occurs; our difficulties in measuring it reflect the limits of our science, not the limits of miraculous healing.

We change constantly, and the principles used in energy medicine can nudge that change in life-affirming directions. In *The Private Life of the Brain,* Susan Greenfield, PhD, reminds us, "We are not fixed entities. Even within a day, within an hour, we are different. All the time, experiences leave their mark and in turn determine how we interpret new experiences. As the mind evolves, as we understand everything more deeply, we have increasing control over what happens to us: we are self-conscious. But this self-consciousness itself is not fixed. ...It will ebb and flow..."[9]

Certain genetic characteristics, like hair color and height, are fixed; the Biblical Psalmist, three thousand years ago, demanded, "Which of you, by taking thought, can add one cubit to his height?" Other groups of genes are continuously influenced by the environment, such as those responsible for our immune and inflammatory responses. Yet intriguing accounts from psychotherapists indicate that even these fixed genes might be mutable. Lee Pulos, PhD, a professor and psychotherapist in Vancouver, Canada, describes treating a patient with multiple personality disorder, a man who was legally blind. When this man snapped into his alternate personality, however, he had twenty-twenty vision. Pulos also reports a case by Lee Bennet-Braun, of a Montreal police officer who made an arrest one evening, and wrote in his report that the subject had brown eyes. The officer checked on the man in his cell three hours later, and noted to his astonishment that the man now exhibited blue eyes. The following morning, the officer visited the suspect again, and found his eyes were green.[10] Other therapists report clients who are diabetic and require insulin injections in one subpersonality, and are not diabetic in another subpersonality. Yet still more bizarre are accounts of women who have several menstrual periods a month, the number depending on which subpersonalities are dominant at the time.

These cases are so rare that I am aware of no systematic study of them, or even a way to aggregate them in order to derive commonalities (and perhaps therapeutic approaches) from them. But they point to the possibility that even those genetic characteristics that we consider fixed and immutable may be susceptible to miraculous change. The more we investigate it, the less certainty the genome presents. These cases point us to the importance of keeping our minds open to the possibility of miraculous change and miraculous cures.

In a universe where the miraculous is available to us every day, where discontinuous positive change is always an option, and in which science shows that DNA follows consciousness, it is high time that we began making space in our experience for routine miracles. Every day, we can choose to take conscious control of our life script. As we write mental and emotional software that codes for health and vibrance, we have the potential to catalyze miracles in our bodies.

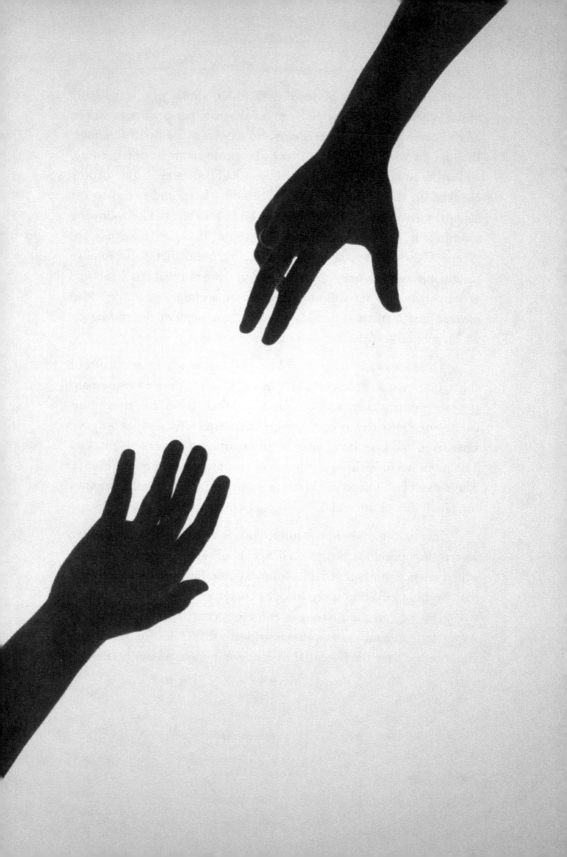

10

Energy Psychology

The fountain of content must spring up in the mind, and he who hath so little knowledge of human nature as to seek happiness by changing anything but his own disposition, will waste his life in fruitless efforts and multiply the grief he proposes to remove.

—Samuel Johnson, Elizabethan lexicographer

"Michelle, a bright, perky, twenty-one-year-old woman, arrived in my office complaining of severe bladder pain. She had to urinate frequently and urgently. I did a complete medical workup but could find nothing out of the ordinary—by the standards of my profession there was nothing wrong with Michelle. Yet it was clear to me that Michelle's pain was real, and her physical symptoms were real. After I had finished looking in her bladder with a cystoscope and found everything to be normal, I ventured, 'Sometimes women with your symptoms have a history of sexual abuse or molestation. Is this possible with you?' In the corner of her eye, the slightest of tears welled up. It turned out that Michelle had been sexually penetrated by an uncle almost daily from the age of three till she was ten years old.

221

"I asked Michelle to think back on these memories and find a part of her body where they were strongest. She said she could feel them acutely in her lower abdomen and pelvis. I asked her to rate them on a scale of one to ten, with one being the mildest and ten being the most intense. Michelle rated her feelings at ten out of a possible ten.

"I then spent forty-five minutes working with Michelle, using some simple yet powerful emotional release techniques. I then asked her to rate her level of discomfort. It was a one—complete peace. I urged her to cast around in her body for the remnants of any of the disturbed feelings she had previously felt. She could not find them, no matter how hard she tried. The emotionally charged memories had been so thoroughly released that a physical shift had occurred in her body. Her bladder condition disappeared. In the three years since that office visit, it has never returned."[1]

Eric Robins, MD, who tells this story in the anthology *The Heart of Healing*, is a urologist at Kaiser Permanente in San Diego, California. He is trained in several Energy Psychology (EP) techniques—powerful therapies that apply the principles of electromagnetic fields to medicine. All work with the body's electromagnetic signaling system to produce healing in the emotions and cells directly and quickly, without the need for extended courses of therapy, and sometimes without even needing to identify the traumas that caused the disturbance. These electromagnetic energy flows are analogous to the energy system treated by acupuncture, a healing modality that has been practiced for thousands of years.

EP doesn't use acupuncture needles. Instead, it uses physical touch to redirect energy. Using energy is an amazingly efficient way to heal. Biologist James Oschman explains, "stored trauma can be resolved as quickly as it was set in place. The body is continuously poised to resolve these afflictions and all of the physiological and emotional imbalances they create. This process goes to the deep energetic level that organizes or incarnates or underlies conscious experience itself. When this happens, the patient may suddenly know that the issue or discomfort will not bother them again."[2]

The first EP technique to be developed was Thought Field Therapy (TFT). Clinical psychologist Roger Callahan formulated this method, beginning in the late 1970s, after he learned another body-based method called Applied Kinesiology. TFT became popular in the 1980s and 1990s. The most widely used form of EP today is Emotional Freedom Techniques (EFT). Other EP methods include the Tapas Acupressure Technique (TAT), PSYCH-K, Eye Movement Desensitization and Reprocessing (EMDR), and WHEE (Wholistic Hybrid derived from EMDR and EFT). These therapies have demonstrated the ability to heal in very short periods of time psychological conditions that can require many months or years of conventional psychiatry or psychotherapy, if indeed they can be healed with those modalities at all.

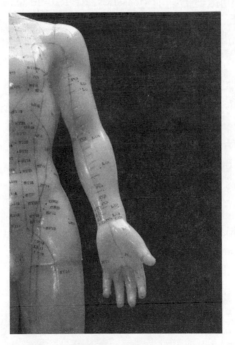

Energy meridians and acupuncture points

Emotional Freedom Techniques

Emotional Freedom Techniques (EFT), used by several million people worldwide, including therapists, nurses, and doctors, is the most popular form of EP. In the 1990s, performance coach Gary

Craig studied TFT with Roger Callahan. He simplified the method and named his variant EFT.

EFT consists of a simple routine. It starts with an affirmation: "Even though I have _____ (this problem), I fully and completely accept myself." While saying this, the person taps a specific acupressure point with the tips of the fingers. Eleven other acupressure meridian end points are then tapped five or more times by the participant with their fingertips, while a "Reminder Phrase" is spoken to keep the problem in mind. The whole procedure takes a minute or two. Although it does not require a therapist, and can be self-administered, finding the root issues prior to tapping takes experience and training. The basics, however, are easily learned by anyone and can be applied to an impressive list of issues. EFT includes a self-assessment system that the subject can use before and then again after the session to determine whether the problem has been cleared or whether further work is required. EFT is often called "tapping" because of its distinctive practice of acupoint tapping.

In a study published in the *Journal of Clinical Psychology* in 2003, therapist Steven Wells and colleagues described the results of a randomized controlled trial of EFT for phobias.[3] The subjects of the study had all been clinically diagnosed as having a phobia to small animals such as spiders, snakes, bats, and mice.

The researchers used several different measures of the strength of the participants' phobia before and after the study. They measured the pulse to see the extent which it rose when an individual contemplated the feared object. They measured the number of steps toward the feared animal a participant could take. They administered stress questionnaires. Subjects in the experimental group received a thirty-minute explanation of the method, which included one brief session of EFT.

The results were remarkable. The participants' levels of fear dropped dramatically, and some were able to walk right up to the very animals that before had triggered crippling phobias. Not only were the results of EFT dramatic at the time, but in a follow-up session six months later, subjects still had a much lower rate of phobic reaction to the objects of their fear. Steven Wells recounts the following story:

> One of the ladies in the study was so afraid of mice that if she saw a mouse or rat, or even thought there was a mouse in the house, she would spend the night sleeping in her car! Needless to say, during pre-testing, she was unable to even enter the room with the mouse.
>
> After treatment, she was able to go right up to the mouse in the container without fear. Meanwhile, not long after the treatment, her daughter bought her granddaughter a pet rat as a present! A television station recording a program on our research went to this lady's home and took some footage of her. She was cradling the rat, and saying that they aren't such bad creatures after all!
>
> There were many similar examples of people who also couldn't enter the room who, after just thirty minutes of EFT treatment, were able to not only open the door but go right up to the creature that would previously have caused them to run from the room. One of these, a lady with a cockroach phobia, felt that her phobia had been holding her back in many areas of her life. Following thirty minutes of an EFT treatment, after which she went straight into the room and picked up the cockroach in the jar to examine it closely, she reported a huge shift in self-esteem and confidence that permeated all parts of her life.[4]

Steven Wells's study was later replicated and extended by Harvey Baker and Linda Siegel of New York's Queens College.[5] They carefully controlled for any factors that could have skewed the original Wells study, such as the expectancy of subjects that a therapy will help them, sympathetic attention from a therapist, and factors common to all therapy. With these even more rigorous controls, the results were the same. Finally, an independent team conducted a third randomized controlled trial, which echoed the results of the previous two studies.[6]

When I first heard of the results being obtained through EFT, I dismissed them as hyperbole; I simply could not believe in such rapid change. After having tried the technique myself, however, tapping on some worries on which other approaches such as meditation were having no impact, I was impressed with the immediate changes I experienced. I trained in EFT and, over the years, have practiced it with thousands of people.

Though the basic EFT routine is very simple, it's necessary to learn EFT's advanced techniques to have a high success rate with difficult mental and physical challenges. Research shows that EFT is very effective for posttraumatic stress disorder (PTSD), though in cases of severe psychological trauma the support of a trained mental health professional is essential.

Tapping on twelve acupoints in sequence looks odd the first time you witness it, but if you look at the natural movements of people under stress, you'll find that they unconsciously stimulate the exact same points. They often touch, tap, or rub certain parts of their bodies. Look at the images on the next page. They're instantly recognizable as natural human gestures made by people under stress. TFT, EFT, and other EP methods simply organize them into a simple routine that can be done on purpose rather than accidentally.

It turns out that certain acupuncture meridians, when tapped rubbed, or needled, release stress. We aren't sure which ones will be most effective at any moment, but since there are only twelve meridian end points, and it takes under a minute, EFT has us stimulate all twelve. Once memorized, the routine can be used for reducing or eliminating stress whenever it occurs.

The medieval Sufi spiritual tradition has many whimsical tales of a trickster called the Mullah Nasruddin. In one of these stories, Nasruddin is a smuggler. Every day he would cross the Egyptian border with his camel. The border guard, knowing his unsavory reputation, would search Nasruddin thoroughly. Day after day, the guard would go over every inch of the Mullah's body, and give his camel the

Unconscious stress-reduction self-interventions

same treatment. But the guard never found an ounce of contraband, no matter how hard he looked.

Many years later, after the guard retired, he was drinking coffee in the marketplace and saw Nasruddin. He called him over and said,

"I no longer have the power to arrest you, but I must know before I die: What were you smuggling that eluded my sharp eyes?"

"Camels," said Nasruddin.

Stress reduction acupoints are like Nasruddin's camels. They're so obvious we don't notice them. But once you've learned them, you'll notice people touching them all the time: children in a classroom, athletes before a competition, witnesses in court, applicants before a job interview, lovers in a quarrel. For hundreds of thousands of years of evolution, these stress-reducing methods have been hidden in plain sight. Until recently, psychologists and biologists had no idea that these common gestures are part of our instinctive response to stress.

Researchers Study Energy Psychology

In a study published in *Counseling and Clinical Psychology Journal,* psychologist Jack Rowe, PhD, of Texas A&M University's psychology and sociology departments, tested people for stress before and after EFT. He administered a standardized test for measuring stress, called the Symptom Assessment 45 (SA-45), to 102 people before, during, and after an EFT workshop. Rowe measured their stress levels one month before the workshop, when the workshop started, when it ended, one month after the workshop, and six months later. He found that the stress levels of participants decreased significantly between the beginning and end of the workshop. But even more promising was the finding that the effect endured, and that when subjects were retested six months later, their stress levels remained much lower than they had been before the event. Such was the strength of the results that there was less than one chance in two thousand that such results could have occurred through chance.[7]

Intrigued, I began to evaluate participants in the EFT workshops I was teaching at psychology and medical conferences. I would administer the SA-45 before a one-day workshop, afterward, and then six months later. The results of five of these workshops were eventually published in a professional journal called *Integrative Medicine.*[8] In total, the study involved 216 healing professionals, making it, at the time, the largest energy medicine study ever published. It's usually referred to as the Healthcare Workers Study.

The data were analyzed by research psychologist Audrey Brooks, PhD, of the University of Arizona, and were astonishing. Participants experienced a 45% drop in the severity of psychological symptoms of anxiety, depression, and other mental health problems. Follow-up data showed that most of the improvements held over time, with those who did EFT more often receiving the most benefit. A 45% drop in symptoms is a big payoff from a small investment of just one day.

The results of that study turned me from an observer, writing with interest about EP, into an advocate. I realized that it was essential to start getting these therapies into the medical system. As that system treats millions of patients every day, this would be the best way to reduce the suffering of huge numbers of people quickly. I knew that getting EFT accepted by the medical establishment would require the publication of a lot of research, especially randomized controlled trials (RCTs), and so I changed my life plan. I moved from reporting on EFT to actively advocating it. I began raising money, forming volunteer teams, and acquiring the skills required to conduct and publish such research. I formed a nonprofit organization called the National Institute for Integrative Healthcare (NIIH.org) to research and implement EP in mainstream medicine and psychology.

I later started a company called Energy Psychology Group to publish books and train practitioners. At our website EFT Universe (www.EFTUniverse.com), we maintain a database of over five thousand case histories written by EFT users. We train thousands of practitioners each year. After ten years of researching and teaching EFT, I wrote the third edition of *The EFT Manual,* the definitive guide to the method.[9] EFT Universe has become one of the most-visited alternative medicine websites on the Internet, with over a million visitors a year.

I introduced rigorous standards based on the quality criteria of the American Psychological Association (APA), and introduced the term "Clinical EFT" to designate the form of EFT validated in scientific research. In 2014, a report published on Examiner.com called Clinical EFT "one of the most successful psychology self-help techniques ever developed."[10] The NIIH has published a stream of RCTs, outcome studies comparing patient outcomes before and after EFT, and review papers summarizing the scientific evidence for TFT, EFT, and other EP methods.

We built on the research conducted by pioneers who conducted earlier studies. One of these examined the EEG (electroencephalogram) patterns of claustrophobic patients when they were confined in a small, metal-lined enclosure similar to an elevator, and compared them with a control group.[11] It found that the claustrophobic subjects had high concentrations of stress-related brain waves, as well as getting high scores on an anxiety test. After tapping, their brain wave profiles resembled those of the non-claustrophobic subjects, and their scores on the anxiety test also dropped. Two weeks later, the results of the experiment still held steady.

Another early study looked at the effects of acupressure on subjects who had received a minor injury that required paramedics to transport them to hospital. Those who had received acupressure showed a significantly greater reduction of anxiety, pain, and heart rate than those who had not.[12] A group of patients who had a fear of needles so strong that they were unable to receive necessary medical treatment went through a one-hour TFT treatment. They showed a significant improvement, with most able both to receive injections and to watch medical shows on television in the subsequent month.[13] In another study, thirty fearful dental patients received a ten-minute EFT intervention. Their levels of anxiety dropped precipitously.[14] Another researcher performed an RCT with a group of forty-eight people afflicted with a fear of public speaking. After TFT, their anxiety decreased significantly, while a control group did not. When the control group was then given TFT, they showed the same improvement.[15] Several studies of test anxiety have been done, measuring student performance before and after they learned EFT.

Students show large drops in anxiety, as well as improvements in test scores.[16,17,18]

In 2008, *Psychotherapy*, the flagship journal of the American Psychological Association, published a survey of the published studies of EP. A noteworthy feature of the review was how dramatically these therapies improve many different psychological problems, including depression, anxiety, phobias, and PTSD.[19] An updated review in 2012 compared acupoint tapping to the standards for "empirically validated therapies" published by a task force set up by the APA's Clinical Psychology group (Division 12). It found: "A literature search identified 51 peer-reviewed papers that report or investigate clinical outcomes following the tapping of acupuncture points to address psychological issues. The 18 randomized controlled trials in this sample were critically evaluated for design quality, leading to the conclusion that they consistently demonstrated strong effect sizes and other positive statistical results that far exceed chance after relatively few treatment sessions. Criteria for evidence-based treatments proposed by Division 12 of the American Psychological Association were also applied and found to be met for a number of conditions, including PTSD."[20]

Researchers are beginning to understand not just *that* EP therapies work but *how* they work. One possibility is that tapping creates a piezoelectric charge that travels through the connective tissue along the path of least electrical resistance. When a traumatic memory is recalled, along with awareness of the site in the body that holds the primary memory of the trauma, tapping introduces a message of safety to the body that is not congruent with the emotionally arousing memory. So while your mind is sending a message of danger, your body is getting a conflicting message of safety. This decouples the memory from the fight-or-flight response. After all, you wouldn't be tapping if you were being chased by a tiger! The immediate early genes that regulate stress are expressed, and the body becomes calm again. The intensity of physical feeling at the site on the body diminishes, discharging the emotional intensity related to the trauma.

In one experiment, the brain scans of subjects suffering from generalized anxiety disorder were examined.[21] Digitized EEG readings were taken before treatment began. They then received twelve EP treatment sessions, after which a second EEG was recorded. The EP group was compared to one receiving the Gold Standard in experimentally validated "talk" therapy, cognitive behavioral therapy (CBT). It also compared them with patients receiving medication. The patients were examined three, six, and twelve months after treatment to determine whether the therapy had produced lasting results.

Before treatment, the EEG scans showed that most areas of participants' brains revealed high or very high levels of dysfunctionality. Only a small portion of their brains, their occipital lobes, showed normal or near-normal patterning. After twelve sessions of EP, most areas were normal or close to normal. Patients given CBT had similar results, but "more sessions were required to accomplish the changes, and the results were not as durable on a one-year follow-up as were the energy psychology treatments."

In patients given drugs, "The brain-wave ratios did not change, suggesting that the medication suppressed the symptoms without addressing the underlying wave-frequency imbalances. Undesirable side effects were reported. Symptoms tended to return after the medication was discontinued." When symptoms are suppressed, the patient may act and feel more normal. But the underlying brain rhythms remain unaffected. Studies by the World Health Organization suggest that antidepressant drugs mask symptoms without removing them, and produce long-term dependence and prolonged depression.[22] No, that's not a typographical error. There is increasing evidence associating antidepressant drugs with prolonged depression.

Drugs that mask symptoms should not be mistaken for a cure. Taking a painkiller when you have a broken arm doesn't heal you. You might feel better, but your underlying condition remains unchanged. As Shakespeare said in *Hamlet,* "It doeth but skin and film the ulcerous place, whiles rank corruption, mining all within, infects unseen."

Energy Cures for Physical Traumas

Besides working well on mental health problems, EFT has established a surprising track record of effectiveness in addressing physical ailments. This is because there is virtually always an emotional component to a physical disease.[23] Cancer patients, for instance, are often psychologically depressed, along with the suppression of their immune system that accompanies chemotherapy. Psychological depression left untreated often contributes to organic disease. Even if a patient has a disease that seems purely physical, such as an acute bacterial infection, releasing emotional stressors reduces the overall burden on the body and, by so doing, supports healing. I have been surprised to find that even colds and flu sometimes disappear after tapping. The following story from the EFT Universe archives illustrates the healing of a physical ailment after using EFT. Note how the woman's carpal tunnel pain and the grief over her sister's death both improve:

> A woman who had suffered from carpal tunnel syndrome for about eight years received some training in EFT. After having had extensive chiropractic and physical-therapy treatment, she thought she was about as healed as she was going to be without surgery. Even though she felt better in general, the chronic pain still wore her down occasionally. After being introduced to EFT and being guided through a tapping sequence for about ten minutes, she had absolutely no pain! She reports, "I couldn't believe it! I kept mentally searching throughout my body for the pain. It just wasn't there! I had actually taken a few minutes to tap on the corner of my eye, my hand, and other simple, easy-to-do places on my body and had shed this pain with which I thought I was destined to live!" Next she applied it to grief that had burdened her for many years. Within minutes, she recounts, "I felt the weight lift from me. I have been able to remember my sister fondly and nostalgically, but with no pain of grief, ever since!"

I have seen the same results from EFT time and time again. While I was writing this chapter, a friend who graciously tends my garden, came in sniffling. "I have allergies," she explained.

"What's the worst?" I inquired.

"Grass seeds," she said, without hesitation.

I asked her to deliberately intensify the feeling. She frowned and said she now had a headache too. The allergy and headache was a seven on a scale of zero to ten, she said. Her nose was so clogged that she sounded stifled.

I did an EFT tapping routine on her. She said her symptoms were now at zero on the scale.

I ran out the door, cut a few stalks of flowering grass, came back in, and presented her with the bouquet as a humorous tribute to healing. While she held them, I did another tapping routine. Then I asked her how she felt, on the same scale of zero to ten.

"I'm a zero!" she said. Her eyes opened wide at the realization. But the sound of her voice showed that more than her eyes had opened: Her nasal passages didn't sound at all clogged as she spoke. She sat on the chair for a while longer, dazed, clutching the paradoxical bouquet in amazement.

Biologist James Oschman says that such situations allow "organized or non-chaotic energy to spread suddenly throughout the organism to create new structures, functions, and order. This concept is important as a frequent observation of practitioners of Energy Psychology, bodywork, energetic and movement therapies is a sudden and beneficial 'sea change' or 'phase change' spreading throughout the organism as trauma or other disorder is resolved, and the whole body reintegrates accordingly."[24]

A nutritionist examined a patient's live red blood cells using darkfield microscopy. She was worried about the degree of clumping found in the patient's blood sample because when red blood cells clump together, they present less surface area to absorb oxygen from the lungs and distribute it throughout the body. An even distribu-

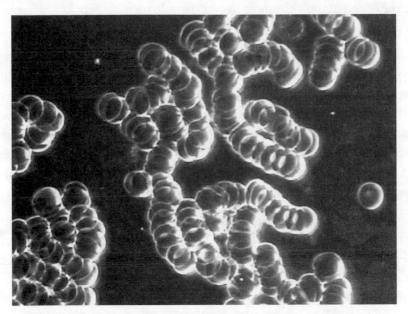

Red blood cells clumped before EFT for cell release

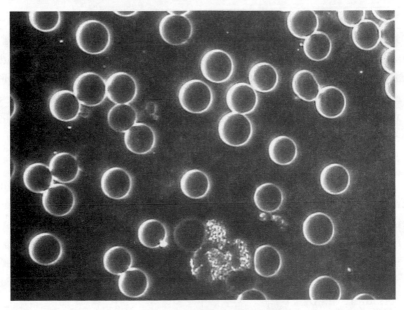

Red blood cells evenly distributed after EFT for cell spacing

tion of red blood cells indicates healthy oxygen absorption, whereas clumping indicates decreased oxygen uptake.

She found that the patient could alter the degree of clumping of her red blood corpuscles by doing EFT, and that the effect showed up immediately when the samples of live cells were examined under a microscope. The top photo in the accompanying pair shows the patient's red blood cells clumped up before doing EFT to release them. The bottom photo, taken twelve minutes later, shows the patient's red blood cells after two rounds of EFT done with the conscious intent of producing even distribution of cells.[25]

Our dominant medical model does not believe that physiological processes such as red blood cell clumping are under the control of a patient's conscious mind. The nutritionist had found by experience that reversing red blood cell clumping usually takes weeks or months of treatment, if it can be accomplished at all. Yet in this case, two rounds of EFT, lasting just a few minutes, were enough to produce an immediate and visible change in the degree of cell clumping.

The EFT Universe website contains stories by hundreds of doctors, psychiatrists, psychotherapists, sports coaches, social workers, and other health professionals about ways in which they have found EFT useful, and of patients who have responded to EFT after conventional interventions had failed. Reports of successful outcomes can also be found in *The EFT Manual,* as well as the books for specific problems, such as *EFT for Weight Loss*[26] and *EFT for Fibromyalgia and Chronic Fatigue.*[27]

By working at the energy level, EFT and other EP therapies can dramatically shorten the time it takes to reverse psychological trauma. To professionals accustomed to lengthy courses of psychotherapy or drug therapies that can be dangerous and have side effects, EP results seem miraculous. In the book *The Promise of Energy Psychology,*[28] coauthor David Feinstein, PhD, lists some of the conditions that have been improved by EFT:

> Performance fears for a nineteen-year-old gymnast, flash-
> backs and insomnia a woman was experiencing following two

automobile accidents during a six-week period, a refinery worker stopping smoking after thirty-five years, a woman's extreme anxiety prior to bladder surgery, a six-year-old girl's psychosomatic pains, a mother's fear of flying that was being communicated to her one-year-old daughter, depression suffered by a single mom with two teenage daughters, a woman's intense lifelong craving for chocolate and ice cream, a thirteen-year-old boy's fear of the dark, a boy with an intense allergic reaction to horses, another boy with severe dyslexia, a woman's pain after reconstructive surgery for a damaged knee.

Among the five thousand stories on EFT Universe contributed by people who use EFT, we find accounts of improvement in a wide variety of problems. These include (again from Dr. Feinstein's book):

> ...headaches, back pain, stiff neck and shoulders, joint pains, cancer, chronic fatigue syndrome, lupus, ulcerative colitis, psoriasis, asthma, allergies, itching eyes, body sores, rashes, insomnia, constipation, irritable bowel syndrome, eyesight, muscle tightness, bee stings, urination problems, morning sickness, PMS, sexual dysfunction, sweating, poor coordination, carpal tunnel syndrome, arthritis, numbness in the fingers, stomachaches, toothaches, trembling, and multiple sclerosis among many other physical conditions.

One of the barriers to acceptance of EFT is the wide variety of problems for which it has been used successfully. Our current medical model assumes a particular treatment for a particular disease. A treatment that is effective for so many problems sounds like a panacea, or quackery. Yet there's a very good reason why EFT works on such a wide variety of issues.

The reason is that they all involve stress. Patients with pain don't just have pain. They also have many emotions connected to the pain. I once worked with a man on crutches. He'd broken his leg in an auto accident two weeks before. His pain was an eight on a scale of zero to ten. I frankly did not believe that EFT would be effective, because it seemed a purely physical injury. Yet it turned out to have many emotional components. He was angry at the driver of the other car. He was upset at the doctor and the hospital. He was mad at his wife, who'd insisted that they drive to an event he didn't want to attend. He was angry at himself for all the times he'd done things he didn't want to do, starting in childhood. We tapped it all away. When we were finished, his pain had gone down to a two. That was his actual level of physical pain. The other six points were the emotional overlay.

You need appropriate medical care for the medical component of your problem. But trying to medicate away the emotional part is misguided. The seminars at which we gathered data for the Healthcare Workers Study included a thirty-minute segment in which we worked on physical pain. The average reduction in those 216 people was 68%. I made a point of never tapping for the pain itself, but only for the emotional components. I wanted to make the point that much of what we perceive as physical pain is really emotional stress. The results represent a two-thirds drop in symptoms, and I suspect that most of the remaining third is actual physical pain. That's the part for which you need appropriate medical care.

Emotional stress is a component of most other problems too. A cancer patient may be fearful of the disease metastasizing, or the side effects of chemotherapy. A man with erectile dysfunction might be embarrassed and ashamed. An athlete's performance might be compromised by memories of earlier defeat in competition. A craving for ice cream might be due to receiving it as a reward in childhood from a parent who later died. Stress is a component of virtually every mental or physical disease. That's why EFT works on so many apparently unrelated problems.

Other Forms of Energy Psychology

Many other pioneers deserve credit for developing EP techniques. Psychiatrist Daniel Benor, MD, is one of the pioneers of mind-body therapy. In the early 1980s, he was the first person to compile a comprehensive database of research studies supporting spiritual healing and energy medicine. He developed a hybrid form of acupoint therapy, drawing on the same principles that underlie

EFT and EMDR. He calls his technique WHEE (Wholistic Hybrid derived from EMDR and EFT). It's very similar to EFT, but taps in an alternating rhythm on both sides of the body. This is called bilateral stimulation, which is also used in EMDR.

EMDR distinguished itself as a method through scientific research conducted from the early days of its development. The first EMDR study was published in 1989.[29] By contrast, both Roger Callahan, who developed TFT, and Gary Craig, who named his tapping variant EFT, maintained that the results of their methods were so compelling and self-evident that formal scientific research was unnecessary. Their extravagant claims of efficacy, combined with a lack of hard data, made many medical professionals skeptical, and delayed the adoption of their methods into primary care. Though EMDR is by no means universally accepted, it has made faster progress due to its adherents embracing from the beginning the need for empirical research.

Changing the Beliefs Underlying the Symptoms

PSYCH-K, developed by therapist Rob Williams, is an EP technique that determines which beliefs are held in your subconscious mind and then shifts them.[30] To identify beliefs, participants are tested on positive statements, which may actually be the opposite of the beliefs embedded in their belief structure. Examples of the statements tested include:

> I give myself permission to do what I love.
> It's okay for others to disagree with me.
> I am able to function independently of others.
> It's easy for me to receive love from others.
> I experience the presence of God within me.
> Money is my friend.
> My body heals itself naturally and quickly.
> It is safe, fun, and easy for me to be slim and healthy.

Rather than focusing on conscious beliefs—everyone believes they want to be wealthy, for instance, even people who never actualize wealth—Williams tests the person's muscle strength (e.g., in the arm) as he or she states each of the beliefs listed. If the muscle tests weak, Williams posits that the subconscious mind doesn't believe the statement, even though the conscious mind may. If the muscle tests strong, it indicates congruence between the conscious statement and the unconscious belief. This method, which goes by terms such as "muscle testing," "energy testing," and "kinesiology" is a puzzle to me because while many practitioners swear by it, research is ambivalent. Some studies show that it works at least partially, while others demonstrate that the results are no better than random chance.[31]

The beliefs for which Rob Williams tests are in six areas challenging to most people: health and the body, prosperity, relationships, self-esteem, personal power, and spirituality. As they run through the lists, participants notice the statements for which their muscles test weak, and then work with them using PSYCH-K's somatic healing tools. Once a negative belief has been healed, the person will test strong when confronted with its positive counterpart.

At a PSYCH-K seminar I attended, I partnered with a woman who came in on crutches. She had suffered for fifteen years, she told me, from a debilitating neurological condition that arose after she was injured in a car accident. Her broken bones had healed, but the pain was so intense that she took large doses of painkillers three times a day, and one at night to allow her to sleep. She had been on this high dosage of painkillers every day for the past fifteen years.

On the final day of the seminar, as people were walking around saying goodbye and giving each other hugs, I noticed she was not using crutches. She told me that she felt fine, and that she had felt so good the previous evening she had forgotten to take her nightly medication. She woke up feeling even better, and had not taken painkillers the entire day. It was now twenty-four hours since her last dose. She had left the crutches in her room. There are hundreds of such stories in the world of PSYCH-K. A former president of the Colorado Association of Psychotherapists wrote: "PSYCH-K is clearly the most amazing tool for effective personal change that I have ever encountered."[32] Other testimonials report recovery from phobias, allergies, depression, overweight, and a variety of diseases.

As Easy as TAT

An easily learned technique that can be applied to a wide variety of anxieties and traumas is TAT, or the Tapas Acupressure Technique, named after its founder, Tapas Fleming.

In TAT, you place three fingers of either hand on the front of your face, and the flat of your other hand at the base of your skull. You touch the ring finger to the thumb, then place the tips of both fingers on the inside edges of the eyes, on either side of the bridge of the nose. There's no need to pinch or apply pressure. The long finger is then placed gently on the forehead. The other hand goes flat on the back of your head, on the bony protuberance where the skull terminates.

You hold this pose while you think of the worst part of the problem that's bothering you, and wait till you feel a physical shift. It usually happens in a minute or two, rarely longer than five. You feel your body relax as the tension drains from you.

Then, while holding the position, you review all the aspects of the traumatic incident in a series of nine steps, with statements such as "All the origins of this problem are now healed," or "All the sources of this problem in my mind, body, heart, life, and all other dimensions of my being are healed now." Each time, you wait to feel a physical shift, such as a deep breath, or shoulder tension dropping.

At a workshop I attended with Tapas Fleming, an audience member asked her an intriguing question: "Isn't it healthy to process emotion? Shouldn't we dig down to the painful roots of the problem and process the emotions till they're gone?" Fleming's reply was typical of EP philosophy: "You don't have to process emotion. Emotion comes from a particular place in the psyche, a particular energy system. When you identify with that place, you're going to feel the associated emotion. But that emotion resides in that place continually. If you travel there, its typical emotions will pour out of you as long as you stay there. If you travel someplace else, you no longer have to process the emotions that exist in that energy system."[33]

Tapas Acupressure Technique (TAT)

This perspective runs counter to modern psychotherapy, which gives great weight to the narrative of early childhood experience, in order to spot repetitive themes. Once enough incidents have been described by a client, the therapist is able to find their commonalities. This big picture results in a diagnosis. A diagnosis is built from a composite of those painful experiences. Once a diagnosis has been made, treatment begins. The kind of treatment prescribed depends on the type of diagnosis made.

EP sees our self-destructive habits and behaviors as *energy systems held in the body*. It dispenses with meaning, theory, conceptualization, generalization, and diagnosis, and simply tries to make you feel better in your body even though you still have the traumatic incidents in your past. It measures the degree to which you go into fight-or-flight when you remember the a traumatic event on a zero-to-ten scale. After tapping, you measure again. If you're successful, you feel much better. After a session, most clients find that they're no longer triggered, even by terrible memories. This treatment focus on the energy system is a much faster path to feeling good than the conventional "event –> diagnosis –> treatment" model.

A group of psychotherapists was interviewed about their use of EP with the survivors of childhood sexual abuse. They considered it to be the most effective treatment available for anxiety and panic, and they reported many improvements in their clients.[34] One professional described her experience in these words: "My life and work have been enriched beyond measure. I have been able to help people in ways I never imagined possible. The speed and depth of change can be astonishing."

EP and allied techniques could someday make many of the risky and invasive interventions of conventional medicine unnecessary, providing "the scientific underpinning for pharmaceutical-free energy medicine."[35]

Evidence-Based Practice

When we started researching EP through the NIIH in 2006, only six studies of EFT and TFT had been published. I developed a systematic research plan, focused on meeting the APA Division 12 standards for empirically validated therapies. Over the next decade, this work plus the efforts of hundreds of volunteers resulted in the publication of more than fifty new studies and review papers. This gave Clinical EFT a sound scientific footing as an "evidence-based" practice.[36] In 2013, we reached a coveted milestone when our training workshops qualified for Continuing Medical Education (CME) credit for doctors and nurses. This accreditation meant that physicians could obtain American Medical Association (AMA) CME credit by training in EFT. Psychologists could also take EFT courses and obtain APA Continuing Education (CE) credit.

Among the research that eventually qualified Clinical EFT as an "evidence-based" practice were studies examining PTSD, depression, anxiety, phobias, and pain. Going far beyond anecdotal reports, these quantified the degree of improvement that participants obtained. Those gains were often substantial. In one RCT of depressed teenage college students, we tested an entire first-year class at a university in Manila. We found thirty who tested positive for depression using a standardized assessment. They then received four ninety-minute group EFT sessions led by a student who had received elementary EFT training. Afterward, average student scores on the assessment were in the "non-depressed" range.[37]

Another RCT looked at PTSD symptoms in a group of teenage boys in a group home to which they'd been sent by a judge after being abused by their families. After a single but comprehensive EFT session, their symptoms normalized.[38] Children and young people seem to response rapidly to tapping. Tapping works with babies as well as older children, according to experienced clinicians. Roberta Temes, PhD, reports, "I've seen babies stop crying in mid-sob when the tapping begins. In an informal experiment in a day care center in New Jersey, I observed one group of nannies lift crying babies to their laps and speak soothingly to them, while other nannies lifted their babies, soothed them with words, and also tapped.... The latter group all stopped crying.[39]

Research also demonstrates that EFT is effective for many physical symptoms. In an RCT of veterans with PTSD, their levels of physical pain dropped by 41% in six sessions.[40] A researcher at Sweden's Lund University developed an eight-week online course applying EFT to fibromyalgia. She found significant improvement in pain, anxiety, and depression among fibromyalgia patients.[41] A third of the participants recovered completely. Note that the Mayo Clinic website states "there is no cure" for this disease.

The Red Cross hospital in Athens, Greece, performed an RCT with patients suffering from tension headaches. Those that received EFT had a drop of more than half in the frequency and severity of their pain.[42] Examining TBI (traumatic brain injury) symptoms in veterans with PTSD, there was a 41% drop after six sessions of EFT.[43] A hospital in Britain's NHS (National Health Service) conducted an evaluation of patients receiving EFT. Their scores for anxiety dropped sharply, while overall mental health and physical functioning improved.[44] Patients suffering from psoriasis, a painful skin rash, also improved after EFT.[45] It helped people suffering from insomnia as well.[46,47] In one group of veterans, insomnia dropped from the severe to the normal range.[48]

One of the most popular searches on the EFT Universe website is for the term "weight loss." There are lots of personal stories of how people have used EFT for weight loss, and research bears them out. In one RCT, participants who completed a group class lost an average of 11.1 pounds over the subsequent year.[49] We've found that people who enroll for Naturally Thin You, an online weight loss class we offer at EFT Universe, lose an average of twelve pounds during the six weeks of the course, and they keep on losing weight thereafter.[50]

Sometimes research produces surprising findings. Many practitioners have assured me that telephone sessions are just as effective as in-person sessions. We decided to test that theory by giving one group of veterans phone sessions and another office sessions. It turned out that the office sessions were markedly more effective at reducing PTSD symptoms. Reductions were 91% in the office group, and only 67% in the telephone group.[51] According to this study, the received wisdom was wrong.

In another PTSD study, we compared EFT delivered by life coaches to EFT delivered by licensed mental health professionals. Here the professionals showed an edge over the coaches (90% versus 83% remission rate) though the difference did not reach the threshold of statistical significance.[52] A graduate student performed an RCT to determine if the tapping part of EFT was a placebo or an active ingredient in its success. A control group did an identical routine but used mindful breathing rather than tapping. The EFT group saw a greater improvement in positive emotions and a reduction in negative ones.[53]

When you put the scientific studies of EFT and TFT together with the thousands of case histories reported on EFT Universe, the outlines of a swift, safe, and effective new healing approach become apparent. It promises us freedom from much of the burden of mental health problems such as phobias, anxiety, depression, and PTSD. Over the coming years, we could see big reductions in these conditions, just as a century ago developed countries virtually eliminated the scourges of typhoid, dysentery, cholera, and polio. A new generation of physicians and psychotherapists is coming of age. I expect an increasing number of them to understand the emotional roots of disease, and to consider releasing the emotional charge of childhood trauma an essential part of any treatment program.

11

Your Happy Genes

Based on what we know of the plasticity of the brain, we can think of things like happiness and compassion as skills that are no different from learning to play a musical instrument or tennis...it is possible to train our brains to be happy.

—Neuroscientist Richard Davidson

Wouldn't it be nice if we had a set of genes that coded for the biochemicals of happiness? Imagine if every one of us possessed a gene collection that, when the right genes were turned off or on, made us happy.

Being happy is what virtually everyone says they want. Even miserable people seem to be happy being miserable. Many human activities revolve around the goal of creating the conditions in which happiness can flourish. Material well-being, safety and security, and physical health all contribute to happiness. Spiritual practices can change our brains in ways that promote happiness.

Yet happiness is not an on-off condition like a light switch. You aren't either miserably depressed or ecstatic, with nothing in between. It's more like a the dimmer on a lamp, in which the position of the slider might be at any point between total lightness and total darkness, and is usually somewhere between those two extremes. In this way it's like our fight-or-flight response. We aren't either in total fight-or-flight mode or totally passive. Most of the time we're somewhere in between. Another spectrum is the production of cortisol and DHEA in the cortex of our adrenal glands. Your body isn't going flat out producing either one or the other. It's producing a ratio of both hormones. Prolonged stress will lead you to produce more cortisol. Prolonged relaxation will lead you to produce more DHEA. At any given moment, you're somewhere between the extremes.

Happiness, neurotransmitters, and stress genes all lie on a continuum

Happiness can also be found along a continuum. At any given moment, we're somewhere on the spectrum between ecstasy and despair. The difference between feeling slightly content and slightly discontent might only be a few clicks along the slider, not very far apart at all. The trick that happy people have learned is to push their emotional state closer to the happy end of the scale, and further away from the dark side. How do our genes figure into these endlessly variable emotional states, and what can we do to nudge our experience closer to the light side of the spectrum?

Genes and Emotional States

When emotional changes occur in the psychospiritual realm, biochemical changes occur in the body. These biochemicals are the products of gene expression. If your body is building more white blood cells, like AIDS patients who have spiritual transformations, or you're boosting your immune markers, like people who master the art of producing coherent heart rate patterns, the genes that code for those physiological changes must be active. When we measure the boost in a feel-good neurotransmitter like serotonin that occurs during positive experiences, it stands to reason that the underlying genes that tell our cells how to produce serotonin must be expressed.

Researchers have now published a sizeable number of reviews of studies that show a link between emotional states and genes.[1,2,3] They have examined the correlations between emotional disturbances such as schizophrenia, depression, panic, and posttraumatic stress disorder (PTSD) and gene expression, especially in the brain. They have come up with startling and compelling evidence that the patterns of gene expression in the brains of these unhappy sufferers are different from those of happier people. Emotions, it turns out, are epigenetic, and can methylate genes in parts of our brain involved in the stress response.

The process is not a one-way street, with emotions turning genes on and off. People with certain genes are more prone to unhappy emotions, though the evidence suggests that most conditions require external epigenetic triggers to stimulate these genes. A 2008 study funded by the National Institute of Mental Health found there are genes that predispose a person to PTSD as an adult. But PTSD is much more likely to occur in these adults if they also have a history of abuse as children.[4] It's an external environmental event, in the form of a traumatic childhood, that provides the epigenetic stimulus to the inner environment that triggers the gene changes. Such studies, using the new technology of DNA microarrays, or gene chips, are allowing scientists to peer into the gene expression in the fight-or-flight structures of the brain, and find out how genes are different in people with various flavors of unhappiness.

Unhappy Emotions, Unhappy Brain

Moshe Szyf, PhD, discovered that nurturing by mother rats provides an epigenetic stimulus to their offspring. Nurturing alters the expression of genes in the hippocampus and other parts of the brain that govern the fight-or-flight response, giving nurtured rats a better ability to manage stressful stimuli.[5] This made Szyf curious about whether human brains would show similar changes. He speculated that schizophrenics who had suffered abuse during their childhoods would also show changes in the hippocampus too.

He dissected the brains of twenty-four people who had donated their organs to science. Eleven of these had happy childhoods. The other thirteen were very unhappy indeed: They were schizophrenics who had committed suicide.

Szyf found that many of the stress-dampening genes in the hippocampi of the unhappy people were switched off. Although the unhappy people possessed all the right genes to dampen their stress response, the genes were methylated, which suppressed their activation. A Canadian study using brain tissue collected during autopsies also found that gene suppression in the brains of people who had committed suicide was much more prevalent than in happy people who had died accidental deaths.[6]

Szyf calls these suppressed genes "frozen assets," because while they are present in the brain, they are not accessible to its owner. In a part of the brain not involved with mood, called the cerebellum, there were no significant epigenetic differences between the happy and unhappy groups. This suggested that the methylation of the mood area was a response to the unhappy childhoods the schizophrenics had suffered.[7]

In a study of 177 boys incarcerated in a juvenile detention center, psychological depression plus a gene that transports the stress neurotransmitter dopamine were linked to unhappy and neglectful mothering.[8] Another researcher compared pregnant women who were being treated for depression using SSRI drugs (a class of antidepressants) with women who were depressed but not receiving the drugs and also compared them to happy women. They found increased secretion of stress hormones like cortisol in the babies three months after they were born, with a corresponding suppression of the infants' stress-dampening genes.[9] This research provides a potent reminder that it's not the presence or absence of genes, alone, that determines whether they build the proteins for which they're designed. We can suppress or facilitate their expression by external environmental influences.

Stress-Induced Genetic Changes

What's particularly interesting is to compare the genes of the same people before and after a stress experience. One study compared the gene expression of medical students to their anxiety scores on a standard psychological test. A measurement of their gene expression was taken just before their licensing examinations, a time of high test anxiety for the students. It was compared with a second gene chip sample and psychological test taken nine months earlier to provide a baseline. The researchers found that during the high-stress period, twenty-four genes were expressed differently. The expression of stress genes tracked the students' scores on the psychological test.[10]

Another set of researchers looked at people who were lonely and depressed, and compared the expression of their entire genome with a happier group. They found 209 genes that were differently expressed in the unhappy people. The nature of the affected genes is particularly interesting. They code for, amongst other things, markers of our levels of immunity from disease.[11] So unhappy people had weakened immune systems and were more susceptible to illness.

A research team found that depression and elevated cortisol correlate with changes in the expression of many of the genes in the limbic system of the brain, which is central to our stress response.[12] Another group examined the link between a gene that codes for cortisol and other aspects of the fight-or-flight response, and the psychological trait of anxiety. Anxious children were more likely to have this gene strongly expressed; the children of parents who had panic disorder, a very high degree of anxiety, showed an even stronger association between behavior and gene expression.[13] To translate what the researchers are saying into plain English (a language carefully avoided in scientific papers), the crazier and unhappier your family is, the more likely it is that you will be anxious and unhappy yourself, with the gene modifications to prove it.

Not only do your genes change with unhappiness, your brain wiring changes, too. Jeffrey Schwartz, PhD, a neuroscientist at the

University of California at Los Angeles, has studied a psychological illness called obsessive-compulsive disorder (OCD). He's tracked the changes that occur in bundles of neurons in the brain when OCD is treated. Successful treatment results, literally, in a rewiring of the neural connections inside the brain. Like a house that adds wiring to the electrical connections that are used most frequently, and strips wiring away from neglected circuits, the plastic brain is in constant motion, responding to stimuli by creating new neural pathways. Unhappiness reinforces our unhappy brain wiring, and vice versa.[14] Science is catching up to where spirituality has been for thousands of years; the Buddha urged us to maintain a calm state of desireless attention to the present moment, reminding us, "We are what we think. All that we are arises with our thoughts. With our thoughts, we make the world."

Psychologist Sees Different Diseases— Biologist Sees Similar Disease

It's interesting to notice that these epigenetic signals were provided by a wide variety of unhappy psychological conditions. Test anxiety is different from loneliness, which is different from PTSD, which is different from schizophrenia, which is different from OCD. Yet the body seems to interpret them all as similar epigenetic stress signals. Psychology has made an art of identifying and differentiating psychological conditions. The American Psychiatric Association's *Diagnostic and Statistical Manual of Mental Disorders,* fourth edition *(DSM-IV),* notes hundreds of classifications of distinct emotional maladies, from "vascular dementia with delirium" (290.41) to "factitious disorder with predominantly psychological signs and symptoms" (300.16).

Although reductionism, the act of differentiating mental disorders into so many categories, has its uses, it's worth remembering that the body doesn't work that way. Whereas all these flavors of stressed-out unhappiness may look different to a psychologist analyzing the mind, they look biochemically similar to a biologist analyzing the body.

The term "stress" was coined by German physician Hans Selye in the 1930s. As he walked the wards of his hospital, he noted that most sick people had certain common symptoms, including aches and pains, looking and feeling unwell, digestive upsets, rashes, and fever. He called this syndrome "stress." When there is enough environmental pressure, whether it's physical, emotional, electromagnetic, or chemical, to produce a surge of adrenaline and cortisol in the bloodstream, then what Selye called "an alarm reaction" follows.[15] Selye went in exactly the opposite direction from the reductionist approach in the *DSM-IV*. He didn't seek the highest common multiple of symptoms; instead he identified the lowest common denominators.

This makes evolutionary sense. When a woolly mammoth charged at your distant ancestor, your ancestor fought back or ran away. Anyone who hesitated was maimed or killed. Any one of a thousand different environmental epigenetic inputs—from a snake to a thorn to a scream to a lion to a spear to a poison ivy bush—would result in a single epigenetic output: activate fight-or-flight. When the woolly mammoth appeared, your ancestor didn't sit down on a log and wonder, "Gee, is this a Specific Phobia (300.29), a Panic Disorder Without Agoraphobia (300.01), or Mood Disorder (296.90)?" and then decide which course of action to take based on that diagnosis. He simply got out of Dodge as fast as his legs would carry him.

Stress Drives Gene Expression

Once Hans Selye had developed his insights into stress as the common denominator to much illness, a Harvard physician became famous for asking the logical next question, "How can we reverse stress?" His name was Herbert Benson, and he developed a method called the Relaxation Response. This stress antidote has practitioners sit quietly for twenty minutes, filling their minds with a positive phrase or belief, and focusing on relaxing their muscles from the feet all the way up to the head. Studies showed that the Relaxation Response was able to help with many different ailments, from high blood pressure to infertility to rheumatoid arthritis to pain. "How could a single simple stress-reduction technique affect so many different conditions?" researchers wondered.

The answer had to wait till the invention of DNA microarrays at the end of the twentieth century, which made possible the study of the Relaxation Response as an epigenetic intervention. Benson took healthy subjects, and compared the differences in gene expression patterns between long-term practitioners of the Relaxation Response and non-practitioners. Then, he put the non-practitioners through an eight-week training, and found that their gene expression profile had changed to substantially resemble that of the long-term practitioners. He then replicated his findings before publishing them.

Among the genes that changed were those involved with inflammation, the rate at which cells regenerate, and the scavenging of free radicals, which are a prime contributor to aging. "For hundreds of years Western medicine has looked at mind and body as totally separate entities, to the point where saying something 'is all in your head' implied that it was imaginary," said Benson of the study. "Now we've found how changing the activity of the mind can alter the way basic genetic instructions are implemented." The Benson study's coauthor says, "This is the first comprehensive study of how the mind can affect gene expression, linking what has been looked on as a soft science with the hard science of genomics." Psychology and spirituality have been regarded as less rigorous than biology and physiology, and the scientific world is having to rethink its priorities as it discovers that invisible human emotions have profound epigenetic effects.[16]

Dean Ornish, PhD, who made the cover of *Time* magazine for his groundbreaking discovery that diet can reverse coronary artery disease, has taken his insights one step further in a gene study published in 2008. He examined the effects of lifestyle change, including an hour a day of a stress-reduction technique such as meditation, on men with prostate cancer. The subjects had decided not to undergo conventional surgery and radiation, or hormone-based cancer treatments. Instead, for three months, they changed their lifestyles. In addition to meditation and other stress management methods, they walked for a half hour a day, and ate a diet rich in legumes, soy, fruits, whole grains, and vegetables. It came as no surprise to the researchers to learn that the men lost weight and lowered their blood pressure. But when the researchers compared prostate biopsies taken before and after, they discovered that an astonishing 501 genes had been changed in just three months. Genes associated with breast cancer and prostate cancer had shut down.

Ornish observes, "It's an exciting finding because so often people say, 'Oh, it's all in my genes, what can I do?' Well, it turns out you may be able to do a lot!"[17] Meditation, prayer, spiritual practice and attendance at a house of worship are all stress-reducing activities. A vibrant spiritual social life also affects life span; the hospitalization rate of churchgoers is half that of non-churchgoers.[18]

Stress, emotions, spirituality, and disease are inextricably linked. Scientific papers have now documented the connection between stress and many organic diseases, including heart attacks, cancer, and the progression of HIV/AIDS.[19] Emotional states such as panic, hostility, depression, and anger all contribute to heart attack risk.[20] The link between cancer and stress is particularly interesting, and has been shown in much research. But a recent study found receptor sites on the outside of cancer cells for adrenaline, indicating a *straight-line biochemical link* between stress and tumors. When we're stressed, our bodies are flooded with cortisol and adrenaline, and this study found that cancers grew 275% faster in stressed mice than in unstressed mice.[21] The scientific consensus is that only 5% to 10% of cancers are hereditary; the rest are due to environmental factors, including stress.

In a paper entitled *Spirituality and Immunity,*[22] Stephen Marini, PhD, lists studies that show the following results of stress at the cellular level:

- Wound healing takes nine days longer.

- Intercellular communication is decreased.

- The immune system is suppressed.

- Poorer inflammation response at the site of injury.

- Increased bacterial infections.

- Increased susceptibility to autoimmune diseases.

- Decreased ability to handle invading toxins.

"We don't have a pill for this," says Moshe Frenkel, MD, medical director of the Place of Wellness, the integrative medicine department at the M. D. Anderson cancer clinic in Houston, Texas, one of the most advanced cancer treatment facilities in the country. "But we do have yoga, meditation, and guided imagery."[23] Using a de-stressing technique doesn't just activate your happy genes, it activates your healthy genes, too!

Telomeres and Life Span

Many of the genes found in these studies were regulatory genes, regulating the expression of other genes and proteins. In a study of fruit flies, the expression of a single regulatory gene triggered the expression of 2,500 other genes. The gene is called PAX6 and it regulates the development of the insects' eyes. Under lab conditions, when induced to turn on, PAX6 led to the growth of an extra eye on the antenna.[24]

Telomeres are the "tails" on the ends of chromosomes. Think of unzipping a zipper on your shirt. At the bottom of the zipper, there's a stopper. This prevents the zipper from unraveling. Telomeres are like stoppers on the ends of chromosomes. To the cell, they signal the end point of the replicating sequence of DNA.

There is a cost to this transaction, however. Each time a cell divides, a pair of molecules falls off the end of the telomere stopper. This makes the telomere a little bit shorter. Throughout the life of a cell, the telomeres shorten with each division, until they are too short to function anymore. At that point, the cell dies. As our bodies age, our telomeres get about 1% shorter each year. Because the process is slow and stable, biologists consider telomere length to be the most accurate possible measure of aging. In a lab, they can measure your biological age, which may be quite different from your chronological age. You might be fifty years old chronologically, but your telomere markers can indicate a biological age of forty or sixty.

Our lifestyle and habits affect the rate at which our telomeres shorten. Poor choices accelerate the process. Stress also shortens telomeres. A study of older adults who had faced many challenges as children revealed that they had shorter telomeres. The difference wasn't trivial; it translated into a life expectancy lower by seven to fifteen years.[25] In a group of studies conducted at the University of California at San Francisco, pessimism, stress, childhood trauma, depression, and other mental health problems were associated with shortened telomeres. One study found that thirty-year-olds with PTSD were nearly five years older than average, biologically speaking.[26] By the age of thirty, a five-year gap represents a big difference between biological and chronological age. Our bodies can be affected by stress even before we are born. If mothers have high levels of the stress hormone cortisol, their offspring have more emotional and cognitive problems after birth.[27] The children of unhappy mothers also have shorter telomeres, inheriting the legacy of stress before they even take their first breath.[28]

Analysis of thirty studies by Dutch professor Ruud Veenhoven found that happiness adds between seven and ten years to your lifespan. He found that happy people were more likely to control their weight, perceive illness symptoms early on, and moderate their smoking and alcohol consumption. "Chronic unhappiness activates the fight-flight response, which is known to involve harmful effects in the long run such as higher blood pressure and a lower immune response," Veenhoven observed.[29]

Not only is happiness healthy, it's contagious. You can catch it from the people sitting next to you. A large scale study of residents of Framingham, Massachusetts, from 1983 on, noted their degree of happiness, amongst other things. Since they had such a large group, the researchers were able to analyze how happiness spread throughout the population. They found that having a friend who's happy increases your chances of happiness by 15%. A second-degree connection, such as the happy spouse of a friend, raises your chances by 10%. And a third-degree contact, such as the friend of a friend, increases it by 6%, after which the effect trails off. And surrounding yourself by more happy friends increases the effect.[30] Since our social networks are largely under our control, this research presents us with yet another practical leverage point over our gene expression. While dumping negative friends and seeking positive ones may be difficult after a lifetime of association, it's a strong signal of an intention to recreate our lives in a healthier mold. And if you find positive people avoiding you after they read the Framingham study, you might be one of the unhappy people they're avoiding, and may need to undertake what Alcoholics Anonymous calls "a fearless moral inventory"!

Choices Reverse Childhood

If you had a lousy childhood, and your stress-dampening mechanisms were epigenetically compromised, are you doomed to a lifetime of unhappiness? Here again research has some encouraging answers for us. When scientists took mice that had been nurtured early on, and deprived them as adults, they undid most of the positive effects of maternal nurturing. But when they took mice that had been neglected as newborns, and provided them with a nurturing environment, the deficits they had shown were partially reversed.[31] Other studies reflect the same possibility. One found twenty-seven genes upregulated by a hearty dose of laughter![32] This suggests that it's never too late to give yourself a happy childhood. Surrounding yourself by nurturing people and conditions can start to reverse the methylation and acetylization patterns in your stress system.

EFT, mindfulness, and other techniques described in this book can have powerful epigenetic effects. A 2014 study found that mindfulness meditation produced rapid and dramatic genetic improvements in the course of just a single day. Dr. Richard Davidson and colleagues examined the gene expression profiles of group of experienced meditators after a day of mindfulness meditation, and compared them to a group that engaged in leisure activities. They found changes in several important classes of genes, including those that regulate inflammation in the body, those that dampen pain, and those that lower cortisol.[33]

In another recent paper, molecular biologist Garret Yount, PhD, of the California Pacific Medical Center (CPMC), traced the molecular pathways by which EFT might affect some of the genes involved in cancer.[34] Dr. Yount and I are working on a study to map the genetic changes that occur after EFT treatment. These studies show that you can take your health into your own hands, meditating and tapping to produce the epigenetic signals required to nudge your gene expression in a positive direction.

Every minute, about one million of your cells die. An equal number of cells are born each minute. Perhaps you implanted lousy epigenetic signals into your old cells through destructive habits and emotions. But your old cells are on their way out. If you start sending new epigenetic signals to the cells that are just getting born, filling your heart with love and your mind with positive thoughts, your new cells might be healthier than the ones they're replacing. Every single molecule in your brain is replaced every two months. Every single cell in your body is replaced every seven years. So as you give yourself a psychospiritual makeover, you give yourself an epigenetic make-over too.

This kind of genetic drift over time shows up in identical twins. They start out with exactly the same genome, and at the age of three, their genes are indistinguishable from one another. But by age fifty, there are many differences in methylation, and hence gene expression.[35] They have made different emotional and spiritual choices, their lifestyles are the habits they've cultivated, they have different stress levels, and every cell in their body has been replaced at least seven times. Though they began life with the same genome, on average identical twins die more than ten years apart! That's a huge difference, indicating that the choices you make have powerful epigenetic effects, at all stages of your life.

The most recent research makes epigenetics even more important than it was before, by showing that conditions can be passed from generation to generation. A stressed mother can pass her patterns of gene expression on to her children. For instance, not only do the daughters of unhappy mothers have a lower birth weight, but the effect extends to their granddaughters as well. Depression, anxiety, and other forms of stress can also be passed down epigenetically generation after generation.[36] There is no change in the genome itself, only in which genes are expressed. The emotions and actions of our parents are epigenetic triggers, inserting chemical tags onto the genes within our cells.

The effects don't last for only one generation. They can last for many. In one startling study, investigators trained laboratory mice to fear a particular scent, that of cherry blossoms. Their offspring then feared the same scent, even though they had never been exposed to it. Not only that, but the offspring of the next generation also feared the scent of cherry blossoms. A particular gene in the sperm of the mice had been chemically tagged by the induced fear, perpetuating the unhappy emotions in their offspring. The fearful experience also produced changes in the brains of the mice affected. The study concluded: "The experiences of a parent, even before conceiving, markedly influence both structure and function in the nervous system of subsequent generations."[37] The researchers call this "transgenerational epigenetic inheritance" and say it provides compelling evidence that memories and emotional predispositions can be passed between generations through epigenetics.

So the scientific evidence continues to pour in, and it is com-pelling. It tells us that where we are on that happiness scale, our emotional state, has a powerful epigenetic effect on our bodies, affecting all the major systems of our body. It also provides us with a list of the practical things we can do to nudge ourselves toward happiness. We can use:

- Positive beliefs
- Spirituality
- Prayers
- Positive images and visualizations
- Electromagnetic shifts

- Optimism
- Intention
- Energy medicine
- Energy Psychology
- Positive attitude
- Nurturing
- Gratitude
- Happy social networks
- Acts of kindness
- Meditation

The exciting implication of this research is that so many of the items in this list are under our conscious control. We can change our attitude by an act of choice. We can stop ourselves speaking an unkind word. We can volunteer for a charity. Every day presents us with opportunities for altruistic acts, if we're awake to the possibility. We can say uplifting words to the people around us, and perform small acts of service. We can pray to whatever deity speaks to our deepest longings. We can meditate. We can join a house of worship, a club, a sports team, or a support group. We can use energy medicine and Energy Psychology to quickly dissipate the emotional charge of traumatic events. We can invent stories and imagine visualizations that are positive. We can turn off our TVs, and read books that enrich our hearts. We can watch inspiring movies and listen to soothing music.

Although these consciousness-based methods are different, they all can affect the stress response. Benson says, "We found that no matter which particular technique is used—different forms of meditation and yoga, breath focus, or repetitive prayer—the mechanism involved is the same." As we use these consciousness-based techniques to shift our emotional state from anxiety to serenity, we affect our gene expression. These are all behaviors we can choose deliberately, inducing happiness, and giving us active control over the genetic markers we place on the game board of life. Your happy genes are present in your body and brain as potentials. What you do with them shapes your destiny.

Soul Medicine as Conventional Medicine

We have to recognize that we are spiritual beings with souls existing in a spiritual world as well as material beings with bodies and brains existing in a material world.

—Nobel Laureate Sir John Eccles[1]

"Tim Garton, a world champion swimmer, was diagnosed in 1989 with stage two non-Hodgkin's lymphoma. He was forty-nine years old and had a tumor the size of a football in his abdomen. It was treated with surgery, followed by four chemotherapy treatments over twelve weeks, with subsequent abdominal radiation for eight weeks. Despite initial concern that the cancer appeared to be terminal, the treatment was successful, and by 1990, Tim was told that he was in remission. He was also told that he would never again compete at a national or international level. However, in 1992, Tim

Garton returned to competitive swimming, and won the one hundred meter freestyle world championship.

"In early July of 1999, he was diagnosed with prostate cancer. A prostatectomy in late July revealed that the cancer had expanded beyond the borders of his prostate and could not all be surgically removed. Once again, he received weekly radiation treatment in the area of his abdomen. After eight weeks of treatment, the cancer had cleared.

"In 2001, the lymphoma returned, this time in his neck. It was removed surgically. Tim again received radiation, though this time it left severe burns on his neck. The following year, a growth on the other side of his neck, moving over his trachea, was diagnosed as a fast-growing lymphoma that required emergency surgery.

"He was told that the lymphoma was widespread. An autologous bone marrow and stem cell transplant was done at this time, but it was not successful. There was also concern that the tumors would metastasize to his stomach. His doctors determined at this point that they could do nothing more for him. He was told that highly experimental medical treatments, for which there was little optimism, were the only alternative. He was given an injection of monoclonal antibodies (Rituxan), which had been minimally approved for recurrent low-grade lymphoma. Rituxan is designed to flag the cancer sites and potentially help stimulate the immune system to know where to focus.

"At this point Tim enlisted the services of Kim Wedman, an energy medicine practitioner trained by Donna Eden. Tim and his wife went to the Bahamas for three weeks, and they brought Kim with them for the first week. Kim provided daily sessions lasting an hour and a half. These sessions included a basic energy balancing routine, 'meridian tracing,' a 'chakra clearing,' work with the 'electrical,' 'neurolymphatic,' and 'neurovascular' points, a correction for energies that are designed to cross over from one side of the body to the other but are not, and a daily assessment of his other basic energy systems, followed by corrections for any that were out of balance. While Tim was not willing to follow Kim's advice to curb his substantial alcohol consumption, or modify his meat-and-potatoes diet, he did introduce fresh vegetable juices into his regimen, plus an herbal tea (Flor-Essence) that is believed to have medicinal properties.

"Kim also taught Tim and his wife a twenty-minute, twice-daily energy medicine protocol, which they followed diligently, both during the week she was there, and for the subsequent two weeks. The protocol included a basic energy balancing routine, and specific interventions for the energy pathways that govern the immune system and that feed energy to the stomach, kidneys, and bladder.

"Upon returning to his home in Denver, in order to determine how quickly the cancers might be spreading, Tim scheduled a follow-up assessment with the oncologist who had told him, 'There is nothing more that we can do for you.' To everyone's thrill and surprise, Tim was cancer-free. He has remained so during the four years between that assessment and the time of this writing. He has been checked with a PET scan each year, with no cancer detected. Was it the energy treatments or the single Rituxan shot that caused the cancer to go into remission over those three weeks? No one knows. Tim still receives Rituxan injections every two months, but he also continues to work with Kim Wedman on occasion for tune-ups."[2]

While the names and other identifying characteristics of patients whose cases are described in this book have been concealed, in this case they have not; Tim Garton gave his permission for this story to be published. Kim Wedman, the energy practitioner who worked with Tim Garton, trained with Donna Eden, author of *Energy Medicine,* and her husband, clinical psychologist David Feinstein, PhD.

Energy Medicine in Hospitals

The demand by patients for CAM, or complementary and alternative medicine, of which energy medicine is a subset, is enormous. A survey by the World Health Organization found that up to 80% of the population in Asia, Latin America, and Africa use CAM.[3] A

2004 survey by the U.S. Centers for Disease Control and Prevention (CDC) found that 62% of adults used CAM in the previous year;[4] the number in a 2008 study was 66%. That study also showed that the majority of patients would like to receive CAM treatments in a primary care facility such as a clinic, doctor's office, or hospital. This wish is taking shape, in fact, as hospitals and clinics increasingly offer CAM services.[5]

Although far from widespread, energy medicine and Energy Psychology (EP) techniques are working their way into mainstream medicine, with increased understanding that unresolved emotional and spiritual maladies underlie many physical diseases. Kaiser Permanente, a giant hospital organization with nine million members, offers "healthy living" classes, including such methods as qigong, yoga, and meditation, at many of its campuses. Kaiser's medical center and hospital in Santa Rosa, California, where I live, uses natural light wherever possible, rather than artificial illumination. To inspire patients to reflect and meditate, it has a labyrinth that patients and their families can walk.

The Portland, Oregon, Kaiser hospital performed a formal trial of weight-loss therapies, comparing the EP method called TAT (Tapas Acupressure Technique) to their current therapies. The TAT group maintained their weight loss after six months, while the group using Kaiser's usual protocol gained back much of the weight they had lost.[6] Kaiser uses EFT in some of its classes, and some of its psychotherapists offer EP to their clients. Sometimes practitioners ask me, "Aren't conventional doctors skeptical about Energy Psychology?" I've given presentations to thousands of medical professionals, including many Kaiser Permanente staff members, and I've found them very open. Most doctors recognize the role that emotions play in disease.

All these activities are good for patients, but they are not purely altruistic on Kaiser's part. A patient at an ideal weight, with a strong mediation practice, and an arsenal of EP techniques for releasing their daily stress, is not just a healthier and happier patient. Such a person is also a lot less likely to need expensive medical interventions, with the result that Kaiser is the lowest-cost health care provider in the San Francisco Bay Area.

The University of Texas has a cancer research and treatment facility in Houston called the M. D. Anderson Cancer Center. In collaboration with a seven-hospital chain called Orlando Regional Healthcare, it has set up the M. D. Anderson Cancer Center Orlando (MDACCO) in Florida.

M. D. Anderson Cancer Center Orlando

Besides offering a wide range of cancer therapies and excellent conventional care, M. D. Anderson has a pioneering Mind-Body-Spirit department that includes an Energy Medicine Program. It was set up and is managed by Patricia Butler, MA, and uses the techniques taught by Donna Eden's "Eden Energy Medicine" certification. Butler provides counseling and EP services to the staff, and also provides energy medicine services to patients on request to reduce the side effects of chemotherapy and radiation. Information on the Energy Medicine Program is found in the "Patient Information Guide" given to every new cancer patient.

During chemotherapy treatments, Butler may sit with patients and do this work while they're hooked up to the chemotherapy drip. She has observed many beneficial effects in patients who combine energy medicine with their conventional treatments. Patients often report feeling much better during and after chemotherapy sessions in which they simultaneously receive energy medicine treatments than chemotherapy sessions in which they don't. "Energy medicine seems to calm the body's energy systems, enabling them to tolerate the presence of chemotherapy drugs," Butler observes. And they often don't require further medications for insomnia or listlessness. She wrote the following account of a typical case:

Sylvia was fifty-five years old when doctors discovered a malignant gastric tumor growing right at the joint between her esophagus and her stomach. With the shock of this news resonating wildly throughout her system, she listened as they recommended chemotherapy and radiation to shrink the tumor followed by surgery to remove what was left behind. Feeling nervous about the outcome, but not knowing what else to do, she followed all of their protocols and underwent the surgery as soon as it was indicated. The good news, she learned afterward, was that the operation had been a success and she was now cancer-free; the bad news was that they'd had to remove her entire stomach to get all of the cancer. They placed a feeding tube in her side to ensure that she would get nutrition, and told her they hoped she could eat normal food one day (albeit with careful new strategies). Although she did her best to recover from both her treatments and the rearrangement of her digestive tract, her quality of life took a real nosedive. The next six months were simply miserable.

Sylvia's follow-up care was transferred to M. D. Anderson Cancer Center Orlando (not her original treatment center), and she learned about the hospital's Energy Medicine Program. She came to see me, wondering if energy medicine could help her begin to feel better and get her life back again. As she began to tell me about her very uncomfortable state, I learned that the worst part for her was the nausea that she'd felt every day since her surgery six months before. Not only was it debilitating, it kept her from being able to eat, and she couldn't have her feeding tube removed until she could eat again. Along with the nausea, Sylvia still felt quite a bit of pain along the incision, at the tube site, and in her lower back. It took 20 mg of methadone three times a day to hold the pain at bay, and she didn't like the way that made her feel. This pile-up of daily pain, nausea, and an inability to eat left her feeling "morbidly depressed," she told me, a term rarely used by non-psychotherapists, but one which captured the destitute emotional state in which she found herself.

Using the energy medicine techniques that I'd learned from Donna Eden, I began to rebalance some basic energy patterns in her body and went after the nausea by holding key acupuncture points with my fingertips. To her astonishment, the nausea began to ease within minutes! When I told her that she could hold these points on herself and get results, she was both delighted and highly motivated to try it. I encouraged her to do this every day, with the idea that she could retrain her energy system to flow in more functional ways, thereby changing her body's nausea response. Then I cleared and balanced her energy vortices, paying special attention to those that were situated near areas of pain. She could feel the pain beginning to soften as I gently spun these energy centers above her body.

By the third session, her nausea surfaced only occasionally, and her pain was described as "mild." At this point, I began using principles from Energy Psychology to identify and clear thought patterns that might be impeding a more complete level of healing. She tapped on acupuncture points while simultaneously thinking about her pain and nausea, and found that it deactivated the negative emotions associated with her thoughts. "I feel good!" she said, with a look of surprise on her face. She could tell that the pattern of her symptoms was becoming more intermittent, and she knew that she was moving in the right direction. I explained that while most patients feel relief in the first session, there is a cumulative benefit derived from multiple treatments as the energy patterns are repeatedly rebalanced and the body's healing systems are coaxed back into action. By the following week, her nausea was completely gone, her apprehension about eating greatly diminished, and she began to eat small amounts of normal food. The week after that, to her great relief, her feeding tube was removed.

When we are in a great deal of pain and discomfort, it's hard to attend to other matters in our lives, and that was true for Sylvia. Her illness and suffering had derailed her from moving through a healthy grieving process over the recent deaths of her parents, but as the layers of her physical symptoms peeled away, she was able to talk about the sadness that she still felt at losing them. To support her energetically through this process, I worked with her lung meridian, which carries the resonance of grief, and she found herself feeling lighter in spirit. Still missing them, but now with a lighter spirit.

Before we ended her energy medicine sessions, she asked me for help with one more thing. "I'm feeling really scared about my next PET scan, and about finding out whether or not the cancer has returned." To soothe her intense anxiety, I had her create a mental videotape of images, thoughts, and feelings regarding the upcoming scan, and asked her to "run it" while I held places on her head called *neurovascular points* that are known to send a calming, soothing energy throughout the body. In less than ten minutes, her worry melted away; she felt ready to get the scan, and decided she'd just hope for the best.

Like other patients with a serious illness, Sylvia brought myriad physical, emotional, and spiritual concerns to our energy medicine sessions. She began to understand that each stress that we cleared from her body-mind would move her to a deeper level of peace, helping to create a more optimal climate for the functioning of her immune system.

I was elated when I received a phone message that her scans were clear. At her tenth and last session, Sylvia summed up her appraisal of energy medicine by saying, "My nausea is gone, my pain medication went from 60 mg to 5 mg a day, I'm eating normal food, and I feel joy in my life again!" She was amazed that it had all been accomplished without the use of further medication. Two years later, Sylvia called to tell me she was still feeling great.

Pat Butler has seen a marked shift in public attitudes toward energy medicine in the past decade. "Patients used to make comments like, 'I don't know if this fits into my religious beliefs,'" she observes, "but not any more. There is a growing awareness that there is a wide set of possibilities for optimal treatment." This awareness is penetrating the research community as well; a group of researchers at the University of Illinois, Chicago, recently wrote that, "instead of trying to fit cancer into a theory employing genetic determinism, we have accepted that dependence upon genetic determinism to explain cancer has become obsolete,"[7] and researchers as well as hospitals are more open to exploring how energy medicine and conventional medicine can both benefit patients with cancer and other serious diseases.

Discerning an Appropriate Treatment Path

Andrew Weil, MD, has developed a simple formulation to allow patients to determine whether conventional or alternative medicine is right for their particular condition. In his book *Spontaneous Healing*, he lays out a set of criteria that allows both patients and medical professionals to "stream" patients into either alternative or conventional therapies. It's important for each of us to have at least a rough idea of whether our condition can be effectively treated by allopathic medicine, whether the best leverage point comes from an alternative therapy, or whether to combine both. In *Soul Medicine*, Norman Shealy, MD, and I describe in detail how to work with your conventional physician and your alternative care provider simultaneously, a course we believe often provides the best of both worlds.

One of the most intriguing experiments in setting up the clinic of the future—one that encompasses both conventional and alternative approaches—is an establishment called the Integrative Medical Clinic of Santa Rosa (California), or IMCSR. Robert Dozor, MD, and his wife, Ellen Barnett, MD, PhD, established their treatment center in 2001. Upon walking into the clinic, the first thing the visitor sees is a wide hall, with a fountain and beautiful artwork,

Fountains, curves, and open space in the waiting room at the Integrative Medical Clinic of Santa Rosa (IMCSR)

Kwan Yin, the Goddess of compassion, on the altar in a corner of the waiting room at IMCSR

Comfortable chairs, plants, and a patient lending library at IMCSR

which then opens up into a large room with comfortable couches, an altar, another fountain, and a holistic health library. On the way, there is a glass-fronted herbal dispensary and a receptionist's desk.

Among the practitioners at IMCSR are a chiropractor (DC), a somatic therapist (CMT), an acupuncturist (LAc), a marriage and family therapist (MFT), a naturopathic doctor (ND), and a psychologist (PhD). In addition, doctors Dozor and Barnett have a compendious knowledge of Ayurveda, Chinese medicine, herbalism, and other alternative medical specialties.

The treatment protocol is coordinated by a computer system that tracks patient files and updates them in real time. During a consultation with the naturopath, for instance, he enters his notes on a screen that is immediately available to all the other practitioners. He might also walk ten steps down the hall to consult with the psychologist or with the family physician. If a patient goes from him to the physician, the physician has an immediate record of exactly what the naturopath's findings and prescriptions were. This system is essential to the coordination of treatment in so many different modalities.

Navigating the Options

Barbara Marx Hubbard, one of the world's preeminent futurists, points out that many of today's occupations did not exist fifty years ago: "Just as many of the new functions that people do today—biotechnician, telecommunication specialist, nanotechnologist, environmentalist, futurist, medical ethicist, desktop publisher—didn't exist in the 1950s, the job descriptions that reflect our emerging evolutionary vocations or callings are yet to be defined."[8] The World Future Society, in a report on "High-Paying Jobs of Tomorrow," lists careers of the future. They include bioinformationalists, who study the results of genetic discoveries and package this knowledge for the developers of practical therapies. Telemedicine technicians connect medical teams with patients or clinicians in remote areas. Cybrarians organize online information, and so on.[9]

One of the most interesting ways in which IMCSR points to the future is that it has required the invention of a new job: an intake specialist, or "Navigator" in IMCSR parlance. This highly skilled person meets with patients and assesses which treatment, or combination of treatments, might work best for them. The mix might change as they visit different practitioners in the building, but the Navigator has responsibility for making the initial determination. Early planning for the IMCSR assumed that a physician would have this responsibility, but the insurance compensation system of the current American medical system means that the physicians are the financial drivers of the clinic; it is their time that generates the most revenue and supports the rest. The structure of the clinic was adjusted accordingly, and the job of Navigator created. In the last decade, many other complex medical systems have invented similar jobs. They may go by the name of "Nurse Navigator" or "Integrative Healthcare Coordinator," but their function remains to match patients with appropriate treatments.

Intention as Quantum Conversation

It is possible to imagine a time in the near future when *paying attention* will be the first thing we do when we get sick. Spiritual and emotional remedies will be the first line of defense, not the last. Sufferers will seek metaphysical solutions *not* when they've *exhausted* all conventional means, but instead *before* they submit to the drugs and surgery of allopathic medicine. Allopathic medicine might become a medicine of last resort, rather than of first. It will be used to treat certain conditions for which it is admirably suited. But others, especially some of the recently recognized and still-mysterious conditions such as autoimmune disorders, will first be treated with noninvasive methods that shift the patient's energy field. Dr. Shealy estimates that surgery or drugs are required by no more than 15% of patients.[10] Many, perhaps most, of the times drugs or surgery are used today are inappropriate. Alan Roses, MD, vice president of genetics for Glaxo, one of the world's largest drug companies, startled the medical world in 2003 when he frankly admitted that most of the industry's drugs are ineffective. Britain's *Independent* newspaper reported that Roses "said fewer than half of the patients prescribed some of the most expensive drugs actually derived any benefit from them.

"It is an open secret within the drugs industry that most of its products are ineffective in most patients, but this is the first time that such a senior drugs boss has gone public. His comments came days after it emerged that the NHS [Britain's universal health service] drugs' bill has soared by nearly 50% in three years."[11] A contemporaneous article by respected medical reporter Susan Kelleher reported how "some of America's most prestigious medical societies take money from the drug companies and then promote the industry's agenda."[12] The result is that many patients take drugs that are worse than the disease for which they are being treated, or "even kill them."[13]

Money infects medicine to the detriment of patients. A comparison of studies of drugs used to treat schizophrenia found that the pharmaceutical company whose drug came out on top in the study was almost always the company that had paid for the study.[14] And even when they're prescribed, doctors are not always doing patients a favor: "Pharmaceuticals temporarily diminish anxiety, panic, and depression; decrease our emotional and physical pain; or kill hostile germs in the body. Yet they leave the root causes of our ailments untouched and diminish our capacity to feel. And our feelings contain vital information that is essential for our health, well-being, and peak functioning."[15]

The closer you scrutinize the alternatives, the more attractive energy medicine becomes. A TAT or EFT session—safe, noninvasive, and usually effective—is a much more compelling first line of treatment than conventional medical therapies for most conditions. It shifts our maladaptive beliefs and irrational fears, rather than suppressing them with prescription drugs.

Precise Energy Leverage Points

The energy diagnosis of the future might be focused on discovering the precise leverage point required to produce healing. Imagine a logjam on a river, hundreds of logs piled up producing a blockage through which nothing can pass. Removing the logs one by one is a tedious process requiring the expenditure of great stores of energy.

But if you find the right log or logs that are the linchpins around which the pressure pattern of the whole jam takes form, and remove it, suddenly all the other logs are released too, without the massive application of work required to remove them all one by one. In the same way, each patient responds differently, and it's worth finding their maximum leverage point. One might benefit most from aromatherapy, another from acupressure, another from somatic therapy. One person's logjam is another person's forest.

Then within each discipline, good therapists notice the particular logs that are holding up the flow. A good acupuncturist may stimulate only the three or four points required to restore balance to the body's energies. A skilled somatic massage therapist will go straight to the zone that releases the most tension the fastest. "How did you know where to touch me?" amazed patients often ask. Adept professionals can quickly spot where the maximum point of pressure is in the mass of logs, and pull out just that one log that releases the rest. When the precise leverage point is discovered, you can focus on healing only those items that are holding you back, the single logs in the logjam that are inhibiting vitality throughout your system.

The skilled diagnostician and prescriber of the future will be trained to spot the possible constellations of jammed logs, and, by going straight to the point of maximum leverage, offer the patient effective relief. Patients who present with various conditions might be trained to discover which thought, linked to which belief, linked to which strong emotion, will release their particular logjam. When precise energy leverage techniques become the front line of medicine, many conditions from which people today suffer will become a thing of the past.

Medicine, wellness, and healing look very different in a quantum world than they did in the mechanistic and reductionist world that preceded it. Each new discovery is another indication of how important consciousness is for healing. We are learning to see our cells and our bodies as malleable, influenced by every thought and feeling that flows through us. Knowing this, we can choose to take responsibility for the quality of thought and feeling we host, and choose those that radiate benevolence, goodwill, vibrance, and wellness. Doing this, we positively affect not just our own well-being, but also that of the entire world of which we are a part—and the great ocean of consciousness in which our individual minds swim.

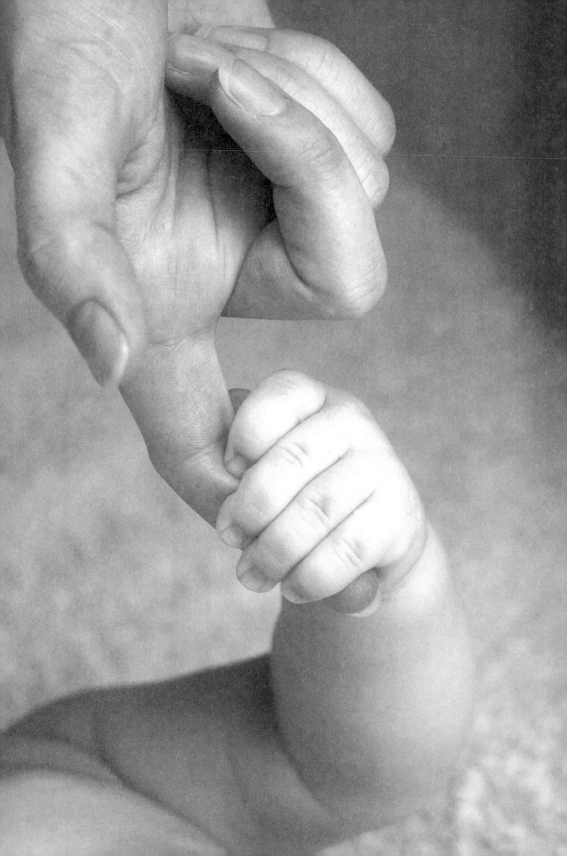

13

Tapping a World of Healing

If you don't break your ropes while you're alive, do you think ghosts will do it after?

—Rumi

"I deployed with 10th Mountain Division to Baghdad from September 2006 to June 2007. I performed a variety of jobs, including guard, medical lab, medic, and pharmacy work. My experience was a typical mosaic of long days, stress, and a variety of emotionally powerful events. In short, I was exposed to the following experiences (some face-to-face and others indirectly through my comrades): IED explosions, small arms fire, rocket attacks, sniper attacks, wounded and dead Americans, allies, and Iraqis (military, enemy, and civilians—including women and children), mass casualty, suicide, self-mutilation, divorce, infidelity, fist fights, rape, captured and beheaded U.S. soldiers, imprisoned terrorists, smell and sights of bloody, decomposing, and burnt tissues, booby traps, destroyed vehicles, and a persistent fear of being attacked.

"Upon my return from deployment, I began my first year of medical school at the Uniformed Services University of the Health Sciences (USU). Even though I completed the first academic year

279

with good grades, I noticed that my quality of life had diminished significantly. I recognized that I was no longer able to be present in the moment and was always observing whatever was happening in my life from a 'witness' perspective. I also replayed many situations in my mind, often thinking of how I could have done them differently. I no longer laughed much and felt burdened by my past, reminiscing about the days when ignorance was bliss.

"A year went by. I spoke about my experiences to a variety of people in attempts to 'release' them or find peace from their recurrent nature. Talking about the experiences helped me a bit, but only on an intellectual level. I understood that what I was feeling was 'a normal reaction to an abnormal situation.' I knew that I had done my best and was a force of good in this world. But my symptoms persisted even after talking about them.

"Then I met an old acquaintance who asked if I was open to letting her try something called EFT to help me gain freedom from my recurring emotions. She said it was an emotional tool and not a mental one. We spent a total of four hours doing the work over two days. The results were immediate. I literally fell back into my body from a defensive posture that I had unknowingly created in my mind. I could feel my body again and could not stop crying and laughing. I could now be present in the moment and not have half of my attention observing the situation as it was happening. I also became less reactive to whistle sounds and sirens that used to initiate in me a flight-or-flight response, as incoming rockets had done in Iraq. Overall, I regained the quality of life that I had prior to deployment.

"It was truly an 'emotional freedom technique.' Since then, I have been on a constant upward spiral and have been able to transform my past into a great strength. We worked through every single memory and emotion that I was not in peace with and 'tapped them out.' I also learned how to self-administer EFT and have been practicing it on myself whenever something new has emerged from my past."

Healing the Wounded Warriors

The previous account was written by Olli Toukolehto, MD, a psychiatrist at Walter Reed Army Medical Center, with whom I am privileged to be working on a project that I believe has immense implications for the future of humankind. Lifting the suffering of one person is a great achievement. If we can lift the suffering of the estimated five hundred thousand troops who have returned from Iraq and Afghanistan, it will change American society. Such a change will point the way toward relieving the suffering of other groups in many countries who are struggling with depression, anxiety, posttraumatic stress disorder (PTSD), and other ailments. A world where these conditions are reduced by even 10% is a world worth striving for. A world in which every child is taught the tools to release the emotional charge of traumatic events will be a very different world from the one we now have.

Dr. Toukolehto, I, and a pool of volunteers created a new nonprofit initiative called the Veterans Stress Project (www.StressProject.org). The number of U.S. troops who have returned from deployment in the Middle East with PTSD is about the same number that returned from Vietnam with PTSD. The Veterans Administration (VA) estimates the latter group to number 479,000.[1] America did a poor job of integrating Vietnam veterans into society and treating the emotional wounds of war. The result of this failure was a catalog of misery. Veterans fell into alcohol and drug addiction, spousal neglect or abuse, unemployment, mental disease, and physical decline. By the mid 1980s, close to half the prisoners in federal prisons were Vietnam veterans. Forty years after the Vietnam war ended, the cost of that failure to society has been immense, both in dollars and in wasted lives.

Those who fail to read history are condemned to repeat it. Following the Iraq and Afghanistan wars, the Veterans Stress Project challenges U.S. society to make different choices this time around. The Veterans Stress Project is the biggest program of our nonprofit National Institute for Integrative Healthcare (NIIH.org). The next biggest program focuses on EFT research.

The Veterans Stress Project

Today, the project site is full of resources for veterans. It connects them with over two hundred coaches and psychotherapists who offer free EFT. Coaches are available in Europe, Canada, and throughout the United States. The website also features video clips of veterans who tell their stories of getting free of PTSD in just a few sessions—sometimes overcoming decades of trauma in just a few hours. Viewers see video footage of veterans trembling with agitation as they tell their traumatic war stories. Some vets cry; one has to leave the room to throw up.

After an EFT treatment, veterans are able to tell the same story calmly. When I show this video to an audience, there is rarely a dry eye in the house. If you want to see what PTSD looks like, and the human face of how effective these therapies are, watch the videos at StressProject.org. We've now offered free courses of treatment to thousands of veterans and their family members.

I also decided to start measuring precisely how much the vets were improving, to quantify the improvements. A pilot study was set up. Some therapists were skeptical about all the work involved in performing a study, which would cost tens of thousands of dollars, thousands of hours, and years to complete. They told me, "We see the obvious changes in clients. You don't need a study to prove them."

The truth is that you do. Studies are the dialog through which researchers communicate and, without quantifiable changes, even the most moving stories of personal change can be dismissed as atypical anecdotes. Imagine your optometrist saying, "I want to perform a new kind of eye surgery on your eyes. I read an interesting story about it online." Would you be reassured? No! You'd want medical evidence that the treatment works and is safe. Any ethical clinician, whether a neurosurgeon, psychotherapist, or social worker, wants hard statistical evidence that a procedure is both safe and effective. That's why clinicians read the latest research in their field, and why new treatments are subject to experimental verification before they are implemented. That reality has led the Veterans Stress project to conduct several studies showing the effects of EFT.

Just Add Lime Juice

It's now more than three hundred years since the first controlled medical trial was performed. In 1747, Dr. James Lind, a surgeon in the Royal Navy, performed an experiment to see if dietary changes could counteract the effects of scurvy. Scurvy left sailors bleeding and inca-pacitated, and killed more of them than the cannons of the Spanish or French fleets. On long ocean voyages, eating a monotonous diet of hardtack biscuits and salt pork, with no fresh food available, many sailors fell victim to scurvy.

Various remedies for scurvy had been proposed over the years previous to Dr. Lind's experiment. The substances suggested for con-sumption by sailors included:

- Two spoonfuls of vinegar daily
- A quart of cider per day
- Half a pint of seawater daily
- Elixir vitriol three times a day
- A daily lump of horseradish, mustard, and garlic
- One lemon and two oranges daily

Since there are six items in this list, Dr. Lind grouped twelve sail-ors suffering from scurvy into six groups of two. He then proceeded to administer the suggested substance for two weeks, in addition to the sailors' normal diet. The group that received the citrus fruit got better much faster. In fact, one of those two sailors returned to active duty after six days, while the other one became nurse to those unfortunate enough to have received one of the other five treatments.

Big Isn't What You Think

Lind's experiment may seem logical to us today, with the ben-efit of three centuries of experience. Yet at the time, it was a radical concept. It also illustrates the experimental principle called *effect size*. If you have a big effect, it takes only a small number of subjects to dem-onstrate it. Lind only had twelve total, and just two in the citrus group. But the effect size was so great that it was obvious in just two people.

We read about pharmaceutical trials with thousands of patients, and we may be very impressed by the "size" of the trial, thinking that because this is a "big" trial the results must be conclusive. Just the opposite may be true. The reason it takes so many participants may be that the effect size is very small. Therefore, it takes a great many subjects to notice a difference between one group and another.

Think of effect size this way: If you want to test whether leg amputation results in a shorter leg, you only need a couple of subjects to give you conclusive results.

But if you want to test whether scratching your fingernail on the desk results in a shorter fingernail, you need to repeat the scrape thousands of times before you notice a result. A small effect size means that it takes lots of repetitions to notice a difference. So trials that involve large numbers of people usually mean that the researchers are trolling for a very small effect. "Big" is a function of effect size, not the number of research subjects.

When researchers say they found a *significant* effect, it usually means that statistical analysis of the data demonstrated that there was just *one possibility in twenty* that the results of the study could be due to chance. Statistically this is expressed as $p < .05$, or a 5% possibility of error. That's the arbitrary consensus threshold at which researchers believe they've found an effect.

When researchers call their findings *highly significant,* they're not just hyping the results. In this context, "highly significant" means that there's just *one possibility in a thousand* that the findings were due to chance, which is a very small possibility indeed. Statistically, this is expressed as $p < .001$. So the amputation study could get "highly significant" findings with just two subjects, while the fingernail study might need thousands just to achieve statistical "significance." Big data equals finding a large effect with a high degree of statistical significance, regardless of whether it involves a cast of characters the size of a family or one the size of a nation.

Erasing PTSD

The first study I did with the modern equivalent of scurvy looked at the psychological health of veterans before and after six sessions of EFT. The EFT sessions were delivered by two different people. One was a licensed psychotherapist who was also a professor at Marshall University Medical School in West Virginia. The other was a life coach who had worked extensively with veterans.

Besides PTSD, we measured a variety of symptoms in these vets before and after their six sessions, including depression, anxiety, hostility, and phobias, and psychotism. We also took follow-up measurements three months later, to see if the effects we'd seen in the initial sessions would hold over time.

The results were amazing. Anxiety dropped by 46% and depression by 49%. PTSD dropped by 50%. The severity of all the vets psychological symptoms collectively dropped by 40%. All of the results were statistically significant. The results for anxiety and depression were highly significant. When we checked them again three months later, the vets had maintained their gains. Like the sailors with scurvy in Dr. Lund's study, the effect size was so great that only seven subjects were required to demonstrate these big improvements.[2] At last we had not just anecdotal evidence, but hard data. The results were published in a peer-reviewed journal, and copies of the study circulated widely at the Pentagon and VA.

By that time, we'd received initial data from the Healthcare Workers Study of 216 professionals such as psychotherapists, doctors, nurses, and alternative medicine professionals.[3] We realized that EFT was effective not only when delivered as individual therapy, but also as group therapy. So in the second study, we examined the effects of treating veterans intensively for a week, rather than six sessions spread out over a month. We also included their spouses or other family members. Most participants were Vietnam veterans, with decades of accumulated emotional trauma. To make sure we had valid scores beforehand, we tested them a month before the study began, and a second time the day before the study began, to make sure that their symptoms weren't just decreasing due to the passage of time.

Their PTSD symptoms dropped by a degree similar to the result we'd seen in the previous study. Both the breadth and depth of their psychological problems such as anxiety and depression dropped significantly. These excellent results held up when we retested them a month later and three months later, despite the fact that they'd gone back to all the daily stresses of their lives.[2]

With these two pilot studies in hand, and with the help of the many selfless volunteers in the Veterans Stress Project, I designed a nationwide study of veterans with PTSD. This was a randomized controlled trial or RCT, the Gold Standard of scientific research. It seemed like an impossibly ambitious project for a handful of volunteers with little research experience to attempt, but we made up for in enthusiasm what we lacked in experience.

Participants were randomly assigned to either a wait list where they continued to receive Treatment As Usual (TAU), which usually consisted of care at a VA hospital. The other half received TAU plus six sessions of EFT. After the wait period, those on the wait list also received six EFT sessions. It took us years to convince the first few veterans to participate in the study, but we eventually recruited fifty-nine of them.

The results were a carbon copy of the earlier pilot study with seven veterans. Those who received no treatment did not improve, while symptoms in the EFT group dropped by over 60%. After treatment, 86% of the veterans no longer tested positive for PTSD.[4] We also tested participants after three months to see if they had maintained their gains, and again after six months. Their symptom levels were flat between the last EFT session and the three-month mark, and between the three- and six-month marks. This type of flat line indicates that the participants were highly unlikely to relapse, and might be permanently free of PTSD. The study was eventually published in a prestigious psychiatry journal, the oldest in the United States.

In the meantime, a colleague of mine working at a hospital in Britain's National Health System (NHS) completed a study comparing EFT to EMDR (Eye Movement Desensitization and Reprocessing). The medical literature shows EMDR to be the fastest PTSD treatment yet developed. The NHS study found that both EFT and EMDR were effective for severe clinical PTSD in just four sessions.[5]

Stress Hormones and Mental Health

As I watched therapists offer EFT, I consistently witnessed their clients relax, even though they were talking about highly emotional events. I watched shoulders drop, breathing return to normal, and pulse rates slow. I wondered, "If that's happening on the outside, I wonder what's happening to their stress biochemistry on the

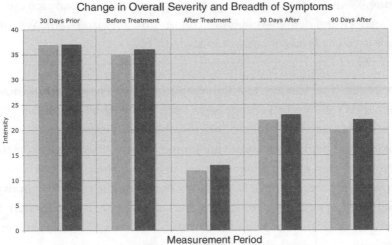

Change in severity and breadth of psychological symptoms

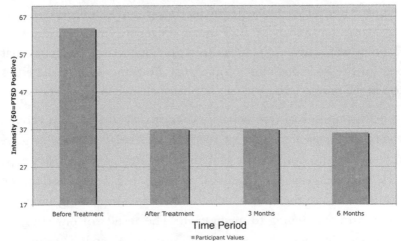

Change in PTSD symptoms in veterans using EFT over time

inside?" So I designed a study to measure their levels of cortisol, the main stress hormone.[6]

We randomized the eighty-three participants into three groups. One received an EFT session; the second a regular psychotherapy session, and the third group simply rested in the waiting room of the clinic. We had them complete psychological tests for conditions such as anxiety and depression before the session and afterward. We also measured the levels of cortisol in their saliva.

To no one's surprise, those who received psychotherapy or rest improved their anxiety and depression scores. Their cortisol, however, didn't show much change, with both groups dropping some 14%. Those who received EFT had great psychological improvements, with anxiety and depression improving more than twice as much as in the psychotherapy group. Their cortisol reflected their reduced stress, dropping an average of 24%. Not only that, but the reduction in psychological symptoms correlated significantly with the reduction in cortisol, demonstrating synchronization between the improvement in physical and psychological markers of stress.[7]

I then teamed up with a molecular biologist at California Pacific Medical Center (CPMC) in San Francisco, Garret Yount, PhD. Dr. Yount had pioneered the objective testing of purported energy therapies, and often found them ineffective. We designed a study to examine the effects of EFT as an epigenetic intervention. Our reasoning was simple: to reduce the supply of cortisol, the genes that code for the hormone must of necessity be being downregulated. A drop in the hormonal by-product implies a change in gene expression.

Treating a drug-free behavioral approach like EFT as though it were a biological signal that triggers molecular changes in gene expression was a new idea at that time, though as science develops quick and inexpensive methods of measuring gene expression, we can now measure the epigenetic effects of stress-reducing activities ranging from gardening to meditation. The results of our study of the epigenetic effects of EFT will be published soon. They're part of a flowering of research into EFT and other EP techniques. Many new studies are in the pipeline, some of which will be published in a peer-reviewed journal I edit called *Energy Psychology: Theory, Research, and Treatment*. With a distinguished editorial board, it provides a place where EP research can receive a fair and impartial hearing (www. EnergyPsychologyJournal.org).

Clearing PTSD in Groups

Once we'd performed the pilot study showing that EFT was effective when delivered as group therapy, we could test it in larger groups. This research would tell us whether this one successful group of eleven people was a statistical fluke, or whether the effects generalized to many other groups as well.

We teamed up with a nonprofit organization that planned a series of seven-day retreats with veterans and their spouses. Over the course of a year, they offered six of these at a rural retreat center in Angelfire, New Mexico. Each retreat included four mornings of EFT and other EP techniques, with the goal of reducing PTSD symptoms. The rest of the time, participants were offered other supportive activities, and had the option to explore CAM (complementary and alternative medicine) techniques such as Reiki, massage, and equestrian therapy. We published our results after 218 veterans and spouses had completed the Angelfire retreats.[7] This made it, at the time, the largest energy medicine study ever published in terms of numbers of participants.

The results were very similar to those of our pilot study. When they arrived for a retreat, 83% of the veterans tested positive for PTSD. What was shocking was that 29% of the spouses did too, a phenomenon called "transferred PTSD." Living with a veteran for a prolonged period of time can severely traumatize a loved one. The good news is that after the seven-day retreat the PTSD scores of most veterans and their spouses had normalized. When we followed up six weeks later, only 28% of veterans and 4% of spouses scored positive for PTSD.

We analyzed the results of each of the six retreats separately, as though each one had been an individual small-scale study. Look at the graph showing participant symptoms. Even though the groups differed in size and composition, the pattern is remarkably similar. This means that the beneficial effects were generalizable across many diverse groups of people.

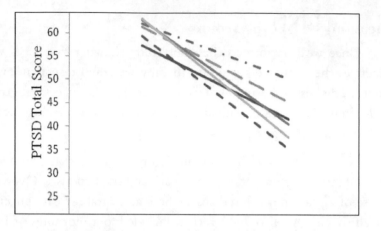

Change in veteran PTSD symptoms by retreat

The question of how generalizable the results of a therapy may be is an important one, because a therapy that works only for women but not for men, or only for seniors and not for teenagers, is of limited use. Researchers at Staffordshire University put this research question to the test by treating two very different groups of students. One group was predominantly male and young, studying sports sciences. The other was predominantly female and older, in a CAM program. EFT was equally effective for both groups.[8] This, plus the very different populations in which EFT has been studied, shows that its effects are generalizable.

That same research team used EFT in an NHS hospital in order to determine the acceptance of EFT by patients and its success in reducing symptoms. This study found a significant improvement in anxiety, with a mean treatment time frame of eight sessions. It also found a large improvement in overall psychological health and physical functioning.[9]

Battle Tap

The success obtained by women in a study of fibromyalgia triggered my thinking, as EFT was offered entirely online in that study. Their pain dropped by 29%, and they showed similar reductions in depression and anxiety. What if we could offer effective online treatments for depression, anxiety, pain, and PTSD? If we can deliver successful solutions online, we reach people a mouse-click away. They can use such software when and where they want help, rather than relying only on the structured environment of a therapy session.

As I brainstormed with various people and groups about this idea, Dr. Toukolehto, whose story you read at the beginning of this chapter, took the bull by the horns. With his father, software engineer Tim Toukolehto, he translated the dream into reality. Putting in hundreds of volunteer hours, they created a virtual online coaching program called Battle Tap. Today, when veterans log on to the Veterans Stress Project website, they can immediately start an online Battle Tap session. The program asks you to name your problem and give it an emotional severity score from zero to ten. It pairs the type of emotion you are feeling with words and video, and guides you through a tapping session. When you are finished, it again scores the emotional intensity of your problem.

Steve, a veteran from Portland, Oregon, tells this story on the Stress Project website: "Using the EFT/Battle Tapping techniques I have learned, I have been able to calm myself when I have been agitated! I have had my ups and downs over the years with my mental health, including drinking. Not all at once, but I now have a long period of sobriety going for me, and I credit the EFT/Battle Tapping method for it!" Steve's experience is typical of veterans who have used Battle Tap.

Even High Performers Improve Dramatically

Here's another research question that dawned on me: If these methods work so well with sick people, how would they work with healthy ones? With the help of colleagues, I designed an experimental way of testing elite athletes. Several stories have appeared in newspapers and magazines in the last few years about athletes using EFT. The *Oregonian* newspaper ran a story about a "most valued player" college baseballer, Jorge Reyes, who was caught tapping during a game by an ESPN camera.[9] *Golfweek* reported on the many pro golfers who use Energy Psychology (EP) to improve their game.[10] Sports psychologists working with top-ranked athletes including major league baseballers, professional football players, and elite golfers have described how they are able to break through performance blocks using EFT. Many of these stories appear in the book *EFT for Sports Performance.*[11]

Once the study was designed, Greg Warburton, LPC, a psychotherapist working with sports teams at Oregon State University, was able to arrange for me to travel there and collect data with the men's and women's basketball teams at the college.

Not only was the study randomized and controlled; it was also blind. "Blinding" means that the athletes didn't know whether they were in the placebo or treatment group. We tested the players' ability to perform free throws and also used an electronic test of how high they could jump. After testing, they were matched into two equally performing groups based on their jump height, then randomly assigned to a group. The placebo group received a reading of tips and techniques written by a famous basketball coach.

The EFT and reading treatments were deliberately kept brief, to just fifteen minutes per player. The player would have their performance measured, then run off the court for a treatment, then run back to get measured again.

The results were striking. The group that got EFT improved slightly in jump height, though the results were not statistically significant. But they improved dramatically in free-throw ability. The difference between the EFT and the control group in free throws after treatment was a whopping 38%.[12]

Greg and I went on to develop a thorough week-long athletic training, designed to revolutionize a team's performance, called EFT Power Training (www.EFTPowerTraining.com). Our reasoning is that once we release the emotional problems that interfere with individuals' athletic performance, all their latent psychospiritual capacities become available to excel at their physical game.

My friend therapist Tam Llewellyn-Edwards then replicated our results with football (soccer) players. Working with women's teams, he randomized them into two groups and measured their ability to perform free kicks into the goal posts. The group that received EFT performed significantly better, and went on to a string of victories in their division.[13]

Researchers at Sheffield Hallam University in England did a research project on a golfer who was having performance difficulties. Using dozens of elaborate electronic measurements of his muscle groups, they assessed exactly what was impeding his golf swing. After EFT, they hooked him back up to their equipment and took a second set of readings. His swing was now fluid, without the tension that had characterized his movements before EFT.[14] In another study at Ursuline College in Ohio, I worked with graduate student Darlene Downs to assess traumatic memories affecting the confidence of female volleyball players.[15] After a twenty-minute EFT session, their anxiety was reduced and their confidence increased. The improvements held at follow-up.

Taking Healing to the World

Let's jump back in time to 1747. Soon after James Lind conducted his landmark study of scurvy, he published his findings.[16] They circulated within the British Admiralty, which now had evidence that a simple and inexpensive supplement of citrus fruit could prevent the major scourge killing the sailors they desperately needed to man their ships. What do you suppose happened then? Church bells pealed and crates of limes were rushed to every ship on the fastest possible carriages?

Unfortunately not. It was another forty-two years before the admiralty acted on Lind's findings and started issuing citrus to sailors. Thousands of sailors died in the interim, and the Royal Navy's capability as a fighting force during the American War of Independence and the Napoleonic Wars was severely compromised by scurvy.

Have things changed much in 250 years? Unfortunately not. The U.S. Food and Drug Administration (FDA) reports that medical advances take an average of seventeen years to reach patients. Only 30% of them even make the transition; the benefits of the other 70% are lost.[17] We sent the results of our PTSD studies to the VA, but were ignored. Eventually, we approached members of congress with our results, and several sent letters to the Secretary of Veterans Affairs and other mental health officials, insisting that they investigate EFT. I also testified about EFT to the House Veterans Affairs Committee and the House Homeland Security Committee. All these efforts were unsuccessful.

Drug therapies face few such barriers to adoption. Between 2002 and 2012, the VA wrote millions of prescriptions for risperidone, a drug touted as treatment for PTSD. In 2012, a study showed that it was no more effective than a placebo. By that time, the VA and Defense Department had spent around one billion dollars on the drug. For that sum, they could have given every veteran with PTSD six EFT sessions. As a society, we seem to be so hypnotized by the promise of drug cures that we often neglect the evidence for safe, noninvasive, drug-free self-help techniques like EFT.

The costs of treating a single veteran with PTSD are estimated to be an astonishing $1.4 million.[18] For that amount, two thousand veterans could go through a week-long group EFT retreat. Yet, as of this writing, despite demand from veterans, congressional pressure, and a mountain of scientific evidence, the VA resolutely refuses to endorse EFT as an approved therapy. Therapists at several VA hospitals have invited me to train them in EFT, but each time we have to raise the funds from private donors because, unlike those risperidone prescriptions, the VA does not pay for them. The unfortunate reality is that while drug companies have millions of dollars to fund the search for their magic bullets, and large government agencies are set up to funnel dollars to conventional academic institutional research, the system starves holistic research of funding. As with the National Institute for Integrative Healthcare, research and treatment is usually offered on a shoestring budget by dedicated volunteers.

Yet we press on. We're driven by a strong belief that these therapies have the potential to change the world by reducing human suffering. Imagine if every child had a way of reducing test anxiety. Imagine if, when conflicts such as those in Kosovo, Palestine, or Rwanda were brewing, teams of volunteers intervened to teach the mobs of angry people how to tap their emotional charge away. Imagine if every workplace was filled with peaceful people who knew how to dissipate the stressful patterns that otherwise enmesh them, robbing their brains and genes of productivity. Imagine if prisoners learned a way to handle the high-octane emotional violence in their environments. Imagine if drivers could effortlessly discharge their stress when traffic became heavy. Imagine if national leaders could make decisions free of the emotional tugs of nationalism, revenge, and communal competition. Imagine if you had grown up in a family in which there had been a quick way of dissipating emotional strife. Such a world is within our reach with this new generation of therapies.

While institutions can take a long time to change, other entities and individuals are more flexible. EFT is used by many top-level athletes. Businesses, too, are motivated to improve their performance, and we're seeing increased interest in EFT training from corporations.

You and I don't have to wait till our workplace, family, community, or government changes. We can start to do these practices every day. By releasing our reactive emotional trauma, we nudge our genes, neurons, and habits a little closer to happiness right now.

14

Medicine for
the Body Politic

*Start by doing what's necessary; then do what's possible; and suddenly
you are doing the impossible.*

—St. Francis of Assisi

"Carl Johnson, a clinical psychologist retired from a career as a
PTSD specialist with the Veterans' Administration (VA), has
frequently traveled over the past decade, to the sites of some
of the world's most terrible atrocities and disasters to provide psychological support using Energy Psychology methods. About a year after
NATO put an end to the ethnic cleansing in Kosovo, Johnson found
himself in a trailer in a small village where the brutalities had been
particularly severe. A local physician who had offered to refer people
in his village had posted a sign that treatments for war-related trauma
(nightmares, insomnia, intrusive memories, inability to concentrate,
etc.) were being offered. Johnson described how, as a line of people
had formed outside the trailer, the referring physician told him, with
some concern, that everyone in the village was afraid of one of the
men who was waiting outside for treatment.

"The others in the line had actually positioned themselves as far away from this man as possible. Johnson asked the physician to invite the man into the trailer. Johnson, who after a career in the VA is seasoned in working with war veterans, recalled that the man "had a vicious look; he felt dangerous." But he had come for help, so with the physician translating, Johnson asked the man to bring to mind his most difficult memory from the war. Everyone in the village was haunted by traumas of unspeakable proportion: torture, rape, witnessing the massacre of loved ones. As the man brought the trauma to mind, his face tensed and reddened and his breathing quickened. Though he never put his memory into words, the treatment began. Johnson tapped on specific acupoints that he determined to be relevant to the trauma. He then instructed the man, through the interpreter, to do a number of eye movements and other simple physical activities designed to accelerate the process. Then more tapping. Within fifteen minutes, according to Johnson, the man's demeanor had changed completely. His face had relaxed and his breathing normalized. He no longer looked vicious. In fact, he was openly expressing joy and relief. He initiated hugs with both Johnson and the physician. Then, still grinning, he abruptly walked outside, jumped into his car and roared away, as everyone watched perplexed.

"The man's wife was also in the group waiting for treatment. In addition to the suffering she had faced during the war, she had become a victim of her husband's rage. The traumas she identified also responded rapidly to the tapping treatment. About the time her treatment was completed, her husband's car roared back to the waiting area. He came in with a bag of nuts and a bag of peaches, both from his home, as unsolicited payment for his treatment. He was profuse and appeared gleeful in his thanks, indicating that he felt something deep and toxic had been healed. He hugged his wife. Then, extraordinarily, he offered to escort Johnson into the hills to find trauma victims who were still in hiding, too damaged to return to life in their villages, both his own people—ethnic Albanians—and the enemy Serbs. In Johnson's words, "That afternoon, before our very eyes, we saw this vicious man, filled with hate, become a loving man of peace and mercy." Johnson further reflected how often this would occur, that when these traumatized survivors were able to gain emotional resolution on experiences that had been haunting them, they became markedly more loving and creative. Although survivors, even after a breakthrough session like this, are still left with the formidable task of rebuilding their lives, the treatment disengaged the intense limbic response from cues and memories tied to the disaster, freeing them to move forward more adaptively.

The 105 people treated during Johnson's first five visits to Kosovo, all in 2000, had each been suffering for longer than a year from the posttraumatic emotional effects of 249 discrete, horrific self-identified incidents. For 247 of those 249 memories, the treatments (using TFT) successfully reduced the reported degree of emotional distress not just to a manageable level but to a "no distress" level ("o" on a o-to-10 SUD scale, after Wolpe, 1958). Although these figures strain credibility, they are consistent with other reports. Approximately three-fourths of the 105 individuals were followed for eighteen months after their treatments and showed no relapses—the original memory no longer activated self-reported or observable signs of traumatic stress."[1]

This story, written by clinical psychologist David Feinstein, PhD, for the peer-reviewed journal *Traumatology*, shows that by helping individuals, Energy Psychology promotes social good. Like emotional CPR, these methods can be used as an emergency medical intervention. If schoolchildren learned these techniques to help them cope with playground stresses, if hospital patients learned them to help them cope with pain, if people in social crises used them to help stabilize their emotions, then panic and powerlessness would no longer thwart sensible action. The reservoir of sane, stable intellectual and emotional power that lies within us would be unlocked and brought to bear on the social problems that lie before us.

Discontinuous Social Change

Just as sudden healing miracles are a possibility for our bodies, sudden social miracles are possible for our culture. We are living at a time of profound social discontinuity. Patterns that have been under the radar for hundreds or thousands of years are coming into the light of healing.

Examples are all around us. For millennia, women were suppressed by society. In most countries, laws prevented them from having social status equal to that of men. Often women were not allowed to own property; often they were treated as property.

LEAFLET No. 1.]

WOMEN'S SUFFRAGE.

Are Women Citizens ?
Yes ! when they are required to pay taxes.
No ! when they ask to vote.

Does Law concern Women ?
Yes ! when they are required to obey it.
No ! when they ask to have a voice in the representation of the country.

Is Direct Representation desirable for the interests of the people ?
Yes ! if the people to be represented are men.
No ! if the people to be represented are women.

All who believe that this state of things is neither just towards women nor advantageous to men are invited to become members of "The Victorian Women's Suffrage Society."

PLATFORM.
To obtain the same Political Privileges for Women as are now possessed by Male Voters, with the restriction of an Educational Test by writing legibly the name of the Candidate on the Ballot-paper.

ELIZTH. H. RENNICK,
Hon. Sec. and Treas

"ATHENA," SHIPLEY STREET,
SOUTH YARRA.

N.B.—Subscriptions received by Miss O'Riordan, Ladies' Club, Collins-street East., and Miss Taylor, 86 Russell-street.

Leaflet printed by the Victorian Women's Suffrage Society

In Western societies this has changed—all in just a century. In 1893, New Zealand became the first country to give women the right to vote in national elections. In Britain, women won the right to vote in 1918 (1920 in the United States), and in the second half of the twentieth century, the women in most of the world's functioning democracies obtained similar rights. In most Western countries, women are now on a roughly equal social, financial, and political footing with men, at least on paper. This means that the vast creative potential of half of humankind, locked up for centuries, has suddenly become available to society. Women's rights are an example of discontinuous social change.

Another example is incest and other forms of child abuse. For most of recorded history, children were entirely under the power of adults, even if they were being dreadfully abused. For centuries, children were routinely employed in mines in Britain, under the most appalling conditions, such as sixteen-hour shifts carrying coal on their backs. Incest was such a taboo that it was not even discussed, and was often presumed not to exist. Suddenly, in the last two centuries, we have witnessed rapid, discontinuous social change.

Child "hurriers" pushing a coal tub in nineteenth-century London

England passed the first child labor laws in 1802, and strengthened them throughout the century. In 1916, U.S. President Wilson pushed a child labor law through congress, only to have it struck down by the Supreme Court. Finally in 1938, the Fair Labor Standards Act came into force. Most Western countries also have movements protesting the importation of goods made with child or slave labor in other countries.

Another is addiction. In the slums of London in the 1800s, a stereotype of the workingman was that he got his wages on Friday, went to the pub, drank most of them away, and returned home to beat his wife and children. None of his neighbors thought that any of this behavior was amiss. Probably in Babylon, four thousand years ago, the same man could have received the same nods for the same behavior. Certain social norms have been static for thousands of years.

Today, that same man might be going to an Alcoholics Anonymous meeting. Whereas for centuries society tolerated addictive behavior, and had few mechanisms for dealing with any but the most violent addicts, today there are many interventions available. There are twelve-step groups for many conditions, from compulsive shopping to gambling to attention deficit disorder (ADD), and for those addicted to nonprescription painkillers. Many individuals have begun to confront addictions that, in past centuries, would have been considered socially normative. Taken collectively, they represent a society that is making a serious dent in its addictions.

Another watchword of today's society is diversity. Today, multinational corporations find ways in which to turn multiculturalism into a benefit, to appreciate the diversity of employees and turn that diversity into a strength. Global companies spend millions of dollars training their employees to understand and appreciate differences.

Yet a hundred years before, the corporate giants of the world—think railroad barons, sugar monopolies, the Dutch East India Company, Rockefellers and Du Ponts, or Henry Ford's production lines—prized uniformity. The rewards of uniformity date back to the ancient Greeks, who grouped their soldiers into *phalanxes*, rather than fighting in individual combat, as early as the seventh century BCE.Uniformity of tactics gave these organized groups of soldiers, referred to in Homer's epics, an edge over their enemies fighting singly.

Individuals Lead Society

Society has undergone another about-face when it comes to the expectation that people with cancer will die. I remember hushed conversations from my childhood that went something like this:

Aunt: "The doctor says it's cancer."

Uncle: "How long does he have?"

The only variable, in their minds, was how long the person would live. Cancer equaled death—no ifs, ands, or buts. It wasn't doctors who began to change that mindset, but patients who refused to die when confronted with terminal diagnoses. There are now hundreds of books, articles, and research studies of exceptional cancer patients: those who, rather than accepting a death sentence, immediately begin taking charge, discovering what they could do to help themselves, and nudging the quantum field, and their cells, in the direction of health.

A similar phenomenon has happened with AIDS. Still officially incurable, there are an increasing number of anecdotes of patients who have later tested HIV-negative, after having been earlier diagnosed with AIDS. In the years after the first AIDS case was diagnosed in the United States in June 1981,[2] most AIDS patients died quickly and horribly. Today there are some half-million people alive in the United States, many in excellent health, who have been diagnosed with AIDS at some point in the previous twenty years.[3] Under the headline "First Case of HIV Cure Reported" (November 2005), doctors at London's Victoria Clinic announced that conclusive tests showed that Andrew Stimpson, who had twice tested positive for HIV infection, was now virus-free. DNA tests were used to confirm that there had been no mix-up in the samples.[4] Society is changing its collective mind about HIV/AIDS being a death sentence, as certainly as it changed its mind about cancer starting a generation ago.

Many of the researchers mentioned in this book have been the target of ridicule, character assassination, or suppression. From 1999 to 2012 the American Psychological Association denied Continuing Education (CE) credits to any organization offering professional training in Energy Psychology. In the early 2000s, a group of self-appointed editorial skeptics rewrote the Wikipedia entry for EFT, branding it as "pseudoscience." Whenever subject matter experts update the Wikipedia entry, for instance by announcing the results of a new study confirming EFT'S effectiveness, the skeptical editors vandalize the text, suppressing the dissemination of these advances in science through this important online resource.

Just as, in the eighteenth century, Ignatz Semmelweiss, a Viennese doctor, was ridiculed for suggesting that surgeons wash their hands before operations, or Edward Lister was pilloried for cleaning his hospital with carbolic acid disinfectant, the pioneers of the new medicine and new psychology have faced the entrenched opposition of their professions. Yet because these therapies work—and are often far more effective than anything conventional medicine has to offer—patients are voting with their feet and their dollars, dragging research along behind them, and creating social mind change on the way.

Epigenetic Influence and Wars Between Nations

A critical finding of gene methylation and acetylization studies is that once nurturing is done by one generation and those genes are expressed, then nurturing behavior and its accompanying gene expression can be passed to the next generation. Nurturing parents produce nurturing offspring, and neglectful parents produce neglectful offspring.

What would happen if an entire population became less fearful and anxious, generation by generation? Would this result in less aggression, both within the society and toward that society's neighbors?

Social scientists have found evidence of precisely these effects when studying conflicts between nations. Robin Grille, a psychologist from New Zealand, has done extensive surveys of the parenting literature of warlike populations.[5] For instance, the most popular Prussian parenting manuals in the nineteenth century stressed that children should be absolutely obedient, and that the most minor infraction should be punished with beating. Beating children several times a day was not uncommon and was not considered cruel. It was the accepted German nineteenth-century paradigm of good parenting.

Swiss psychiatrist Alice Miller points out that these children were rigidly obedient to authority, fighting the Franco-Prussian war (successfully for the Germans), and then World Wars I and II (unsuccessfully for the Germans) as faithful soldiers of any current government. Miller provides four centuries of historical examples of societies that practiced mass childhood cruelty subsequently producing generations of brutal and martially minded adults.[6]

The largest scale human experiment demonstrating the epigenetic effects of diet on psychology was unintentionally performed by the Germans in WWII. During the "Dutch Hunger Winter" of 1944, the Nazi occupation government stopped food going into Holland. More than twenty thousand Dutch citizens died of starvation. Epidemiologists have studied the effects of this social catastrophe on subsequent generations. They found that the offspring of women exposed to famine during this time had a much higher incidence of schizophrenia as adults, the result of the epigenetic effects on the fetus of dietary deprivation.[7]

Grille believes that societies that introduced enlightened elements of child nurturing became less violent and martial in subsequent generations, and more prone to direct their energies into a quest for justice and equality. This led to social innovations.

In the American colonies in the eighteenth century, children were often raised to be independent and outspoken. Visitors remarked on finding confident children who were not afraid to speak their minds. These were the mothers and fathers of the authors of the Declaration of Independence and the Bill of Rights.

The nurturing of children has other intergenerational social consequences. The author of the best-sellling book *Freakonomics* proposes a novel and provocative explanation for the dramatic decrease in violent crime in America from the early 1990s onward. The roots of this phenomenon long baffled social analysts. How could crime in a country drop by such a huge percentage in such a short time? Explanations like better policing or longer incarceration are inadequate to explain such a marked shift.

The answer comes from an unlikely source: the establishment of legal abortion on demand.[8] When unwanted children could be aborted, many accidental or unplanned pregnancies were ended this way. Women who were economically or psychologically unable or unwilling to raise their babies had the option of abortion. Many exercised their new legal right.

This meant that most of the babies born were wanted by the mother, father, or both. These children presumably received better nurturing than the unwanted children of the pre-abortion era. The availability of abortion created an abrupt decrease in the number of neglected babies, and an abrupt increase in the number of nurtured babies. We now know that nurturing initiates epigenetic signals that produce less fearful and anxious adults. Twenty years after the legalization of abortion, when both groups had grown up, the pool of violent adults had shrunk, leading to the sudden and precipitate drop in the crime rate. Without knowing it, society, by legalizing abortion, made an epigenetic intervention that resulted in less violence a generation later. Nurtured children produce a more peaceful society.

The Epigenetic Social Cycle

One of the best-known proponents of early childhood nurturing is Michel Odent, MD, a legendary French obstetrician. Odent groups together the child's time in the womb, birth, and the first year into what he calls the "primal" period, which he believes is formative of many key adult attributes. He says that when "researchers explore behavior, a personality trait, or a disease that can be interpreted as an 'impaired ability to love,' they always detect risk factors in the perinatal period." He cites studies that show that, "the main risk factor for being a violent criminal at age eighteen was the association of birth complications, together with early separation from or rejection by the mother.[9]...From studies among mammals as diverse as rats, hamsters, sheep, goats and monkeys one can conclude that there is always, immediately after birth, a short 'sensitive' period which will never be repeated, and which is critical to mother-baby attachment and subsequent development."[10]

A chain of social events which I call the epigenetic social cycle is discernible here. Nurturing of children produces beneficial gene changes, which produces increased nurturing of subsequent generations, and a less violent and safer society. This in turn leads to the synthesis of fewer stress proteins in individuals, and greater production of cell repair hormones such as DHEA. Less stressed individuals are in turn more likely to contribute to social peace.

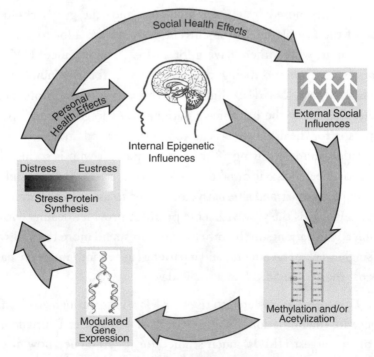

The epigenetic social cycle

The same epigenetic social cycle can also lead to a descending spiral of fear, anxiety, and violence. The failure of a society to nurture its children creates an epigenetic intervention that suppresses their ability to handle stress. They are more fearful and anxious, and more prone to offensive or defensive violence. A violent society is unconducive to childhood nurturing, leading to further epigenetic gene modulation and even greater stress. This leads to increased violence.

These cycles are by no means evident to the fields of medicine and psychology at the moment. Epigenetics is too new for its impact to be assimilated and understood. Epigenetics explains the success of interventions that look like magic to the existing medical and psychotherapeutic models, and is likely to take several years, or even decades, to penetrate into daily practice, even though the social benefits of positive interventions are clear.

The Reaction of the Old Guard

It will be fascinating to see how conventional medicine handles the challenges posed by energy medicine and Energy Psychology. Some of the key players in the current system have a lot to gain by embracing it, while others have a lot to lose. For instance, HMOs, hospitals, and doctors being paid fixed rates for the number of patients they see (called "capitation" in the jargon of the profession) benefit financially the healthier a patient is. Average amount spent per person for "health" care was $8,508 in the United States in 2010.[11] A provider who is receiving $8,508 from a patient who is so healthy that he or she makes one or no doctor's visits in a year, and uses only a few complementary and alternative therapies to assist in maintaining peak health, ends the year with a big profit. A provider dealing with a chronically ill patient, on the other hand, can spend more than $8,508 in a single week of treatment, and a patient rushed into intensive care can cost more than $8,508 in a single day.

This figure is projected to rise by 5.8% a year through 2022, a far higher rate than inflation. That's one reason why Kaiser Permanente, one of the largest HMOs, much-studied for its efficiency, now offers

Qigong classes, meditation classes, chiropractic, acupuncture, addiction recovery classes, and other strategies to make people happier and healthier. Some Kaiser practitioners also use Energy Psychology techniques. It's not just good health care; it's good business. Such organizations are net winners when people are healthy. Chronic disease is estimated to cost the U.S. economy a staggering 1.3 trillion dollars each year. Forty million Americans could avoid chronic disease by making modest lifestyle improvements, and the economic impact of disease would be reduced by 1.1 trillion dollars.[12] So society as a whole is a net winner when people get unstressed and happy, and take care of their bodies.

Others are net losers when quick and effective new therapies arrive. Psychotherapists with patients who have been seeing them weekly for many years, working on life issues, at an average visit cost of one hundred dollars, lose an ongoing revenue stream of five thousand dollars a year when a patient settles an issue with Energy Psychology in a session or two. Such therapies pose a financial threat. They also suffer from a credibility gap. A therapist may rightly be skeptical that a patient's chronic agoraphobia, for example, can be cured in an hour, when years of therapy have produced only modest gains.

Long-term, however, therapists often report financial benefits from using Energy Psychology, quite aside from the professional satisfaction of seeing patients get better. "The financial benefit comes in being able to charge more for sessions, and overcoming the likelihood that people avoid therapy because it takes too long," says Fred Gallo, PhD, who coined the term "Energy Psychology" and has authored several books on the subject.[13]

When the healing professions see their revenue streams threatened, they sometimes act in ways that protect their pocketbooks but hurt their patients. In the early 1900s in New York, Mary Mallon, an immigrant from County Tyrone, Ireland, later to be known as Typhoid Mary, infected dozens of people with typhoid fever, several of whom died. Though she was herself healthy, she passed the infection along in the course of her work as a cook for wealthy families, often through her favorite dish of iced peaches. Typhoid fever, caused by a strain of *Salmonella* bacteria, is spread by poor hygiene, and in Mary's case, denial, since she believed she was healthy. She maintained her innocence even when doctors confronted her with evidence to the contrary—and to be fair, there was no scientific consensus at the time that a person could carry a disease without an active infection. Mary strenuously resisted efforts by Dr. Josephine Baker of the New York City Health Department to have her removed from circulation. Dr. Baker tried twice to have her quarantined, in one case sitting bodily on "Typhoid Mary" till the police could cart her away.

Typhoid Mary, from a contemporary publication[14]

Dr. Baker also trained mothers to wash their hands, limiting the spread of the epidemic. She also insisted that older siblings, who often cared for their younger brothers and sisters, maintain good hygiene, too.

Dr. Baker's success in controlling the spread of typhoid and cholera roused the ire of the traditionalists of her day. Thirty Brooklyn pediatricians petitioned the mayor to pull the plug on her activities, because the supply of sick children being brought into their lucrative practices was drying up. Today, a conventional medical system under threat from many fronts has to confront new therapies that can heal patients much faster—and, in many cases, more cheaply—than conventional approaches. Some react with ridicule, scorn, dismissal, and an unscientific refusal to honestly consider the facts. Yet surfing through the Energy Psychology websites reveals the names of thousands of physicians, social workers, psychiatrists, and psychologists who have eagerly trained in these new methods for the benefit of their clients and patients.

Energy tapping is to the twenty-first century what hand-washing was to the nineteenth. It's a technique that's so simple, accessible, and low-tech that it doesn't seem possible it can deliver the results it promises. It requires no expensive gadgetry, elaborate explanations, board certification, years of professional training, university degrees, or membership in prestigious societies. It seems preposterous to those with an investment in today's medical system that energy tapping could have such powerful results. Yet clinical practice is proving the worth of this method every day, and science is rapidly providing a base of evidence for the efficacy of this simple intervention.

Clearly, as a society, we should be studying the best examples of healing we can find, even if they seem like quackery or storytelling at first glance, and apply those principles for the benefit of all sick people. And we must sharpen our focus on a paradigm of health that seeks optimal vibrant wellness, instead of one that allows unrecognized low-level malaises to mature into full-blown diseases, which we must then treat, often causing misery to the patient while squandering large sums of money.

Emotional Peace in the Wake of War

Two thousand years ago, Jesus said, "Blessed are the peacemakers." Yet it is only in the last century that we have seen institutions emerge to study and develop the skills to make peace. The League of Nations was a first faltering step on an international scale. The United

Nations is far from perfect, yet has catalyzed peace in many regional conflicts that would have been worse without UN intervention.

One of those is Kosovo. Though a province of Serbia, only a minority of the population was Serbian. When the Kosovars became politically restive, the Serbian army went in. Civilians were attacked, and in some cases massacred. The Serbian army used rape "as an instrument of intimidation," as it had earlier done in Bosnia and Croatia. Thousands of Kosovars fled. The Serbians ignored appeals from the European Union and the UN to stop the killing and violence. Only when the United States under President Bill Clinton began a high-altitude bombing campaign were the Serbs eventually deterred.

Kosovar refugee with deserted village of Milic in background[15]

The volunteer team of Energy Psychology practitioners who went to Kosovo wrote that survivors experienced complete recovery from "the posttraumatic emotional effects of 247 of the 249 memories of torture, rape, and witnessing the massacre of loved ones" that were treated. The chief medical officer (surgeon general) of Kosovo wrote the following letter of appreciation:

> Many well-funded relief organizations have treated the posttraumatic stress here in Kosovo. Some of our people had limited improvement, but Kosovo had no major change or real hope until...we referred our most difficult patients to [the international treatment team]. The success from TFT was 100% for every patient, and they are still smiling until this day [and, indeed, in formal follow-ups at an average of five months after the treatment, each was free of relapse].[17]

Similar results have been shown in work with Hurricane Katrina survivors, Pakistani earthquake survivors, and those dealing with the effects of other disasters. Charles Figley, founder of Green Cross, which addresses the psychological needs of disaster victims, has said that, "Energy Psychology is among the most powerful interventions available to us."[18]

In June 2006, Sarah Bird and Paul O'Connor, Irish humanitarian volunteers, traveled to Kashmir to help earthquake victims. They were shocked at what they saw: "Eight months after the earthquake Mussarafabad is still a hellhole for the people who lost everything. They are still living in tents, shanties, and hut-like structures. There was huge devastation here; the mountain swallowed up whole communities and the figure they are talking about unofficially is closer to 200,000 deaths." They worked with schoolchildren, as well as in the hospitals. They had many profound encounters, of which this is typical:

> We went to see the head psychiatrist on our arrival and he had a woman in with him who was seeing him for the first time. She had lost her children and hadn't been able to sleep since the earthquake. She was complaining of severe headaches.

313

When we went into his room she was softly banging her head on his desk. After about five minutes of this I could not watch anymore and I asked him if I could sit with her. I just tapped her hand until she raised her head and then held her head in the TAT pose until she relaxed. The doctor was translating; she said she felt lighter but the head was still bad. So we tapped some more and you could see her visibly relax. The doctor gave her some medicine for the head but also told her to use TAT every day!

Fred Luskin, PhD, whose Stanford Forgiveness Project has taught thousands of people how to let go of wounds and resentments, has offered similar trainings in other troubled parts of the world. "Luskin says resolving such resentment 'replaces hostile feelings with positive ones that make your body feel calm and relaxed, which enhances health.' In one of his studies, seventeen adults from Northern Ireland who lost a relative to terrorist violence received a week of forgiveness training. Their mental distress dropped by about 40%, and they saw a 35% dip in headaches, back pain, and insomnia."[19]

EMDR has a Humanitarian Assistance Project which has worked in the Middle East, in New York after September 11, and in many other trouble spots around the globe. The following story comes from the efforts of a team in Palestine:

> In one memorable instance, a Palestinian father of four underwent EMDR as part of [the EMDR Humanitarian Assistance Project]. When he began the session, he was filled with homicidal rage toward all Israelis. At the end of the session, he reported feeling "much better" and spoke these words: "You must always remember: where there is life, there is hope." In the eighteen months since his session, this man has tirelessly worked to establish EMDR programs for children in West Bank refugee camps. He has given permission for his story to be told in order that others might also have hope.[20]

The effects of such improvements in people's lives has great benefit to society as a whole. "A study that tracked the clinical outcomes of 714 patients treated by seven therapists using Thought Field Therapy (TFT) in an HMO setting[21] found that decreased subjective distress following the treatment was far beyond chance with thirty-one of thirty-one psychiatric diagnostic categories, including anxiety, major depression, alcohol cravings, and PTSD."[22] Just imagine if every patient had access to such therapies as a routine part of treatment. Savings from the social costs of alcoholism and depression alone would far outweigh the costs of treatment. Ill will between warring factions and groups could be treated before it reaches out to devastate the whole society. And conflicts could be defused before they become conflagrations, with all the resulting human tragedy.

Another organization that uses Energy Psychology and energy medicine interventions to treat disaster victims in developing nations is called Capacitar. Capacitar founder Patricia Mathes Cane, PhD, has worked in most Central American nations, including Guatemala, which was ravaged by a thirty-five-year civil war. During the war, there were instances in which the entire population of men and boys in a village was shot, and the bodies buried in mass graves.

The degree of psychological trauma of the survivors, mostly women, is hard to overstate. Dr. Cane has found Energy Psychology techniques, especially TFT, to be invaluable in treating such people. She has written several workbooks, in both English and Spanish, to guide relief workers and others in these situations. She believes that Energy Psychology techniques are actually culturally more appropriate for such populations than traditional psychotherapy.

In her book *Trauma Healing and Transformation*, she writes, "Often the client-therapist model does not fit the needs of grassroots people, who for most of their lives have been disempowered by state, church, educational, and medical institutions."[23] Self-treatment can avoid triggering the power dynamics inherent in the psychotherapy techniques with which most therapists and their clients are familiar.

Women of the Mayan village of Solola, Guatemala, using TFT[24]

The story of the angry violent man that begins this chapter is drawn from an important journal article on the treatment of people in disaster zones. It surveyed twenty years of experience by many practitioners who, like Patricia Cane, reported marked improvements after Energy Psychology treatments. Whether the disasters were human-caused, like civil wars, or naturally occurring, like earthquakes, those using these treatments with survivors reported the lifting of troublesome memories, stress reduction, and an increased ability to put the past behind them and get on with their lives. The report recommends moving Energy Psychology to the front line of disaster relief.[25]

Wanted: One Thousand People

Under the impact of changes in consciousness, our social DNA is changing as surely as our physical DNA does.

The cells of the immune system are few in number compared to the trillions of cells in our bodies. Yet they play a dominant role in keeping the whole organism healthy. Every cell in the body does not have to be an immune system cell in order to fight off infection. It only takes a few.

In the same way, it does not require that all of the individuals in a society wake up in order for the whole of that society to wake up. It does require a critical mass, but that mass can be surprisingly small. Remember that the Renaissance, a cultural earthquake that completely transformed medieval society in just twenty-five years, was sparked by *a mere one thousand people.*[26]

Like the few who sparked the Renaissance and changed the world forever, today we are witnessing a new revolution fomented by just a few thousand courageous volunteers who are aware not just of the effect of their own thoughts and feelings on their genetic expression, but of themselves as the change agents for society. By transforming their own consciousness, they are spearheading the transformation of the whole. They model what a transformed person can look like; they are the social genes that activate the immune machinery of an entire society.

Are you one of them? If you are one of the many thousands of people who have read this book, you have already self-selected yourself as one of those social catalysts. To an individual gene, the task of getting a trillion-celled organism to change looks formidable, even though we know that the organism must awaken if it is to survive. Awakening is urgent.

Yet once you realize you're acting in concert with a system, that you are not isolated, that your mind and your experience are subject to quantum entanglement in a multiverse of possibilities, then everything changes. The little effects you have in your daily life become part of one large effect. That effect is large enough to change the world. It already has. And the results of humanity becoming a conscious co-creator in the great ecology of being are beyond our wildest dreams.

Ten Principles of Epigenetic Medicine

The winds of grace are always blowing, but you have to raise the sail.
—Ramakrishna

Today, as I write these words, I'm sitting on a bench in a park on one of Northern California's sunny winter days. My laptop and a notepad sit on my lap. I watch as my youngest son, Alexander, plays in the sand with his bucket, spade, trains, and cars. "I'm digging for buried treasure!" he exclaims excitedly, as his toy rake hits a buried object. Then, as he unearths it, he says, "That's garbage!"

A toddler runs up, his drooly smile proudly revealing two brand new teeth. He picks up Alexander's toy train and begins waving the pieces about. Suddenly, he discovers that the engine and the tender snap together. He snaps them and unsnaps them over and over again. He's just discovered a major secret to the way the world works.

Meanwhile, Alexander has run to the slide. After a few minutes, he and a diminutive little girl discover that they don't have to slide down the slide in a seated position. They experiment with going down sideways, head first, and on their backs. They have to show me each new trick. First Alexander counts: "One, two, three, twenty-eight, seventeen, nine, hurry, watch me!" and then he slides down.

As I contemplate the discovery of epigenetic control of genes and watch the joyful play in front of me, I realize how much scientific discovery resembles the playful children in the park. We humans discover how things fit together. We experiment with hypotheses, some of which fail. Even after we've made an exciting new discovery, we are not content. We immediately push forward into new territory. When our knowledge crosses one horizon, we quickly push forward to another, with scarcely a backward glance.

Applying the discoveries of epigenetic control of the genes, and hence cellular function, offers great potential for medical breakthroughs. It allows us to seek therapies that intervene at the level of consciousness by changing beliefs and behaviors that interfere with health. Changing energy patterns before they manifest as disease works at a level of cause that is of a higher order than matter. While metaphysicians have advocated such a focus for millennia, modern research is now giving us an understanding of the genetic changes that occur in response to changes in energy and consciousness. This opens up the prospect of using consciousness deliberately, as a planned medical intervention.

Like the toddler who has discovered that the two parts of the train snap together, science has taken the first tiny steps in charting the mechanisms of epigenetic control. Now, a huge new panorama of research presents itself. Undoubtedly, there are widespread positive effects that come from belief change and meditation. Yet researchers cannot be content with understanding only that there is a generalized benefit to these practices. They must begin to chart the precise pathways by which such therapies have their effects, so that the power of consciousness can be harnessed with precision.

Epigenetic medicine seeks these precise pathways. It's not enough to prescribe meditation for depressed patients, even though we know that meditation can be useful in alleviating depression. We need to develop a battery of interventions that we are reasonably certain can be effective, and that are reasonable for the patient to perform. Though they can affect all body systems simultaneously, consciousness-based epigenetic shifts aren't as mechanistic as taking a drug; they require a degree of self-awareness that is not required of the patient popping a pill along with the morning's toothbrushing routine.

Epigenetic medicine based on consciousness works seamlessly with conventional medicine, alternative medicine, and integrative medicine (medicine that combines the best of conventional and alternative approaches). For instance, molecular *biomarkers,* "signatures of genes or proteins that are specific to a disease,"[1] allow diagnosis of many conditions long before they might show up on an X-ray or manifest as symptoms. Testing for biomarkers is also noninvasive and safe. Biomarkers have the potential to allow early detection of cancer and other diseases, and biomarker-based tests are expected to become widespread in the coming decades. Dr. Leroy Hood, cofounder of Amgen, the world's largest biotechnology company, and in whose laboratory the DNA sequencer originated, forsees a day when "with just a single pinprick, a nanotechnology device will quickly measure and analyze one thousand proteins in a droplet of your blood."[2]

DNA screening is now widely used. There are "more than two dozen online genetic testing services springing up to take advantage of advances in genomics.... Tests for nearly 1,300 ailments have been developed so far."[3] Newer tests are being developed that use techniques even more sophisticated than gene chips. DNA testing is joining hands with nanotechnology to produce tests that can determine the expression not just of a gene, a sequence of DNA, but also of individual molecules, the "building blocks of gene expression."[4]

One of the most exciting new contributions of technological medicine is natural orifice transluminal endoscopic surgery (NOTES).

Surgical instruments have been developed that allow surgeons to pass their instruments through the mouth and other body cavities through a tube, and perform surgery without breaking the skin. Many of these procedures require only a local anesthetic, rather than riskier general anesthesia. Patient recovery time can be greatly shortened.

Tiny robots have been developed to work inside the body. The Pillcam, introduced in 2001, is a camera the size and shape of a pill. It is swallowed, and takes photographs as it moves through the digestive tract, giving physicians valuable diagnostic information. Other robots being developed for surgery are controlled by electromagnetic fields from outside the body. The surgeon moves the robot by altering the charge of the externally generated field. This avoids the need for miniature internal devices to be equipped with batteries, which would add weight. Scientists from the Swiss Federation of Technology are developing these devices to perform microsurgery inside the eye.[5]

Pillcam

An abundant source of information is already being generated by MRI scans—and ignored. Every clinician is familiar with the images from inside the body generated by MRIs. But there is a wealth of information in the electromagnetic fields outside the body as well, as is apparent from the accompanying illustration of an MRI scan. Currently, this information is discarded, since medicine is so geared to the physical body. Future science may look at the information-rich area outside the body, too. It could develop electromagnetic profiles of energy disturbances and blocks in these fields outside as a diagnostic tool.

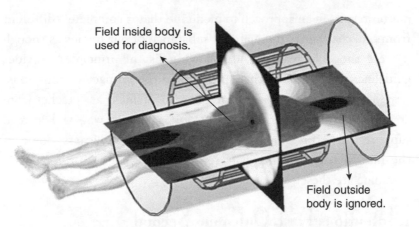

Field inside body is used for diagnosis.

Field outside body is ignored.

Internal and external fields of a patient in an MRI scanner

As these new technologies become more sophisticated, consciousness-based epigenetic interventions could be developed to target conditions that they uncover. Used in conjunction with epigenetic visualizations and energy therapies that have proven effective, gene, MRI, nanotechnology, and biomarker tests could go hand in hand with integrative medicine in a comprehensive treatment plan.

Imagine if each of us constructed a set of visualizations that was uniquely geared to our psychological structure. Imagine going to your preventive medicine physician or psychiatrist and having a caring expert help you identify your unique psychological triggers, levers that can aid you in maintaining health. You walk out of the office visit with a prescription pad of beliefs, concepts, prayers, and visualizations that have been scientifically verified to boost your immune system. You then spend ten minutes a day on this routine. In this way, epigenetic medicine has the potential both to treat disease and to help keep you healthy.

We already have an outline of the potential effectiveness of epigenetic medicine in our studies of nurturing in animals and adults, from researching the brains of both happy and unhappy people, by examining the beliefs of sick patients, and all the other ways in which we humans can use our consciousness to affect our well-being. Recognizing that we are conscious energy systems giving rise to matter results in an approach to medicine that is completely different from one that treats the material substance of our bodies as though it were the only reality. The following list of principles provides guidelines for treatment that spring from the primacy of consciousness. They are the foundation for a new medicine that detaches from an obsession with making matter look a certain way, and instead supports the expression of health through consciousness. Some of the interweaving and mutually reinforcing principles of epigenetic mecidine are these:

1. Intentions First, Outcomes Second

The literature of medicine is littered with the word "outcomes." The eventual material result, the "outcome," is the end point that studies use to determine the efficacy of a particular treatment. A good outcome means that the symptom has disappeared. The medicine of consciousness, on the other hand, focuses first on the well-being of the soul, and then on the epigenetic effects of that well-being on the cells of our bodies. Symptoms are perceived as guides to understanding the needs of body and soul, not as nuisances that must be made to disappear.

"Cancer was the best thing that ever happened to me" is a paradoxical refrain that echoes through the annals of survivors' stories. The "outcome" for such a patient may still be cancer, but the inner experience may be healing. Illness can be full of gifts, if we shift our perspective to the present moment and detach from an obsession that our bodies be in a certain state.

The quantum soup has an infinite number of possibilities. Rather than get too attached to any one outcome and cling neurotically to our preferred result, we can instead state our intentions clearly, then let go. Reinhold Niebuhr's serenity prayer used by AA and other twelve-step programs is a powerful mantra of non-attachment: "God, grant me the serenity to accept the things I cannot change; courage to change the things I can; and the wisdom to know the difference." It isn't whether you live or die in the end that counts, it's how healed your life is at any moment. Western medicine, with its focus on outcomes, must shift to realize the truth of the Zen dictum: "The journey is the destination."

In another paradox, it is often by letting go that we gain something. Setting a clear intention in our consciousness is often a better way to get what we want than manipulating the events around us to attempt to produce it. Clear intentions open us up to streams of quantum possibility that our ego-bound imaginations cannot grasp.

2. Healing Is a Process, Not an Event

Modern medicine has an underlying structure that perceives illness as an event. The event starts with "symptoms," and ends with a "cure." Center stage in the event is the prescribing of a drug or performing of surgery. But health is not an event. It is a process. It is not a rock, but rather a river. Lifestyle changes such as diet and exercise can address systemic problems, but involve a change in life-process day after day after day. Weight loss isn't going on a diet (an event), or being twenty pounds lighter (an event). Weight loss is what I eat and how I exercise today and always (a process).

Joining a gym is an event, and an event-centered perception of health encourages people to do this. Many people join gyms every year. But "up to 65% of new gym members drop out in the first six months,"[6] and more thereafter, as a result of seeing health as an event rather than a process. A process is something we incorporate into our lifestyle, like having a habit of going to the gym every Monday, Wednesday, and Friday, and completing a set routine.

The same applies to spirituality. At last Easter's sermon, attendance at my church was dramatically greater than usual, as is typical for holidays. Starting his sermon, the minister laughed and said, "Now I'm going to talk to all of you that I last talked to last Easter, and won't see again till next year." Old Catholic joke: "A Catholic goes to church three times in his life, and two of those times he's carried." The three events are the sacraments of baptism, marriage, and the funeral.

Going to church on holidays is a symptom of seeing worship as an event. A daily prayer practice is a process that enfolds every event of the day. It is in these regular daily choices that the possibility wave of quantum potentials is consistently collapsed down into the probability of health.

Researcher William Collinge has a useful visual aid to conceptualize the healing process. He represents it as wavy line with a series of ups and downs. There is a turning point, imperceptible at the time, that marks a shift to higher highs and an upward trend.

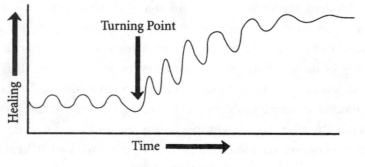

The healing pattern[7]

The giant U.S. Kaiser Permanente hospital system now offers its nine million members a variety of lifestyle classes to help them lose weight, kick cigarette, drug, and alcohol addictions, and acquire beliefs and energy techniques that improve their happiness and health. Retraining patients lowers Kaiser's medical costs. Shifting to a process view of healing, in which patients make a daily flow of healthy choices, lowers the probability of catastrophic medical events.

3. Heart-Centered

Are you in love with your doctor? Is your doctor in love with you? Do you feel a warm glow whenever you think of your doctor? Do you believe that your doctor feels kind and warm feelings toward you? A heart-centered connection (though not a romantic one) is an essential aspect of the healing encounter.

The quality of interaction can be as important, or more important, than the content of interaction. Simply being met by another human being, heart to heart, at the level of soul and emotion, can be a profoundly healing experience. This is the state that people in love find themselves in, and it triggers a cascade of powerful hormonal responses. No matter how smart your doctor's head is, her or his heart comes first. In fact, in the ancient Hindu creation myth told in the *Upanishads,* the heart appeared first, and "from the heart came the mind."[8] A sound heart was seen by these ancients as the source of a sound mind. Modern medicine could take a leaf from their book.

If every medical encounter began with a heart connection, and did not proceed until that connection had been established, the content of those encounters might be much more powerful. In a landmark paper by Andrew Weil, MD, and Ralph Snyderman, MD, published in the *Archives of Internal Medicine* in 2002, the authors conclude with a list of six reforms that build on the platform of sound science, yet also focus broadly on the well-being of patients. They urge "far more meaningful patient-physician relationships...[that]...provide compassion, [and] provide close attention to our patient's spiritual and emotional needs..."[9]

4. Being-Focused

People's state of being might have as much to do with their health as the puncture wound in their arm. Larry Dossey, MD, recounts the story of doing his rounds in a coronary care unit and asking patients (all men) why they were there. They had seemingly succumbed to sudden and unforeseen heart attacks. But the majority of answers they gave were based in their life situations, not their medical histories. Typical responses were "I couldn't stand to see my boss's face one more day" or "I feel trapped in my marriage. I can't abide being with my wife" or "My kids fight constantly. I would do anything to get away from their constant bickering." Their heart attacks had resulted in them getting away from the conditions that were intolerable to them—at the cost of their health. Ongoing focus on the quality of a person's being might prevent them having to produce extreme symptoms to catalyze a change in their lives.

Our presenting symptoms may have a great deal more to do with our state of being than with our medical histories. They may hold keys to our wellness that can make or break our medical histories. To fix the medical problem, while leaving the soul unaddressed, at best defers the consequence.

Some practices—a rich social network, consistent spiritual practice, an authentic vocation, the ability to speak one's feelings, meditation—have been shown by research to build a more powerful sense of personal well-being. The physician of the future might first look for the practices that can most bolster the patient's soul, like James Dillard writing on his prescription pad, "Long talks with your rabbi," in order to banish the shadow of death from the consulting room and generate a healthy, creative, peaceful state of being.

5. Treat Whole Systems

Energy therapies typically treat the whole human being, reducing stress generally, and having a positive effect throughout the body. They are *generalist*. By contrast, conventional therapies are *reductionist*, attempting to reduce the problem to the smallest possible target.

The reductionistic approach has its apex in the drug industry. Big Pharma looks for magic bullets. These are molecules that affect other molecules in predictable ways. Such molecules are valuable because they can be patented and sold. America's War on Cancer, which began in the early 1970s and has consumed billions of dollars in a search for the magic bullet that will kill cancer cells but leave healthy cells intact, has tested hundreds of potential magic bullets on long-suffering human beings.

By contrast, a holistic approach looks at ways to affect trillions of cells and thousands of protein molecules simultaneously. The methods described in this book are holistic methods, affecting all the body's organ systems at the same time. These stress-reduction methods are the opposite of a magic bullet. They are a magic wand capable of creating head-to-toe physical transformation in moments. Reversing the fight-or-flight response causes the blood to flow back out of the peripheral muscles and into the digestive tract, improving digestion. Blood is available to the reproductive organs, enhancing sexual function. Breathing deepens and muscle activity slows, providing all the tissues of the body with more oxygen. Blood flows back into the frontal lobes of the brain, enhancing cognition. Blood pressure and blood sugar both drop.

Let's see now: We've just improved digestion, sexual function, mental acuity, circulation, and cell rejuvenation, and all at the same time. That's the magic of stress reduction, as it *affects all the body's systems simultaneously.* If there were a drug that did this, it would truly be a miracle drug. Yet every human being has the ability to summon up such healing magic by de-stressing themselves using any one of a dozen proven effective methods. By shifting our emotional balance toward happiness, we initiate the epigenetic signals that shift our gene expression toward health.

One of the problems resulting from scientists identifying a particular gene or neurochemical associated with an emotion is that there will be a "gold rush" to turn it into a patentable drug, and the holistic implications of epigenetic research will be lost in the commercial stampede.

Serotonin suffered this fate. When the role of this molecule in regulating mood was discovered, Big Pharma began work on magic bullets that block the natural breakdown of serotonin. This class of drugs is called selective serotonin reuptake inhibitors (SSRIs). Now prescribed to millions of people to combat anxiety and depression, the drugs do indeed produce greater quantities of free serotonin in the brain. But SSRIs have some negative side effects, and only after two decades of widespread use have the data become available to link them to increased risk of suicide and other troubling symptoms.

By contrast, natural methods of raising serotonin, such as meditation, yoga, energy medicine, and optimism, can be neglected in favor of a pill. Research into Energy Psychology, meditation, and other free techniques is not going to bring great commercial rewards to anyone. It draws no drug company sponsors with deep pockets. Holism is rarely the road to riches. Yet of all the patients showing up at doctor's offices not feeling well, only 10% have an identifiable organic disease. The other 90% feel sick or believe they're sick, but in ways that defy simple reductionist definitions.[10] Their bodies are often demonstrating symptoms of the system-wide degradation that comes from long-term stress, and the holistic approach, by working as globally and nonspecifically as their complaints, has a reasonable chance of making them feel better.

The reductionist approach, seeking a molecular target among the body's one hundred thousand proteins, sees your body as a complex machine like your car. If your car isn't running well, you find the source of the problem and insert a fix. Perhaps one of the springs is soft, and isn't holding up that corner of the car properly as you drive. Reductionist biotechnology would isolate the required compound and synthesize a pill that's analogous to the car's spring. Since you can't synthesize the protein as precisely as the body's formulation, you design an analog.

For a car, that might be a huge and powerful new spring. Suddenly, that one corner of the car is higher and harder than the others. The biotechnologists then design another fix to take care of the problematic side effects of the first fix. They invent big, rigid tires and install them. Now you can no longer feel the nonstandard spring as you drive. But you can't feel the road, either, because of the new tires. The engine starts to work much too hard, and a "service engine" light pops up on the dashboard. Unfortunate side effect. So another fix is found, a panel to fit over the annoying light. And so on, till patients are taking a multitude of drugs to mask the side effects of drugs previously prescribed, and the real initial problem has not been solved at all.

This approach shows up all over medical research. In a comprehensive study funded by the National Institute of Mental Health,

1,915 subjects receiving an SSRI antidepressant drug were examined for frequency of suicidal thoughts. A correlation was found between two genes and suicidal thoughts. The study concluded by suggesting that gene testing be done to determine which patients had these two genes, so that they could be more closely monitored by their clinicians after being prescribed SSRIs.[11] That's a logical reductionist conclusion: Prescribe a second procedure to limit the negative side effects of the first drug.

A holistic perspective might draw different conclusions. The study found that patients with these genes were no more likely to have attempted suicide than other patients prior to treatment with SSRIs. In other words, SSRIs appeared to trigger suicidal thoughts in people with one or both of these genes. So a holistic approach might be to teach these same patients ways to raise their serotonin naturally and reduce their stress levels, in addition to the prescription drug remedies available. This possibility was never suggested by the prestigious panel that authored the study.

As we learn about the molecules that regulate gene expression, the temptation to turn these into pills is hard for reductionist medicine to resist. A gene called CRHR1 codes for a stress hormone called CRH. A researcher found that by breeding mutant mice that lacked the gene, he reduced CRH levels, and the stress and anxiety levels of the mice went down. So he proposed removing CRH from anxious human beings, assuring readers that this would be "unharmful."[12] But legions of pharmaceutical scandals have shown us that tinkering with the body's biochemistry usually has unintended consequences. Only after millions of people have taken a drug for years do the side effects begin to show up. And drug solutions often lead us to neglect the many safe, free, non-pharmaceutical alternatives available. Our limited new knowledge of genetics risks leading us down the same long and expensive blind alley as the search for the magic bullet to cure cancer did forty years ago.

Which would you rather see our children do: learn stress-reduction techniques, which they can use any time to epigenetically activate their happy genes, or have them turn to the medicine cabinet for happy pills? And then another pill to regulate the unhappy side effects of the happy pill? Drug research will continue, and can bring great benefits. But drugs and other forms of reductionist medicine can never substitute for the behavioral and lifestyle skills that improve our health and well-being by reducing stress generally.

Holistic medicine approaches every symptom as an expression occurring within an integrated energy system, and finds the leverage points that bring that whole energy system back into balance.

6. Healing Before Disease

Energy medicine is not only the place to start treatment of a problem; it is the place to start *before* there is a problem. A person whose energy systems have been optimized and are functioning well has established a baseline that makes it much harder for disease to take root. Whatever the conditions of our lives, no matter what difficulties we are experiencing in our health, our relationships, our work, the techniques found in energy medicine can optimize entire systems in our bodies, minds, and emotional realms. Because it breaks from a mechanistic model of cause and effect, energy medicine opens our minds, hearts, and bodies to the possibility of radical, discontinuous change. Experiments tell us that healing is not localized in time or space; so we can pray for our own childhoods, we can pray for distant people, and we can pray for the wellness of our planet. A morning prayer creates a healing context for the day to come.

Once we get in the habit of attuning to our inner state of health, we may notice energy disturbances before they manifest as disease. A daily energy self-scan can give us valuable information about areas that are out of balance. Our focus eventually shifts from looking for disease to raising our threshold of wellness.

7. Magnify the Body's Inherent Self-Healing Powers

Sometimes a person needs only a nudge in the right direction to get unstuck from a recurrent pattern and initiate the process of the body's restoration of homeostasis. The first thing a wellness counselor can do is look for those leverage points that might help the process get going. So rather than first looking for outside interventions, the guide of the future will look for the interventions inherent in the patient that the patient might not have seen or might not be utilizing. One of the reforms advocated by Weil and Snyderman is: "Involve the patient as an active partner in his or her care, with an emphasis on teaching each patient the best way to improve his or her health."[13]

A doctor is often with the patient one or two hours a year. The patient is with the patient the other 8,758 hours. Who do you suppose has the most influence on the patient's wellness on a daily basis? Recognizing the enormous healing powers of the body—and finding ways to engage them—presupposes an entirely different model from the classic image of the patient being fixed by a doctor or hospital. A patient accustomed to allopathic medicine might be baffled by an acupuncturist who inserts a needle far from the site of the symptom. Many alternative therapies look for the one log that is producing the logjam, and shift just that one. Once it is shifted, the rest of the jam takes care of itself and the body's full power comes to bear on re-creating homeostasis.

8. Stream to Appropriate Treatment Paths

Some conditions are obvious candidates for conventional medical treatment. Others are unlikely to respond to this approach. Trying to treat chronic fatigue syndrome with allopathic medicine is misguided; trying to treat a gunshot wound with alternative medicine is foolhardy. In *Spontaneous Healing*, Andrew Weil offers this simple advice: "Do not seek help from a conventional doctor for a condition that conventional medicine cannot treat, and do not rely on an alternative provider for a condition that conventional medicine can manage well."[14] He makes the following distinctions in "what allopathic medicine can and cannot do for you:

CAN:

Manage trauma better than any other system of medicine.

Diagnose and treat many medical and surgical emergencies.

Treat acute bacterial infections with antibiotics.

Treat some parasitic and fungal infections.

Prevent many infectious diseases by immunization.

Diagnose complex medical problems.

Replace damaged hips and knees.

Get good results with cosmetic and reconstructive surgery.

Diagnose and correct hormonal deficiencies.

CANNOT:

Treat viral infections.

Cure most chronic degenerative diseases.

Effectively manage most kinds of mental illness.

Cure most forms of allergy or autoimmune disease.

Effectively manage psychosomatic illness.

Cure most forms of cancer."[15]

This list needs updating, as more and more conditions are being moved from the allopathic column to the complementary and alternative medicine (CAM) column as better research is published. For instance, conventional hormone replacement therapies have been shown to have negative side effects in the fifteen years since Weil penned this list (the National Women's Health Network calls hormone replacement "a triumph of marketing over science"[16]), whereas alternative medicine, through exercise and diet-based approaches, plus supplementation if necessary, has been shown to stimulate the body's hormonal production and balance. Electromagnetic stimulation, for instance, has been shown by Norman Shealy to boost the production of DHEA, the most common hormone in the body, vital for cell regeneration.[17] Shealy also draws attention to a category that he calls "semi-orphan diseases," those for which conventional medicine is only partially effective. Among the conditions he lists are rheumatoid arthritis, lupus, multiple sclerosis, and chronic hepatitis.[18]

If a provider and patient have these kinds of clear distinctions in mind, it becomes possible to seek appropriate treatment and avoid wasting time, money, and effort on inappropriate treatment. The new category of specialist, like the "Navigator" at the Integrative Medical Clinic, is trained in helping patients (and practitioners) understand these distinctions. Such navigators could become a routine part of the beginning of any treatment plan.

Many holistic practitioners get patients who have not been helped by conventional medicine. Many have been chopped by surgery and debilitated by prolonged prescription drug use. Most of the chronic pain patients who show up at Dr. Dillard's practice or Dr. Dozor's integrative clinic have already gone through the medical mill. By the time they give up on conventional medicine and decide to see an integrative practitioner, they may be suffering the consequences of needless surgeries or have immune systems depleted by inappropriate drugs. The alternative physician then has to deal, not just with the original problem, but with the side effects of conventional treatment. I can see this changing in a few years, as patients become more aware of the benefits of alternative medicine. Holistic treatment might be the first option they choose, not the last.

"Doc, I've tried everything! Acupuncture, herbs, EFT, Reiki, prayer, yoga...Now I'm ready for drugs and surgery!"

9. Revisioning Death

One of the great services that authors like Bernie Siegel, MD, Elisabeth Kübler-Ross, MD, and Stephen Levine have done is to shake up the idea, so prevalent in our medical institutions, that death equals failure. I remember talking to a grief counselor many years ago about the exciting ideas in Bernie Siegel's book *Love, Medicine & Miracles*.[19] He was skeptical. "It is terrible for a client," he objected, "if they try all that touchy-feely stuff and it doesn't work."

Underlying his objection was the assumption that living meant that the "touchy-feely stuff" worked and dying meant that it did not. Siegel and others have reintroduced into public consciousness the idea of a healed death.

My mother showed me this firsthand. She developed cancer in her left eye and her liver. She had some conventional medical treatments such as radiation (chemotherapy was not indicated for her particular condition) and also tried alternative therapies such as shark cartilage. She fit the profile of a person whose life was usually in turmoil, often self-created. That chaos regularly spilled over to affect the lives of the people around her.

In the two years before she died, she sought to make amends for the anguish she'd caused others. She traveled to visit many of the people she had grown up with, and, in person, asked for forgiveness. Her father was still living, and she traveled halfway across the world to see him. She visited her sisters and her childhood friends. Layer by layer, all the heavy weights of a lifetime of resentment and anger dropped off her shoulders. In one of the last conversations I had with her, she agonized over a person she could not locate. She said, "There was a girl in my high school whose name was Helen Freund. I hated her, and she hated me. I've tried to track her down so I can say I'm sorry, but I can't find out where she lives now." She started to cry. I sat her on my knee, and said gently to her, "Mom, I think it's okay if you can't find Helen Freund. I'm sure she's forgiven you for whatever happened, and I know you've forgiven her."

My mother's heart and soul recovered, but her body did not. She eventually died. But she died at peace and, in every way that mattered, she died healed. She and my father lived in my sister's spacious home for those last two years, surrounded by friends and family, and she died in the bed where she had slept. It was very early morning when she died, before dawn, but she started up just before the end. Her last words were, "I see the light. Do you see the light?"

When she died, she was honored by hundreds of people. The atmosphere leading up to her funeral was filled with grief, and the rest of the family had decided on an open casket affair, which hardly added to the sense of cheer. So to emphasize the joy she'd come to find in life, I had a large-screen TV set up next to the casket. On it, I played a continuous loop of video of her I'd taken a couple of years earlier. In the video, she was telling jokes, laughing uproariously, and waving her hands around to illustrate her points. It presented the vital spirit of a life fully lived.

The doctor of the future may not say, in hushed tones, "I lost a patient." The patient's ego and body might have died, and a medical ego that sees death as the enemy might indeed see a reflection of its own death in the death of another. But when we understand the survival of consciousness beyond death, and that death does not mean failure, we can celebrate the continuation of spirit even as we mourn the loss of a body. Everyone dies; our challenge is to live a life of passion, creativity, joy, inspiration, and healing in however many years we have. Death is a change of state, and not the enemy of healing.

10. Understand the Global Context of Healing

Fantastically healthy people cannot thrive on a dying planet. As a society, we have to wake up to the ways in which our personal health fits into the picture of global healing, and vice versa. This will lead to sustainable, rational approaches to health care, rather than medical systems that pay no attention to the waste and cost they incur.

In addition to the financial waste, burgeoning bureaucracies, and unneeded medical tests, procedures, and prescriptions, our landfills are overflowing in part due to the huge volumes of medical waste generated by the large number of disposable objects (and their sterile packaging) used in treatment and diagnosis. Their biotoxicity is also an added hazard to our water supplies and to those who handle this waste. Cod caught by fishermen in the North Sea, off the coast of Scandinavia, have been found to contain traces of the SSRI drugs used to treat depression. The fishermen did not report if the fish were happier; they certainly dramatized the problem of overprescribing medications.

A field called ecologically sustainable medicine (ESM) has developed, complete with a journal.[20] ESM advances medicine with environmental integrity by offering affordable and renewable medical choices, saving resources and money, while preserving the health of the environment.

Among its goals, ESM advocates the emphasis of wellness in medical practice, the choice of ESM treatments as a first resort, awareness of the environmental impact of medicine, recognition of the importance of ecological health in medical ethics, and awareness of the psychological and cultural benefits of sustainable medicine.

The practice of sustainable medical care necessitates fundamental changes in the delivery of medicine. Whether practicing family medicine, oncology, chiropractic, acupuncture, massage, psychotherapy, or any other medical technique, providers can emphasize prevention, precaution, efficacy, and wellness. As a result, the healing professions become more sustainable.

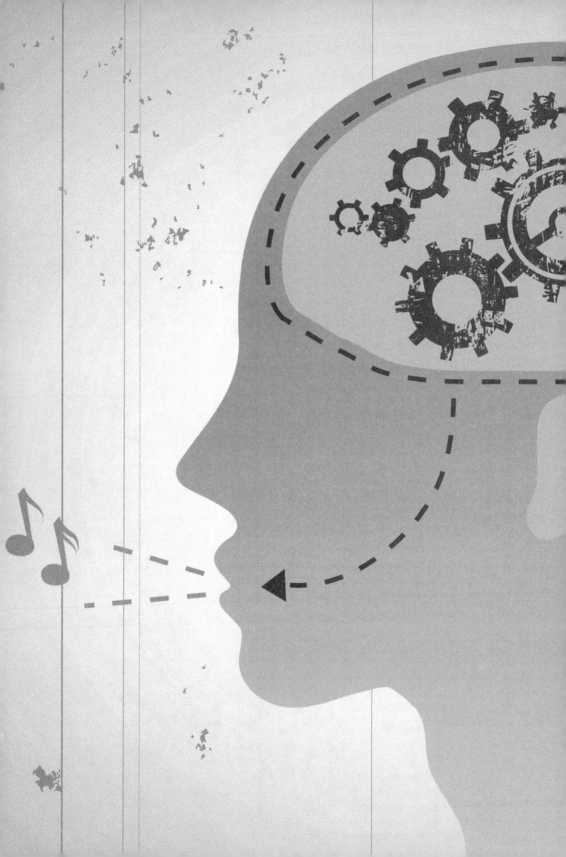

16

Practices of Epigenetic Medicine

As human beings our greatness lies not so much in being able to re-make the world, as in being able to re-make ourselves.

—Mahatma Gandhi

Epigenetics bears promise far beyond our current field of vision. The journal *Science* defined epigenetics as "the study of heritable changes in gene function that occur without a change in the DNA sequence."[1] That's a good definition of epigenetics as applied to the transmission of information across generations, once seen as the primary function of genes. But it misses the potential of the positive genetic shifts we can create *right now,* in our own bodies, by deliberately making changes in our consciousness that have epigenetic effects.

As I have read the research in this field, it has challenged me in my own life and behavior. There are days when I feel unaccountably grouchy. I know that if I spread my misery into the world around me, I become an agent of negative epigenetic change, activating stress genes in people around me. So I make a conscious choice to say and do certain things. I might say an affirmation and do an EFT routine. I might meditate for a few minutes, enter a state of heart coherence, or say a prayer. I might take a ten-minute nap. I might force myself to say a kind thing to another shopper in line at the grocery store. I might visualize my work life a year in the future, and see myself looking back on the solutions I found to the problems that so vex me today.

These are all deliberate conscious interventions. My grocery store conversation engages the healing power of altruism. My nap gets my feelings back in synch with my clock genes. An affirmation neutralizes harmful beliefs. EFT balances the electromagnetic field of my body. Saying positive words reminds me that I can cultivate the habit of kindness. My visualization reduces my stress, reminding me that "This too shall pass." Each of these things requires only a few minutes. Taken together, they can turn a bad day into a good day, and give me an experience of peace of mind and health of body. Knowing the power of epigenetic control makes one much less casual about words, thoughts, and actions.

Gene splicing seeks beneficial effects by manipulating the composition of genes in the laboratory. Imagine a medicine of the future where *the laboratory in which your genes are being modified is your own mind*, moment-by-moment, with every thought and every action you undertake. Imagine a virtuous cycle in which heart-focused intention sends an epigenetic signal deactivating your fight-or-flight mechanism. That improves your mood, which reinforces the strength of your heart-focused intention, which sends a signal to build cell repair hormones like DHEA. Where does the cycle stop? No one knows. The human health span (health span = healthy life span), using only the factors known today and not the fruits of future research, might extend to 140 years.[2] This figure seems completely outside the bounds of possibility to most medical practitioners today—perhaps as improbable as proposing to a Utah frontier surgeon in 1900 that, within a century, human life expectancy would almost double from the forty-two-year average that prevailed at the time.

The idea that our DNA can be triggered by our feelings, thoughts, and intentions acting in our energy fields might be as axiomatic to the next generation of treatment professionals as today's understanding that aspirin thins the blood. As this idea is researched and developed, an entirely new medicine might take shape. This medicine might look completely different from today's medicine. Weaving together complementary and alternative medicine with advances in technological medicine, it will shift personal and social well-being to an extent we can barely imagine today.

Recently, Jay Olshansky, PhD, professor of epidemiology and biostatistics at the University of Illinois at Chicago, debunked the idea that human life expectancy might increase significantly in the years to come. In a *New York Times* article that holds that "the era of large increases in life expectancy may be nearing an end," he asserts that "there are no lifestyle changes, surgical procedures, vitamins, antioxidants, hormones, or techniques of genetic engineering available today with the capacity to repeat the gains in life expectancy that were achieved in the twentieth century."[3] I can see how he would reach that conclusion working from his list. But missing from that list are energy medicine, consciousness-based therapies, spiritualilty, and all the other methods in this book. When you factor these into the equation, you get a much more encouraging result.

A typical medical visit today goes something like this: A patient makes an appointment, driven to the practitioner by some ailment or complaint. The doctor listens, asks questions, performs an examination, gives advice, and writes a prescription for that ailment.

If the ailment does not go away, or if it disappears but resurfaces in some other form, then further steps may be taken. Tests may be performed. Surgery or more powerful drugs may be prescribed. An escalation of treatment occurs, until the patient "responds."

The first doctor visit is relatively quick and cheap. By the time treatment escalates, for instance into chemotherapy and radiation for cancer, or a hip replacement for degenerative bone disease, the solutions are neither quick nor cheap—and they may have severe consequences for the quality of life of the patient. This is "back-loaded" treatment, with few of the costs on the front end of the treatment cycle, and a very high total cost in terms of both dollars and quality of life.

An integrative medical approach is quite different. There are more costs, and more attention, on the front end. During the first visit, attention is given to all aspects of the patient, to see how the presenting condition fits into the larger picture. Those larger picture issues are then addressed. If the patient's lifestyle can be shifted, perhaps given nudges by a number of different healing modalities, then many of the medical problems that characterize poor ongoing lifestyle choices may be avoided. The diabetic, for instance, who embraces a low-glycemic diet, plus an exercise program, may eliminate the need for later costly and devastating interventions such as the amputation of gangrenous limbs. The attention and costs of appropriate holistic intervention result in a much higher quality of life for the patient—and much lower costs over the whole treatment cycle. Every dollar that a company invests in wellness and prevention programs saves three dollars in later disease-care costs.[4] Here is what such a treatment plan might look like:

1. Start Treatment with Energy Medicine

Energy medicine functions at the high level of general wellness. It is nonspecific, tuning up every cell, organ, and system of organs. As such, it is the place to *start* treatment, not a place to go once the remedies offered by allopathic medicine have been exhausted, as so many patients do. Energy systems underlie cellular architecture; they are the first place to start building a foundation for vibrant health.

If you have a serious or life-threatening medical condition, conventional treatment might be the perfect solution. "When you've been hit with a poisoned arrow," advised the Buddha, "take the arrow out before you start praying for healing." The American College of Emergency Physicians offers the following guidelines for recognizing a medical emergency that requires immediate care:

- difficulty breathing or shortness of breath
- chest pain or pressure lasting two minutes or more
- fainting
- sudden dizziness or weakness
- changes in vision
- confusion or disorientation
- any sudden or severe pain
- uncontrolled bleeding
- severe or persistent vomiting or diarrhea
- coughing or vomiting blood
- suicidal or homicidal feelings[5]

But most visits to hospitals are not for any of these conditions. In 90% of instances, no identifiable organic ailment can be found.[6] Deciding what constitutes a condition that requires treatment, and for which conditions treatment can be deferred for a time, requires information and self-awareness. Early treatment for certain conditions, such as prostate cancer, makes little difference to the outcome.[7]

Low back pain is another common condition for which a variety of safe treatments based on exercise and consciousness are available. It is pervasive, afflicting some 65 million Americans, "affecting nearly 80% of the adult population at some time during their life. It represents the single most common cause for disability in persons under age forty-five."[8] Studies show that the practice of hatha yoga by back pain sufferers can reduce "pain intensity, reliance on pain medication, and disability."[9] Yoga has also been shown to reduce the stress level of cancer patients, ease insomnia, and improve emotional well-being.[10] And the book *EFT for Back Pain* is full of examples of sufferers who've quickly overcome back pain by addressing the underlying emotional issues.[11] These are the first places to start when dealing with low back pain, rather than jumping to drugs, which may mask the symptoms without addressing the causes.

The medical encounter of the future might start with a prayer as certainly as the medical encounter of today starts with a clipboard and a white coat. It might involve Energy Psychology, meditation training, or another epigenetic intervention. Only once safe and non-invasive techniques had been exhausted would risky and dangerous medical interventions be considered.

2. Attachment Doctoring

Without some extra effort, we simply cannot relate effectively to other human beings at the fast pace of modern life. For the gifts of deep human connection to appear, we have to set aside our busy lives and slow down—at least for a time—in order to engage in the meaningful relationships that Weil and Dossey advocate. Andrea Bialek, MD, whose business card says "holistic gynecologist" and who specializes in menopause, has a busy practice assisting women looking for alternatives to hormone replacement therapy. She says, "A woman will say she has no sex drive, and I may suggest she and her husband go to a bed and breakfast and see what happens when they're happy, healthy, and relaxed."[12] That lovemaking improves on vacation is a truism among marriage and family therapists. When a couple has no agenda for two or three days, no telephones, obligations, or children to deal with, and each person slows down to a pace where they can listen carefully and speak meaningfully, then gradually match the pace of their mate, a new level of healing becomes possible.

Most medical settings today allow the doctor very limited time with the patient. In the wise words of the authors of *A General Theory of Love:* "Medicine lost sight of this truth: attachment is physiology. Good physicians have always known that the relationship heals. Indeed, good doctors existed before any modern therapeutic instruments did, in the centuries when the only prescriptions were the philters deriving their potency from metaphoric allusion to the healer's own person. The extraordinary results of the lab tests and procedures, the mastery they provided over the wily enemy of disease, proved seductive. Western medicine embraced the effective machines and ceded its historic soul."[13] Establishing a relationship, and *setting a human pace* for the healing encounter, reclaims this historic soul.

Matching our pace to that of another, especially when we're living fast-paced lives, can take some effort. It is one of the jobs of a parent to notice the pace at which a child comprehends, and match that pace. This is one of the disciplines that can make child-rearing a joy for busy people; it forces them to downshift to second or first gear. It requires paying primary attention to the physical connection with the person you're with, and is part of what prenatal psychologists call "attachment parenting."

The same is true for the healing encounter. The client in front of the doctor doesn't want to rattle off a list of symptoms for evaluation, and is not assessing the doctor by how fast she comes up with a prescriptive solution. The client is suffering, and needs understanding and empathy. Tuning in to people in order to understand their afflictions cannot be done at the same pace as drag racing. This "attachment doctoring" is one that establishes relationship first. Alternative medicine is good at this. Again, from *A General Theory of Love*: "The 'alternative' healers proliferated in response to the demand for a context of relatedness. These limbically wiser settings are friendlier to emotional needs—they involve regular contact with someone who participates in close listening, and often, the ancient reassurance of laying on hands. Alternative medicine sees these activities as quintessential rather than incidental to healing."[14] A paper recently published by a Johns Hopkins University researcher, Bruce Barrett, summed up a survey of the remarkable internal pharmacy we have at our disposal with the following eight recommendations that caregivers can use to engage it: "speak positively about treatments, provide encouragement, develop trust, provide reassurance, support relationships, respect uniqueness, explore values, and create ceremony. These clinical actions can empower patients to seek greater health and may provide a healthful sense of being cared for."[15]

The healing encounter of the future will be done at the pace of the Integrative Medical Clinic's Navigator—a wise and compassionate ear who can hear the patient's state of being, and then steer him or her in an appropriate direction—not at the pace of the HMO physician, who might have just twelve minutes per patient.[16] The actual therapy session might be quick; I'm happy going to a naturopath who listens to my symptoms and writes a prescription, and with a chiropractor who lays me on the table and makes four adjustments in as many minutes. But the initial encounter has to be conducted at a pace that allows the evaluator to tune into the patient deeply and notice what's happening on every level with that person.

3. Scaled Interventions

In a *scaled* application of treatments, the most benevolent and least invasive therapy is used first. This approach supposes an escalation of interventions, using the simplest ones as the first line of treatment, and employing more drastic means only if the previous treatment is not effective—and using technological medicine only when

"I'd prefer alternative medicine."

and if it becomes absolutely necessary. If a patient learns to meditate, begins an adequate exercise program, and makes appropriate dietary shifts, many illnesses take care of themselves. Norman Shealy lists a number of conditions in his books where innocuous, small-scale changes can reverse the course of diseases that are difficult, costly, and life-disruptive to treat with conventional means.[17] In the late 1970s,

I was acquainted with an eccentric old doctor, Henry Wasserman, a professor at New York University whose area of interest was medical ethics. He was horrified at what he discovered in his profession. The most passionate thing he ever said to me in his raspy, cynical, Yiddish-accented voice was, "I have learned enough in this job to give you one piece of solid advice: Never go near a hospital unless you are near the point of death." Though he may have had a jaundiced view of doctoring, it's clear that all of us have huge leverage available to us through the power of our awareness, and that consciousness is the first place to go for healing.

Marc Micozzi, MD, PhD, co-editor of the anthology *Consciousness and Healing*, refers to a continuum of approaches, from the most invasive, to the least invasive.[18] A continuum approach is also used by the National Pain Foundation. They advise patients to use a "Pain Treatment Continuum." This is a step-by-step plan "for the logical use of pain treatments that suggests using less invasive, less costly therapies before resorting to more invasive and more costly therapies."[19] They strongly advise relaxation, psychological awareness, and healing behaviors before resorting to more invasive therapies.

The plan "suggests either using one therapy or more than one therapy at a time, abandoning those that do not work, and advancing

Noninvasive Therapies	Invasive Therapies
Exercise	Medication management
Psychological pain management	Anesthetic blocking techniques
Physical and occupational therapies	Spinal cord stimulators
Biofeedback	Implanted pumps
Chiropractic manipulation	Peripheral nerve stimulators
Nutritional therapy	Surgery
Massage therapy	Chemical, surgical, or thermal nerve destruction
Psychotherapy	
Complementary medicine	

to more invasive therapies, as in climbing a ladder." It starts with exercise, progresses through psychotherapy and over-the-counter medication, and, when all else fails, ends with highly invasive interventions such as "anesthetic nerve blocks, epidural steroid injections, implanted catheters, neurodestructive techniques, spinal cord stimulators, and morphine pumps."[20]

An example of a noninvasive, quick, and cheap intervention for anxiety is a self-administered thirty-second EFT routine. It involves absolutely no risk, yet it holds the potential to produce big shifts. If the problem does not shift after small-scale interventions, it might be necessary to scale up. That might mean enrolling in a class, taking a retreat, training in a specific technique, or trying several different energy therapies in quick succession to see if one of them brings relief. Finally, if all else fails, it might be necessary to scale up to an anxiety-reducing drug. But strong interventions like this should be the last resort, not the first. Hippocrates advised us to "First, do no harm," and that is a good first principle to start with in designing a "step-by-step plan" to address our healing issues.

4. Thrive Through Chaos

People often have elaborate sets of reasons as to why they cannot be well. Brad Blanton, PhD, a psychotherapist who wrote *Radical Honesty: How to Transform Your Life by Telling the Truth* and a number of other books, calls these our "tragic stories."[21] He explains how we get wrapped up in them and neglect the very things that are healthy and serving us in our lives right now.

Tragic stories prevent us from seeking our full potential, let alone realizing it. In *The Beethoven Factor*, Paul Pearsall, PhD, talks about how many great works of art, literature, and science have been produced despite the chaos in the personal lives of their creators.[22] Although he cites dozens of examples, he picks Beethoven as the archetypal creator of beauty amongst personal tragedy. Forsaking the traditional label of "survivors," he calls these people "thrivors," people who don't just make do, but go on to extraordinary accomplishment despite psychological, spiritual, and physical setbacks, tragic stories that any of them might have used as a valid excuse to give up hope and accept a limited life. In a condensation of *The Beethoven Factor* that Dr. Pearsall prepared for *The Heart of Healing,* in a section entitled "A Thrivors' Hall of Fame,"[23] he assembled the following partial list of thrivors, some of them world-famous, others obscure:

William Carlos Williams: He suffered a severe stroke and subsequent emotional breakdown, only to later write great poetry and win the Pulitzer Prize for his work *Pictures from Brueghel.*

Nelson Mandela: He emerged from years of imprisonment and torture to become a leader for freedom, democracy, and the rights of the oppressed.

Pierre-Auguste Renoir: Unable to walk, and with fingers twisted by arthritis, he attached a paintbrush to his hand and painted some of the world's most memorable works, including, at age seventy-six, "The Washerwoman."

Henri Matisse: Suffering from heart failure, gastrointestinal disease, and with his lungs failing, he placed paintbrushes on a long stick and painted from his bed. His style created an entirely new field with a unique combination of color and form.

Enrico Dandolo: While serving as a peace ambassador to Constantinople in 1172 CE, he was blinded in both eyes by the emperor's guards. Twenty-nine years later, and at age ninety-four, he led Venice to victory over Constantinople, and at age ninety-seven was appointed chief magistrate of Constantinople.

Sister Gertrud Morgan: She devoted her entire life to establishing and running an orphanage in New Orleans named Gentilly. When she was sixty-five years old, a hurricane destroyed her orphanage. She then returned to her interest in painting and went on to have her works displayed in museums around the world.

Ding Ling: (A pseudonym used by the Chinese novelist and radical feminist Kian Bingzhi.) She was imprisoned from the age of sixty-six to seventy-one, during the Cultural Revolution of the 1970s in China. Upon her release, she went on to write some of her most highly praised works. She wrote an inspiring novel describing her experience of banishment to China's northern wilderness.

Helen Keller: Blind, deaf, and mute from age nineteen months, she wrote and published, at age seventy-five, her book *Teacher* in honor of the woman who helped her thrive through her suffering.

Jesse J. Aaron: A descendant of slaves, with a Seminole Indian grandmother, he, too, worked as a slave. Throughout his life, he cared for his disabled wife and had to spend all of his meager funds on surgery to save his wife's sight. In poverty, he offered a definition of what I am calling the Beethoven Factor. He wrote, "It was then that the Spirit woke me up and said, 'Carve wood.'" He went on to become one of the most respected wood sculptors in the world.

The new model of wellness focuses on what's working in patients' lives, and what their potentials are, as well as treating the issues that trouble them. But the places of wellness will be the starting point, not the end point. I had a mentor, Bill Bahan, DC, when I was taking my first classes in energy medicine in my late teens. One of his favorite sayings was "What's right with you is the point. What's wrong with you is beside the point."[24]

Our lives are often messy, ambiguous, perplexing, and incomplete. Yet the doctor of the future will see, in every patient, in whatever state, the presence of the dimension of wholeness. That archetype becomes the starting point for every treatment, for every step on the journey of recovery, regardless of whether the body and ego survive. Even if they do survive, it is just for a limited season, for eventually, *every* body and *every* ego will die. If our medical model is not wrapped up in attachment to how long that period is, and instead focuses on what's vibrant, alive, and vital in the person right now, it has a far more promising starting point for creating wellness. Once we let go of our tragic stories, the ground of healing is open to us. We can thrive in the midst of chaos.

5. Discover What Triggers Your Quantum Field

Years ago, I was a frequent visitor to a spiritual community in the Catskill Mountains of New York. It embraced a rigid lifestyle: meditations in the chapel before breakfast, study and classes in the morning, work in the afternoon, and worship at night.

There was another spiritual community close by, founded by Swami Muktananda. One day I visited there. The Swami was not in residence, but I talked to the chief administrator. "What techniques does the Swami advocate?" I asked, as we swapped notes about how our two communities were structured. "Oh, he might tell a student that he is forbidden to meditate at all," he replied. I was aghast. "Why would he say that?" I wondered.

"Perhaps the student has been meditating for hours each day for many years, and has become detached from the material world. Another student, who has never meditated, he might have them sitting in the lotus position day and night."

The Swami was skilled at noticing people's habitual tendencies, and giving his students the opportunity to express their divinity in ways that were unfamiliar to them. Each of us needs to find our own answer to the question: "What activates the expression of my inner wisdom?"

The answer is absolutely unique for you, and you have to figure out what is best for your particular constellation of body, mind, and heart. It may look very different from the culture's vision—or even from your own beliefs.

For instance, in the early 1990s, many of my friends belonged to gyms and they sometimes tried to recruit me. But I lived twenty minutes' drive from the nearest gym. Driving there, dressing for exercise, working out, showering, and driving back, all collectively took about two hours. I just couldn't work that commitment into my day on a habitual basis. But what I could do was work out for twenty minutes a day at home. So I bought some home exercise equipment—a rebounder, a weight machine, an ab wheel, and some free weights, and used them regularly.

Working out at a gym fit well for my friends. My routine worked for me. Once you set the intention of being healthy, you have to discover what it is that works for you. Later, I moved to a house five minutes from a gym, joined, and began going regularly—and sold my home exercise equipment.

For me, forty-five minutes of meditation each morning before I work out is essential. It is like a drug, or rather an antidote to the slothful, addictive, and intellectually lazy tendencies I have. It took me years to realize this and give myself that time in the mornings.

I take a peculiar mix of supplements every day. They're the ones I notice work well with my physiology. I review the list and make changes every so often. My regimen might not work for you; yours might not work for me. Understanding our bodies and listening to their signals is a vital part of wellness.

What colors make you feel comfortable? What music soothes your heart? What images nourish your soul? What people do you have in your life that affirm the best in you? What events stimulate your creativity? Setting up our lives so that our highest potentials are continually affirmed by our external environments, and so that our outer world provides epigenetic stimulation for our inner world, is an invitation to the multiverse to dance with us.

Eve Bruce, MD, is a plastic surgeon who discovered indigenous healing during a trip to South America and was eventually initiated into the Yachak tribe as a shaman. She published a book about her experiences called *Shaman, M.D.* She beautifully articulates the call and response of the quantum universe: "In our culture we seem to have many answers. When asked why we had an accident or a disease, or in the face of global climate change, we give many answers—faulty tools, faulty user, genetics, biochemical and anatomic mishaps, pollution, the shrinking ozone layer. Yet these are answers to the question how, not why. 'Why' questions lead to a message. What is the message? What is spirit telling us through the language of our physical existence? How can we connect more fully to our physical existence and begin to hear God? The answers are within ourselves. We need only to ask, open up to the answers, and pay attention."[25]

Once you state your intentions, once you invite the universe into a conversation about your well-being, listen intently for the answers. Find the mix that is just right for you. Don't be too swayed by the latest fads, but tune in to the whispers of your soul and the storehouse of advice it contains.

6. Allow for the X Factor

I used to write an operations plan for a ten-million-dollar book publishing and distribution company each year. It was a famous exercise within the company, involving every employee. The result was a 150-page operating manual that described the blueprint for the coming year. But I also had a section called "The X Factor" with a couple of blank pages behind it. "You never know what's going to come up," I told curious and skeptical inquirers, "and while you can plan for every conceivable eventuality, there will always be occurrences you did not foresee." Quantum healing is a lot like that. You state your intentions, you fuel them with passion, and then you wait upon the universe to see what X factors it throws your way. Energy moves in mysterious ways, and you cannot graph the paths it might take.

Exceeding the Limits of Vision

Every human being is inclined, in the words of nineteenth-century philosopher Arthur Schopenhauer, to "take the limits of his own field of vision for the limits of the world." In 1899, Charles Duell, then U.S. Commissioner of Patents and Trademarks, urged the U.S.

Congress to abolish his office, with the conviction that "Everything that can be invented, has been invented." His position seemed reasonable at the time: After all, for transportation, we had railroads that traversed continents, and steamships that could cross the Atlantic in less than a week. For communication, we had telegraphs that could relay messages in Morse code around the world.

Yet within a half a century of his prediction, a flood of inventions—the airplane, the automobile, the telephone, the computer—had made nonsense of his prediction.

Today we are at a similar place in the history of healing. Modern technological medicine has given us great benefits, and the breakthroughs will accellerate. But it is dawning on us that the solutions we find outside of ourselves might be dwarfed in magnitude by the solutions that come from within our own consciousness.

For most of the last half of the twentieth century, scientists assumed that consciousness arose as the result of increasing complexity in living systems. They believed that as living systems evolved from bacteria to simple animals to complex animals to mammals with large brains, they gradually evolved this phenomenon called "consciousness" to cope with the increasing complexity of life. This unexamined assumption pervades the writings of scientists. Stephen Jay Gould, one of the fathers of modern evolutionary biology, wrote: "Humans arose, rather, as a fortuitous and contingent outcome of thousands of linked events, any one of which could have occurred differently and sent history on an alternative pathway that would not have led to consciousness."[26]

In the jargon of science, consciousness is regarded as an "epiphenomenon of matter." Matter comes first, then consciousness. In this conviction, consciousness is something that arises out of the interaction of trillions of molecules within your body. This view was encapsulated by Sir Francis Crick, a co-discoverer of the double helix structure of the DNA molecule, in his 1994 book *The Astonishing Hypothesis:* "'You,' your joys and your sorrows, your memories and your ambitions, your sense of personal identity and free will, are in fact nothing more than the behavior of a vast assembly of nerve cells and their associated molecules. As Lewis Carroll's Alice might have phrased: 'You're nothing but a pack of neurons.'"[27]

Sir Francis's famous "Central Dogma of Molecular Biology" states that the code for life lies in the DNA, and that consciousness lies a long way down the biological chain:

DNA > RNA > Protein

His hypothesis certainly is astonishing, but for reasons other than the ones Sir Francis imagined. For science has taken us by the shoulders, turned us around, and pointed us resolutely in the direction opposite to his hypothesis. We now realize that consciousness underlies and organizes matter, and not the other way around. We have discovered that changes in consciousness precipitate changes in matter. We have realized that it is consciousness that is primary, and matter secondary. Consciousness is epigenetic, triggering biological expression:

Consciousness > DNA > RNA > Protein

The changes in our bodies produced by consciousness reveal the most potent tool for healing we have ever discovered. To a culture accustomed to looking for solutions "out there," it seems inconceivable that the answers might lie within. Yet scientific research, the very method we use to study the world "out there," now boomerangs back at us, pointing us to a much more challenging frontier. It reveals that the world "out there" is influenced by every shift we produce "in here." The stack of research piles higher every year. It shouts to us that the tools of our own consciousness—faith; prayer, intention, optimism, belief, vision, charity, energy—hold promises of health, longevity, and peak performance that the interventions "out there" are hard-pressed to match.

An ancient Sufi story tells of the angels convening at the dawn of time to discuss where to bury the meaning of life, a secret so sacred that only the most worthy of initiates should be allowed access to it.

"We should put it at the bottom of the ocean," one exclaims.

"No, the highest mountain peak," argues another.

Eventually, they turn to the wisest angel and ask where the most secret place might be. The angel replies: "There is one place no one will look. We will hide it in the human heart."

Medicine, wellness, and healing look very different in a quantum world than they did in the mechanistic and reductionist world that preceded it. We see levels of causality and epigenetic control that supersede the code in our DNA. The leading edge of scientific research opens up a new creative realm, in which the intangible energy of our thoughts and emotions affects the tangible physical universe itself.

Each new discovery is another indication of how important consciousness is for healing. We are learning to see our cells and our bodies as malleable, influenced by every thought and feeling that flows through us. We can claim responsibility for the quality of thought and feeling we host, selecting those that radiate benevolence, goodwill, love, and kindness. Doing this, we are doing more than conscious epigenetic engineering on our bodies; we are loving the whole world into health.

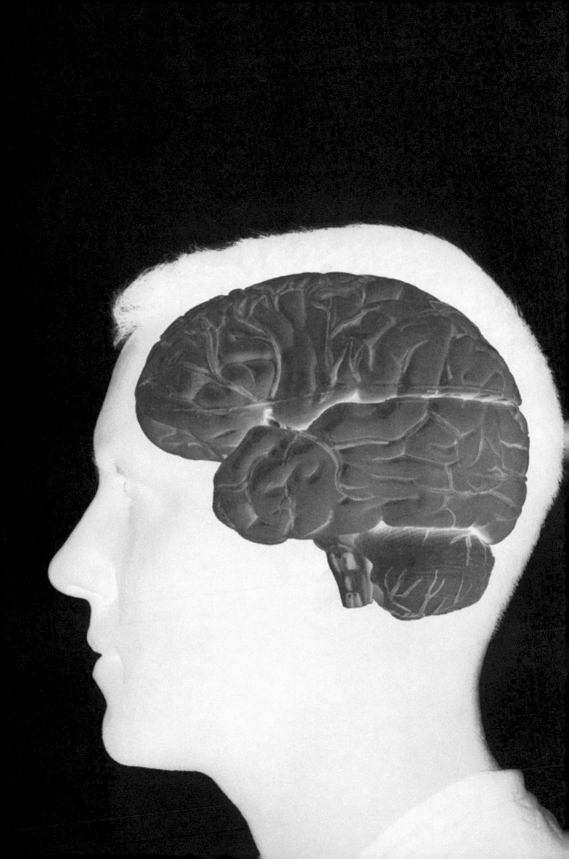

Appendix A: EFT Basic Recipe

1. **Where in your body** do you feel the emotional issue most strongly?

2. **Determine the distress level** in that place in your body on a scale of 0 to 10, where 10 is maximum intensity and 0 is no intensity:

    10, 9, 8, 7, 6, 5, 4, 3, 2, 1, 0

3. **The Setup:** Repeat this statement three times, while continuously tapping the Karate Chop point on the side of the hand (large dot on hand diagram below).

    "Even though I have _____ (name the problem), *I deeply and completely accept myself."*

4. **The Tapping Sequence:** Tap about seven times on each of the energy points in these two diagrams, while repeating a brief phrase that reminds you of the problem. Take a deep breath between points.

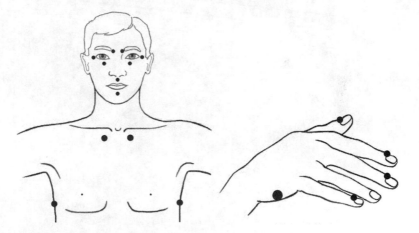

5. **Determine your distress level** again on a scale of 0 to 10 again. **If it's still high, say:**

    "Even though I have some remaining _____ (problem), *I deeply and completely accept myself."*

6. **Repeat from Step 1** till your distress level is as close to 0 as possible.

    Watch free Tap Along videos and download the EFT Mini-Manual at www.DawsonGift.com.

Appendix B:
Five Minute Energy Routine

The Five Minute Energy Routine packs many of the principles of energy medicine and Energy Psychology into a compact, practical form. It can be used in the morning to center yourself before starting your day, or when you're feeling stressed. This set of techniques also works well any time you are feeling tired or scrambled, can't think clearly, feel hysterical or out of control, feel droopy and out of energy, or need a pick-me-up. It represents the distilled wisdom of a quarter century of practice by the gifted energy healer Donna Eden, and is presented with more discussion in her book *Energy Medicine*. This abbreviated version is used with her permission; for a better understanding of the derivation of the techniques, as well as a host of other methods for use in specific situations, *Energy Medicine* is a valuable guide.

The Five Minute Energy Routine consists of seven postures and movements, and takes under five minutes to perform. Note how you feel in your body before doing the routine, and how you feel afterwards. Most people who practice the routine feel a marked shift in the five little minutes required to complete the process. The routine includes:

1. The Three Thumps
2. The Cross Crawl
3. The Wayne Cook Posture
4. The Crown Pull
5. Neurolymphatic Massage
6. The Zip Up
7. The Hook Up

Here's how you do the routine:

1. The Three Thumps

Tap or thump the indicated collarbone points with the tips of your four fingers, or the front of your fist, for about twenty seconds. Then tap over your thymus gland.

Collarbone points

Thymus point

2. The Cross Crawl

The Cross Crawl looks like marching in place. You swing your left arm up whilst raising your right leg, and vice versa. Move your arms in an exaggerated arc up and down, whilst also crossing the midline of your body.

Cross Crawl

3. The Wayne Cook Posture

Sit down and place your right leg over your left knee. Wrap your left palm around your right ankle. Wrap your right palm around your instep. Breathe slowly in through your nose, and out through your mouth for the duration of this pose.

Do the mirror image of this posture.

Place your thumbs on the bridge of your nose, with your fingertips together, and take three deep breaths.

Right foot hold   *Left foot hold*

Center hold

4. The Crown Pull

Place your fingertips on the centerline of your forehead. Using moderate pressure, pull them apart. Repeat this pull several times, each time moving your fingers up, till you've moved over the top of your head, and are pulling at the back of your skull.

Crown pull

5. Neurolymphatic Massage

Massage the following places with your fingertips:

Under your collarbone

Where the fronts of your arms connect to your torso

Down the front of your breastbone

Under your breasts

Under your ribcage, an inch to each side of your breastbone

The outside edge of each thigh, from the hips to the knees

The back of your neck, from the base of your skull, then traveling as far down as you can reach.

6. The Zip Up

Place your fingertips on your pubic bone.

Take a deep inbreath, whilst moving your hand up the center of your body, to your lower lip.

Repeat two more times.

7. The Hook Up

Place a fingertip in your navel.

Place a fingertip of your other hand between your eyebrows.

Pull up gently with both fingertips as you take a deep breath.

That's it! Five minutes have gone by, and most people find themselves rejuvenated. After you've tried out the Five Minute Energy Routine once or twice, you'll find it useful anytime you need a quick boost, to center yourself at the beginning of your day's activities, or when you're about to enter a situation you suspect will be stressful. And beyond the immediate benefits, the routine, when practiced regularly, is designed to establish healthier "energy habits" throughout your body.

Appendix C:
About the National Institute for
Integrative Healthcare

The National Institute for Integrative Healthcare (NIIH.org) is a 501(c)(3) nonprofit organization dedicated to research and training in energy medicine and Energy Psychology. NIIH has funded, designed, or partnered in more than a dozen randomized controlled trials of EFT and other energy therapies, in the belief that these techniques will dramatically advance the fields of medicine and psychology in the coming decades.

NIIH has three main programs, dedicated to helping veterans with PTSD (the Veterans Stress Project), researching energy therapies (the Foundation for Epigenetic Medicine), and providing humanitarian assistance to those in need (EFT Global).

The Veterans Stress Project

Soon after the first group of U.S. troops began arriving back from the conflict in Iraq, NIIH set up a clearinghouse to connect veterans with effective PTSD therapy. The Veterans Stress Project (www.StressProject.org) matches veterans with therapists and life coaches who offer EFT and similar therapies at little or no charge. The Stress Project trains veterans in the skills they need to manage stress and PTSD symptoms. The website features the stories and videos of many veterans who have benefited from these methods. It lists therapists and life coaches by state and country so that veterans can quickly locate practitioners who can help them. Many practitioners work by phone, providing comprehensive international coverage for veterans suffering from PTSD, depression, anxiety, and other mental health conditions.

Battle Tap

Battle Tap is a state-of-the-art virtual online tapping coach for veterans and their family members. It guides them through EFT sessions using an interactive interface. Users record their issues and the intensity of their emotional distress on the website, after which the software matches their emotions with video, audio, and written instructions, guiding them through a tapping session. The advantage of Battle Tap is that veterans don't have to make appointments with practitioners at set times; they can get help anonymously, whenever and wherever they choose. Battle Tap is available on the home page of the Stress Project website as well as its own site, BattleTap.org.

The Foundation for Epigenetic Medicine

The Foundation for Epigenetic Medicine is the research arm of NIIH. It has conducted many studies and contributed to several review papers published by peer-reviewed medical and psychology journals. The foundation has published several studies of the effects of EFT treatment on PTSD, pioneering research in this field. This work has led to EFT meeting the standards of the American Psychological Association's Division 12 Task Force on Empirically Validated Treatments as an "evidence-based" practice. The foundation conducts psychological research into conditions such as anxiety and depression and biological research on stress hormones and gene expression. Contact information for volunteer opportunities and financial contributions can be found on the NIIH website.

EFT Global

EFT Global is a volunteer organization providing humanitarian relief to victims of human-caused and natural disasters. EFT Global trains practitioners in the skills required to interface with relief organizations and provide culturally appropriate help to disaster victims. EFT Global has sponsored humanitarian projects in several countries.

Public Policy

NIIH has contributed to the public policy debate and legislation in the U.S. and Great Britain. It has provided the research required to present EFT and TFT to Britain's National Institute for Clinical Excellence (NICE) and the American Psychological Association (APA). NIIH has also sent representatives to testify before U.S. congressional committees, and meet with individual members of Congress. This has contributed to the drafting of legislation aimed at making these officially sanctioned therapies in the U.S. Veterans Administration (VA).

Other NIIH Services

The NIIH website provides links to sites listing energy medicine and Energy Psychology practitioners. It also links to educational institutions that offer courses in these therapies. The site has links to books and trainings in these methods, as well as to EFT Power Training (www.EFTPowerTraining.com). EFT Power Training uses the most highly qualified coaches and trainers, with the goal of revolutionizing performance in measurable ways in very short time frames.

Grants, Bequests, and Funding

Without the resources of a government or drug company, NIIH relies on the donations of concerned individuals. Please consider making tax-deductible donations to NIIH a regular part of your giving or tithing program. You can find a donation button at NIIH.org.

Endnotes

CH. 1 EPIGENETIC HEALING

1. Rossi, E. (2002). *The psychobiology of gene expression: Neuroscience and neurogenesis in hypnosis and the healing arts* (p. xvii). New York, NY: Norton.
2. Ibid., 9.
3. Kandel, E. (1998). A new intellectual framework for psychiatry? *American Journal of Psychiatry, 155,* 457.
4. Kemperman, G., & Gage, F. (1999). New nerve cells for the adult brain. *Scientific American, 280,* 48.
5. Greenfield, S. (2000). *The private life of the brain: Emotions, consciousness, and the secret of the self* (p. 9). New York, NY: John Wiley.
6. Eldridge, N. (2004). *Why we do it: Rethinking sex and the selfish gene* (p. 15). New York, NY: Norton.
7. Editorial staff. (1998, July 10). *Weekly* (p. 3), publication of the University of Southern California Health Science Campus, Los Angeles, CA.
8. Team finds gene mutations behind glaucoma. (2007, August 11). *Los Angeles Times.*
9. Nelkin, D., & Lindee, M. S. (1995). *The DNA mystique: The gene as a cultural icon* (p. 193). New York, NY: Freeman.
10. Justice, B. (2000). *Who gets sick?: How beliefs, moods, and thoughts affect your health* (p. 63). Houston, TX: Peak.
11. Idler, E., & Kasl, S. (1991). Health perceptions and survival: Do global evaluations of health really predict mortality? *Journal of Gerontology, 46*(2), S55.
12. Dossey, L. (2006). *The extraordinary healing power of ordinary things: Fourteen natural steps to health and happiness* (p. 21). New York, NY: Harmony Books.
13. Wright, W. (1998). *Born that way: Genes, behavior, personality* (p. 13). New York, NY: Knopf.
14. Dugatkin, L. (2000). *The imitation factor: Evolution beyond the gene* (p. 8). New York, NY: Free Press.
15. Ratner, C. (2004, April). Genes and psychology in the news. *New Ideas in Psychology, 22*(1), 29–47.
16. Wilson, E. O. (2000). *Sociobiology: The new synthesis* (25th Anniversary Ed., p. 575). Cambridge, MA: Harvard University Press.
17. Eldridge, *Why we do it,* 22.
18. Crick, F. (1970, August 8). Central dogma of molecular biology. *Nature, 227,* 561.
19. Ho, M-W. (2004, March 9). Death of the central dogma [Press release]. Institute of Science in Society, London, UK.
20. Fisher, C. (2007). *Dismantling discontent: Buddha's path through Darwin's world* (p. 177). Santa Rosa, CA: Elite Books.
21. McCallum, I. (2005). *Ecological intelligence: Rediscovering ourselves in nature* (p. 5). Cape Town, South Africa: Africa Geographic.
22. Oschman, J. (2006). Trauma energetics. *Journal of Bodywork and Movement Therapies, 10,* 21.
23. Rossi, *Psychobiology,* 66.
24. Cousins, N. (1989). Beliefs become biology. *Advances in Mind-Body Medicine, 6,* 20.
25. Richardson, K. (2000). *The making of intelligence* (p. 50). New York, NY: Columbia University Press; summarized in Rossi, *Psychobiology,* 50.
26. Grauds, C.& Childer, D. (2005). *The energy prescription: Give yourself abundant vitality with the wisdom of America's leading natural pharmacist.* New York, NY: Bantam.
27. Cool, L. C. (2004). The power of forgiving. *Reader's Digest,* May 2004, 92.
28. Childre, L., & Martin, H. (2000). *The HeartMath solution* (p. 57). San Francisco, CA: HarperSanFrancisco.
29. Study: Happy marriage heals. (2005, March 8). *USA Today.*
30. Holt-Lunstad, J., Birmingham, W., & Jones, B. Q. (2008, April). Is there something unique about marriage? The relative impact of marital status, relationship quality, and network social support on ambulatory blood pressure and mental health. *Annals of Behavioral Medicine, 35*(2), 239.
31. Robles, T. F., Shaffer, V. A., Malarkey, W. B., & Kiecolt-Glaser, J. K. (2006). Positive behaviors during marital conflict: Influences on stress hormones. *Journal of Social and Personal Relationships, 23*(2), 305–325.
32. Cahill, L., Prins, B., Weber, M., McGaugh, J. L. (1994, October 20). Beta-adrenergic activation and memory for emotional events. *Nature, 371*(6499), 702.

33. Grauds & Childer, *Energy prescription,* 38.
34. The RNA revolution: Biology's big bang. (2007). *Economist,* June 14, 2007, 87.
35. Rossi, *Psychobiology,* 229.
36. Pennisi, E. (2001). Behind the scenes of gene expression. *Science, 293,* 1064.
37. Epigenetics [Special issue]. (2001, August 10). *Science, 293*(5532).
38. Dossey, L. (2001). *Healing beyond the body: Medicine and the infinite reach of the mind* (p. 235). Boston, MA: Shambhala.
39. Gauqelin, M. (1974). *The cosmic clocks: From astrology to a modern science.* New York, NY: Avon.
40. Shealy, C. N., & Church, D. (2006). *Soul medicine: Awakening your inner blueprint for abundant health and energy* (p. 177). Santa Rosa, CA: Elite Books.
41. Snyderman, R. (2005). Creating a culture of health. *Spirituality and Health Magazine,* October–December, 2005, 46.
42. For an extended discussion of these figures and their sources, see Shealy & Church, *Soul medicine,* Chap. 17.
43. Dworkin, R. (2005). Science, faith and alternative medicine. *Policy Review, 108.*
44. Shealy & Church, *Soul medicine,* 234.
45. Bader, C., Dougherty, K., Froese, P., Johnson, B., Mencken, F. C., Park, J. Z., & Stark, R. (2006, September). *American piety in the 21st century. Selected findings from the Baylor Religion Survey* (p. 45). Waco, TX: Baylor Institute for Studies of Religion.
46. Astin, J., A., Shapiro, S. L., Eisenberg, D. M., & Forys, K. L. (2003). Mind-body medicine: State of the science, implications for practice. *Journal of the American Board of Family Practice, 16*(2), 131.
47. Shealy & Church, *Soul medicine,* 235.
48. Judah Folkman, MD, quoted in C. Kalb, Folkman looks ahead. *Newsweek,* February 19, 2001, 44.

CH. 2 YOU: THE ULTIMATE EPIGENETIC ENGINEER

1. Rabinoff, M. (2007). *Ending the tobacco holocaust* (p. 212). Rosa, CA: Elite Books.
2. Marcus, G. (2004). Making the mind: Why we've misunderstood the nature-nuture debate. *Boston Review,* December/January 2004.
3. Kelly, E., & Leyden, P. (Eds.). (2002). *What's next? Exploring the new terrain for business* (p. 204). Cambridge, MA: Perseus.
4. Bultman, S. J., Michaud, E. J., & Woychik, R. P. (1992, December 24). Molecular characterization of the mouse agouti locus. *Cell, 71*(7), 1195.
5. Watters, E. (2006, November). DNA is not destiny: The new science of epigenetics rewrites the rules of disease, heredity, and identity. *Discover, 27*(11).
6. Weinhold, R. (2006, March). Epigenetics: the science of change. *Environmental Health Perspectives, 114*(3).
7. Learning without learning. *Economist,* September 23, 2006, 89.
8. Steinberg, D. (2006). Determining nature vs. nurture: Molecular evidence is finally emerging to inform the long-standing debate. *Scientific American Mind,* October 2006, 12.
9. Marcus, Making the mind.
10. Felitti, V. J., Anda, R. F., Nordenberg, D., Williamson, D. F., Spitz, A. M., Edwards, V., Koss, M. P., & Marks, J. S. (1998, May). Relationship of childhood abuse and household dysfunction to many of the leading causes of death in adults. The Adverse Childhood Experiences (ACE) Study. *American Journal of Preventive Medicine, 14*(4), 245.
11. Ironson, G., Stuetzle, R., Fletcher, M. A., & Ironson, D. (2006). *View of God is associated with disease progression in HIV.* Paper presented at the annual meeting of the Society of Behavioral Medicine, March 22–25, 2006, San Francisco, CA. Abstract published in *Annals of Behavioral Medicine, 31*(Supplement), S074.
12. Ironson, G., Kremer, H., & Ironson, D. (2007). Spirituality, spiritual experiences, and spiritual transformations in the face of HIV. In J. Koss-Chiono & P. Hefner (Eds.), *Spiritual transformation and healing.* Walnut Creek, CA: Altamira Press.
13. Ibid.
14. Donnelly, M. (2006). Faith boosts cognitive management of HIV and cancer. *Science and Theology News,* May 2006, 16.
15. Ironson, G., Solomon, G. F., Balbin, E. G., O'Cleirigh, C., George, A., Kumar, M., Larson, D., & Woods, T. E. (2002). The Ironson-Woods Spirituality/Religiousness Index is associated with long survival, health behaviors, less distress and low cortisol in people with HIV/AIDS. *Annals of Behavioral Medicine, 24*(1), 34.

16. Ironson, G., Stuetzle, R., & Fletcher, M. A. (2006). An increase in religiousness/spirituality occurs after HIV diagnosis and predicts slower disease progression over 4 years in people with HIV. *Journal of General Internal Medicine, 21,* S62–S68.

17. Interview with author, January 30, 2007.

18. Grauds, C., & Childer, D. (2005). *The energy prescription* (p. 45). New York, NY: Bantam. Quoting *Journal of Gerontology, 55A,* M400.

19. Bader, C., Dougherty, K., Froese, P., Johnson, B., Mencken, F. C., Park, J. Z., & Stark, R. (2006, September). American piety in the 21st century. Selected findings from the Baylor Religion Survey (p. 26). Waco, TX: Baylor Institute for Studies of Religion.

20. Ironson, Kremer, & Ironson, Spirituality, spiritual experiences, and spiritual transformations.

21. Bower, B. (2007, January 27). Mind over muscle: Placebo boosts health benefits of exercise. *Science News Online, 171*(4).

22. Oxman, T. E., Freeman, D. H., Jr., & Manheimer, E. D. (1995). Lack of social participation or religious strength and comfort as risk factors for death after cardiac surgery in the elderly. *Psychosomatic Medicine, 57*(1), 5.

23. Powell, L. H., Shahabi, L., & Thoresen, C. E. (2003, January). Religion and spirituality: Linkages to physical health. *American Psychologist, 58*(1), 36.

24. Astin, J. E., Harkness, E., & Ernst, E. (2000). The efficacy of "distant healing": A systematic review of randomized trials. *Annals of Internal Medicine, 132*(11), 903.

25. Jonas, W. B. (2001). The middle way: Realistic randomized controlled trials for the evaluation of spiritual healing. *Journal of Alternative and Complementary Medicine, 7*(1), 5–7.

26. Casatelli, C. (2006). Study casts doubt on medicinal use of prayer: Cardiac patients show no improvement after intercession. *Science and Theology News,* May 2006, 10.

27. McTaggart, L. (2002). *The field: The quest for the secret force of the universe* (p. 189). New York, NY: HarperCollins.

28. Dossey, L. (1996). *Prayer is good medicine: How to reap the healing benefits of prayer* (p. 104). San Francisco, CA: HarperSanFrancisco.

29. Wallis, C. (2005). The new science of happiness. *Time,* January 15, 2005.

30. Grauds & Childer, *Energy prescription,* 136.

31. McClelland, D., & Kirshnit, C. (1988). The effect of motivational arousal through films on salivary immunoglobulin. *Psychology and Health, 2,* 31–52.

32. Rein, G., Atkinson, M., & McCraty, R. (1995). The physiological and psychological effects of compassion and anger. *Journal of Advancement in Medicine, 8*(2), 87–105.

33. Bower, B. (2003, July 26). Giving aid, staying alive: Elderly helpers have longevity advantage. *Science News, 164*(4), 51–52.

34. Donnelly, Faith boosts cognitive management, 16.

35. For a database of meditation studies, see the Institute of Noetic Sciences website, specifically http://www.noetic.org/research/medbiblio/index.htm

36. Dozor, R. (2004). Integrative health clinic meets real world. In D. Church (Ed.), *The Heart of Healing* (p. 312). Santa Rosa, CA: Elite Books.

37. Weil, A. (2006). *Dr. Andrew Weil's Self Healing Newsletter,* July 2006, 2.

38. Ellison, K. (2006). Secrets of the Buddha mind. *Psychology Today,* September–October 2006, 74.

39. Hirschberg, C. (2005). Living with cancer. In M. Schlitz & T. Amorok (with M. S. Micozzi), *Consciousness and healing: Integral approaches to mind-body medicine* (p. 163). St. Louis, MO: Churchill Livingstone.

40. Rhodes, D. R., Yu, J., Shanker, K., Deshpande, N., Varambally, R., Ghosh, D., . . . Chinnaiyan, A. M. (2004, June 22). Large-scale meta-analysis of cancer microarray data identifies common transcriptional profiles of neoplastic transformation and progression. *Proceedings of the National Academy of Sciences, 101*(25), 9309.

41. Trudeau, M. (2007, February 15). Students' view of intelligence can help grades. *NPR News: Your Health.* Retrieved from http://www.npr.org/templates/story/story.php?storyId=7406521

42. Weil, A. (2006). Attitude is everything with aging. *Andrew Weil's Self Healing Newsletter,* September 2006, 1.

43. Shealy, C. N. (2005). *Life beyond 100: Secrets of the fountain of youth* (p. 37). New York, NY: Jeremy P. Tarcher/Penguin.

44. Pettingale, K. W., Morris, T., Greer, S., & Haybittle, J. L. (1985). Mental attitudes to cancer: An additional prognostic factor. *Lancet, 1*(8431), 750.

45. Greer, S., Morris, T., Pettingale, K. W., & Haybittle, J. L. (1990). Psychological response to breast cancer and 15-year outcome. *Lancet, 335*(8680), 49–50.

46. Childre, L., & Martin, H. (2000). *The HeartMath solution* (p. 90). San Francisco, CA: HarperSanFrancisco.

47. Ibid., 55.

CH. 3 THE MALLEABLE GENOME

1. Silvia Hartmann was the therapist.

2. Feinstein, D., Craig, G., & Eden, D. (2005). *The promise of energy psychology: Revolutionary tools for dramatic personal change* (p. 109). New York, NY: Jeremy P. Tarcher/Penguin.

3. Rossi, E. (2002). *The psychobiology of gene expression* (p. 36). New York, NY: Norton.

4. Wen, X., Fuhrman, S., Michaels, G. S., Carr, D. B., Smith, S., Barker, J. L., & Somogyi, R. (1998). Large-scale temporal gene expression mapping of central nervous system development. *Proceedings of the National Academy of Sciences, 95*(1), 334.

5. Chen, E. (2006, November). Detection of differentially expressed genes using DNA microarray in acute tremor by electro-acupuncture treatment: the role of meridian system to conduct electricity and to transmit bioinformation. *Journal of Accord Integrative Medicine, 2*(6), 156.

6. Bentivoglio, M., & Grassi-Zucconi, G. (1999). Immediate early gene expression in sleep and wakefulness. In R. Lydic & H. A. Baghdoyan (Eds.), *Handbook of behavioral state control: Cellular and molecular mechanisms* (p. 235). New York, NY: CRC.

7. Tolle, T. R., Schadrack, J., & Zieglgänsberger, W. (Eds.). (1995). *Immediate-early genes in the central nervous system.* New York, NY: Springer-Verlag.

8. Marcus, G. (2004, December/January). Making the mind: Why we've misunderstood the nature-nuture debate. *Boston Review.*

9. Glaser, R., Kennedy, S., Lafuse, W. P., Bonneau, R. H., Speicher, C., Hillhouse, J., & Kiecolt-Glaser, J. K. (1990, August). Psychological stress-induced modulation of interleukin 2 receptor gene expression and interleukin 2 production in peripheral blood leucocytes. *Archives of General Psychiatry, 47*(8), 707.

10. Glaser, R., Lafuse, W. P., Bonneau, R. H., Atkinson, C., & Kiecolt-Glaser, J. K. (1993). Stress-associated modulation of proto-oncogene expression in human peripheral blood leukocytes. *Behavioral Neuroscience, 107*(3), 525.

11. Castés, M., Hagel, I., Palenque, M., Canelones, P., Corao, A., & Lynch, N. R. (1999, March). Immunological changes associated with clinical improvement of asthmatic children subjected to psychosocial intervention. *Brain, Behavior, and Immunity, 13*(1), 1.

12. Morimoto & Jacob, quoted in Rossi, *Psychobiology,* 236.

13. Ibid., 236.

14. Rossi, *Psychobiology,* 237. Diagram used with permission.

15. Ibid., 68. Diagram used with permission.

16. Ibid., 57.

17. Werntz, D., Bickford, R. G., & Shannahoff-Khalsa, D. (1987). Selective hemispheric stimulation by unilateral forced nostril breathing. *Human Neurobiology, 6*(3), 165.

18. Rossi, *Psychobiology,* 68.

19. Ibid.

20. Ibid., 103.

21. Ibid., 103.

22. Ibid., 202.

23. Kemperman, G., & Gage, F. (1999). New nerve cells for the adult brain. *Scientific American, 280,* 48.

24. Rossi, *Psychobiology,* 229.

25. Ibid., 191.

26. Maguire, E. A., Frackowiak, R. S., & Frith, C. D. (1997). Recalling routes around London: Activation of the right hippocampus in taxi drivers. *Journal of Neuroscience, 17*(18), 7103–7110.

27. Damasio, R., Grabowski, T. J., Bechara, A., Damasio, H., Ponto, L. L., Parvizi, J., & Hichwa, R. D. (2000, October). Subcortical and cortical brain activity during the feeling of self-generated emotions. *Nature Neuroscience, 3*(10), 1049.

28. Raheem, A. (1991). *Soul return: Integrating body, psyche, and spirit* (p. 81). Boulder Creek, CA: Aslan.

29. Moyer, C. A., Rounds, J., & Hannum, J. W. (2004, January). A meta-analysis of massage therapy research. *Psychological Bulletin, 130*(1), 3.

30. Botox lifts brows—and spirits. (2006). *Washington Post,* May 22, 2006.

31. Nakamura, T., Kiyono, K., Yoshiuchi, K. Nakahara, R. Struzik, Z. R., & Yamamoto, Y. (2007, September 27). Universal scaling law in human behavioral organization. *Physical Review Letters, 99*(13), 138103.

32. Rossi, *Psychobiology,* 304.

33. Ibid., 47.

34. Kandel, E. R. (1998). A new intellectual framework for psychiatry? *American Journal of Psychiatry, 155*(4), 457.

35. Squire, L., & Kandel, E. (1999). *Memory: From mind to molecules.* New York, NY: Scientific American Press.

36. Rock, D., & Schwartz, J. (2006, Summer). The neuroscience of leadership. *Strategy + Business Magazine, 43.*

37. Lüscher, C., Nicoll, R. A., Malenka, R. C., & Muller, D. (2000, June). Synaptic plasticity and dynamic modulation of the postsynaptic membrane. *Nature Neuroscience, 3*(6), 545.

38. Ibid.

39. Matus, A. (2000). Actin-based plasticity in dendritic spines. *Science, 290,* 754.

40. Kandel, New intellectual framework, 457.

41. Vogel, G. (2000). New brain cells prompt new theory of depression. *Science, 290,* 258.

42. Sheline, Y., Wang, P. W., Gado, M. H., Csernansky, J. G., & Vannier, M. W. (1996). Hippocampal atrophy in recurrent major depression. *Proceedings of the National Academy of Sciences, 93*(9), 3908.

43. Lisman, J., & Morris, G. (2001). Why is the cortex a slow learner? *Nature, 411,* 248.

44. Doidge, N. (2007). *The brain that changes itself: Stories of personal triumph from the frontiers of brain science* (p. 251). New York, NY: Viking.

45. Seligman, M. (2004). *Authentic happiness: Using the new positive psychology to realize your potential for lasting fulfillment.* New York, NY: Free Press.

46. Rossi, *Psychobiology,* 125.

47. Bittman, B. B., Berk, L. S., Felten, D. L., Westengard, J., Simonton, O. C., Pappas, J., & Ninehouser, M. (2001). Composite effects of group drumming music therapy on modulation of neuroendocrine-immune parameters in normal subjects. *Alternative Therapies in Health and Medicine, 7*(1), 38–47. Quoted in Rossi, *Psychobiology,* 244.

48. Rossi, *Psychobiology,* 126.

49. Shors, T., Miesegaes, G., Beylin, A., Zhao, M., Rydel, T., & Gould, E. (2001). Neurogenesis in the adult is involved in the formation of trace memories. *Nature, 410*(6826), 372.

50. Waelti, P., Dickinson, A., & Schultz, W. (2001). Dopamine responses comply with basic assumptions of formal learning theory. *Nature, 412*(6842), 43.

51. Rossi, *Psychobiology,* 140.

52. Whitehouse, D. (2003, July 1). "Fake alcohol" can make you tipsy [Summary of article in *Psychological Science,* published by the American Psychological Association]. *BBC News.* Retrieved from http://news.bbc.co.uk/2/hi/health/3035442.stm

53. Carey, B. (2007, July 31). Who's minding the mind? *New York Times.*

54. Motluk, A. (2005, August). Placebos trigger an opioid hit in the brain. *New Scientist, 22,* 23.

55. Brain maps perceptions, not reality. *Science Daily,* November 4, 2003. Retrieved from http://www.sciencedaily.com/releases/2003/11/031104063920.htm

56. Ibid.

57. Davidson, R. J., Kabat-Zinn, J., Schumacher, J., Rosenkranz, M., Muller, D., Santorelli, S. F., . . . Sheridan, J. F. (2003). Alterations in immune function produced by mindfulness meditation. *Psychosomatic Medicine, 65*(4), 564.

58. Orme-Johnson, D. W., Schneider, R. H., Son, Y. D., Nidich, S., & Cho, Z. H. (2006, August). Neuroimaging of meditation's effect on brain reactivity to pain. *Neuroreport, 17*(12), 1359.

CH. 4 THE BODY PIEZOELECTRIC

1. Retrieved January 19, 2009, from itp.nyu.edu/~nql3186/electricity/pages/pliny.html

2. Fukada, E., & Yasuda, I. (1956). On the piezoelectric effect of bone. *Journal of the Physical Society of Japan, 12,* 1158.

3. Shealy, C. N., & Church, D. (2006). *Soul medicine* (p. 187). Santa Rosa, CA: Elite Books.

4. Oschman, J. (2003). *Energy medicine in therapeutics and human performance* (p. 5). Boston, MA: Butterworth Heineman.

5. Childre, L., & Martin, H. (2000). *The HeartMath Solution* (p. 15). San Francisco, CA: HarperSanFrancisco.

6. Szent-Györgyi, A. (1957). *Bioenergetics* (p. 139). New York, NY: Academic Press.

7. Biscar, J. P. (1976). Photon enzyme action. *Bulletin of Mathematical Biology, 38,* 29.

8. Coetzee, H. (2000). *Biomagnetism and bio-electromagnetism: The foundation of life* [Originally published in *Future History,* Vol. 8]. Los Gatos, CA: Academy for Future Science.

9. Kirschvink, J. L., Kobayashi-Kirschvink, A., & Woodford, B. J. (1992). Magnetite biomineralization in the human brain. *Proceedings of the National Academy of Sciences, 89*(16), 7683.

10. Shealy & Church, *Soul medicine,* 191.

11. Magnetism and behavior. *Economist,* August 30, 2008, 76.

12. Grad, B. (1965). Some biological effects of "laying on of hands." *Journal of the American Society for Psychical Research, 59,* 95.

13. Ibid., 95–127.

14. Grad, B., Cadoret, R. J., & Paul, G. I. (1964). The influence of an unorthodox method of treatment on wound healing in mice. *International Journal of Parapsychology, 3,* 5.

15. Otto, H. A., & Knight, J. W. (1979). *Dimensions in wholistic healing: New frontiers in the treatment of the whole person* (p. 199). Chicago, IL: Nelson-Hall.

16. Zimmerman, J. (1985). New technologies detect effects of healing hands. *Brain Mind Bulletin, 10*(3), 136.

17. Seto, A., Kusaka, C., Nakazato, S., Huang, W. R., Sato, T., Hisamitsu, T., & Takeshige, C. (1992). Detection of extraordinary large bio-magnetic field strength from human hand during external qi emission. *Acupuncture and Electrotherapeutics Research, 17*(2), 75.

18. Maret, K. (2005, Spring). Seven key challenges facing science. *Bridges, 16*(1), 14.

19. Rubik, B., & Flower, G. (1993, January 14). *Electromagnetic applications in medicine.* NIH-OAM Panel Report, National Institutes of Health, Office of Alternative Medicine.

20. Gordon, G. (2008). *Protein iteration and cellular response to extrinsic electromagnetic forces.* Keynote paper presented at the International Conference on Informatics and Biomedical Engineering, May 16, 2008, Shanghai, China.

21. Sandyk, R., Anninos, P. A., Tsagas, N., & Derpapas, K. (1992). Magnetic fields in the treatment of Parkinson's disease. *International Journal of Neuroscience, 63*(1–2), 141.

22. Liboff, A. R. (2004). Toward an electromagnetic paradigm for biology and medicine. *Journal of Alternative and Complementary Medicine, 10*(1), 41.

23. University of Illinois, Chicago. (2006). The paradox of increasing genomic deregulation associated with increasing malignancy. Retrieved January 15, 2009, from www.mechanogenomics.com

24. The human epigenome: Life story, the sequel. (2005). *Economist,* December 24, 2005, 104.

25. Magnetic stimulator tested for depression. (2006). *United Press International,* January 31, 2006.

26. Graham Spence, quoted in D. Eden (2000), *Energy Medicine: Balance your body's energies for optimal health , joy, and vitality* (p. 299). New York, NY: Bantam, 2008.

27. Beck, R. (1986). Mood modification with ELF magnetic fields: A preliminary exploration, *Archaeus, 4,* 47–77.

28. Schumann, W. O. (1957). Elektrische eigenschwingungen des hohlraumes erde-luft-ionosphare. *Z. angew. u. Phys, 9,* 373.

29. Retrieved February 3, 2009, from www.lifetechnology.org/schumann.htm.

30. Roffey, L. E. (2006, April). The bioelectric basis for "healing energies." *Journal of Non-Locality and Remote Mental Interactions, 4,* 1.

31. Shealy & Church, *Soul medicine,* 87.

32. Kelly, R. (2000). *Healing ways: A doctor's guide to healing* (p. 153). New York, NY: Penguin.

33. Shealy & Church, *Soul medicine,* 190.

34. Ibid., 190.

35. Ibid., 194.

36. Roffey, Bioelectric basis, 1.

37. Rossi, *Psychobiology,* 190.

38. Schlebush, K. P., Maric-Oehler, W., & Popp, F. A. (2005). Biophotonics in the infrared spectral range reveal acupuncture meridian structure of the body. *Journal of Alternative and Complementary Medicine, 11*(1), 171.

39. Hyvärinen, J., & Karlsson, M. (1977). Low-resistance skin points that may coincide with acupuncture loci. *Medical Biology, 55*(2), 88–94.

40. Soh, K. (2004, November). Bonghan duct and acupuncture meridian as optical channel of biophoton. *Journal of the Korean Physical Society, 45*(5), 1196.

41. Hyvarien & Karlssohn, Low-resistance skin points. (1995). Quoted in *New England Journal of Medicine, 333*(4), 263.

42. Kober, A., Scheck, T., Greher, M., Lieba, F., Fleischhackl, R., Fleischhackl, S., Randunsky, F., & Hoerauf, K. (2002). Prehospital analgesia with acupressure in victims of minor trauma: A prospective randomized, double-blinded trial. *Anesthesia and Analgesia, 95*(3), 723.

43. Allen, J., Schnyer, R., & Hitt, S. (1998). The efficacy of acupuncture in the treatment of major depression in women. *Psychological Science, 9*(5), 397.

44. Molsberger, A. F., Boewing, G., Diener, H. C., Endres, H. G., Kraehmer, N., Kronfeld, K., & Zenz, M. (2006, April). Designing an acupuncture study: The nationwide, randomized, controlled, German acupuncture trials on migraine and tension-type headache. *Journal of Alternative and Complementary Medicine, 12*(3), 237.

45. Rosenfeld, I. (2006). Does acupuncture really work? *Parade,* July 9, 2006, 17.

46. Cho, Z. H., Hwang, S. C., Wong, E. K., Son, Y. D., Kang, C. K., Park, T. S., . . . Min, K. T. (2006). Neural substrates, experimental evidences and functional hypothesis of acupuncture mechanisms. *Acta Neurologica Scandinavica, 113*(6), 370.

47. Korotkov, K., Williams, B., & Wisneski, L. A. (2004). Assessing biophysical energy transfer mechanisms in living systems. *Journal of Alternative and Complementary Medicine, 10*(1), 49.

48. High technology meets ancient medicine. (2002). *Alternative Medicine,* March 2002, 93.

49. Association for Comprehensive Energy Psychology. (2006). *ACEP Certification Program Manual.* Ardmore, PA: ACEP.

50. Matthews, R. (2006). Harold Burr's biofields: Measuring the electromagnetics of life. Paper submitted for publication.

51. Burr, H. S. (1972). *The fields of life: Our links with the universe.* New York, NY: Ballantine.

52. Suarez, E. (2004). C-reactive protein is associated with psychological risk factors of cardiovascular disease in apparently healthy adults. *Psychosomatic Medicine, 66,* 684.

53. Childre & Martin, *HeartMath,* 15.

54. Langman, L., & Burr, H. S. (1947). Electrometric studies in women with malignancy of cervix uteri. *Obstetrical and Gynecological Survey, 2*(5), 714.

55. Liu, H., Park, W. C., Bentrem, D. J., McKian, K. P., Reyes Ade, L., Loweth, J. A, . . . Jordan, V. C. (2002). Structure-function relationships of the raloxifene-estrogen receptor-alpha complex for regulating transforming growth factor-alpha expression in breast cancer cells. *Journal of Biological Chemistry, 277*(11), 9189.

56. Tiller, W. A. (1997). *Science and Human Transformation: Subtle energies, intentionality, and consciousness* (p. 120). Walnut Creek, CA: Pavior.

57. Gardner, S. E., Frantz, R. A., & Schmidt, F. L. (1999, November). Effect of electrical stimulation on chronic wound healing: A meta-analysis. *Wound Repair and Regeneration, 7*(6), 495.

58. Benveniste, J., Arnoux, B., & Hadji, L. (1992). Highly dilute antigen increases coronary flow of isolated heart from immunized guinea-pigs. *FASEB Journal, 6,* A1610.

59. Benveniste, J., Jurgens, P., Hsueh, W., & Aissa, J. (1997). Transatlantic transfer of digitized antigen signal by telephone link. *Journal of Allergy and Clinical Immunology, 99,* S175.

60. Swanson, C. (2003). *The synchronized universe: New science of the paranormal.* Tucson, AZ: Poseidia.

61. Gariaev, P. (2009). Brief introduction into WaveGenetics, its scope and opportunities. Retrieved from http://eng.wavegenetic.ru/index.php?option=com_content&task=view&id=14. Gariaev, P. P., Friedman, M. J., & Leonova-Gariaeva, E. A. (2008). Crisis in life sciences: The Wave Genetics response. Retrieved from http://www.emergentmind.org/gariaev06.htm

62. Bennett, D. (2002, February). Body talk. *New Scientist, 173*(2331), 30.

63. Ibid.

64. Retrieved July 13, 2008, from www.anatomyfacts.com/Research/photonc/htm#edn23

65. Heimburg, T., & Jackson, A. D. (2007, May 1). The thermodynamics of general anesthesia. *Biophysical Journal, 92*(9), 3159–3165.

66. Johng, H. M., Yoo, J. S., Yoon, T. J., Shin, H. S., Lee, B. C., Lee, C., Lee, J. K., & Soh, K. S. (2006, August 30). Use of magnetic nanoparticles to visualize threadlike structures inside lymphatic vessels of rats. *Evidence-Based Complementary and Alternative Medicine 4*(1), 77–82.

67. Shin, H. S., Johng, H. M., Lee, B. C., Cho, S. I., Soh, K. S., Baik, K. Y., Yoo, J. S., & Soh, K. S. (2005, May). Feulgen reaction study of novel threadlike structures (Bonghan ducts) on the surfaces of mammalian organs. *Anatomical Record, 284*(1), 35.

68. Soh, K. S., Kang, K. A., & Ryu, Y. H. (2013). 50 years of bong-han theory and 10 years of primo vascular system. *Evidence-Based Complementary and Alternative Medicine, 2013,* 587827.

69. Soh, K. S. (2004, November). Bonghan duct and acupuncture meridian as optical channel of biophoton. *Journal of the Korean Physical Society, 45*(5), 1196.

70. Ballegaard, S., Jensen, G., Pedersen, F., & Nissen, V. H. (2008). Acupuncture in severe stable angina pectoris: A randomized trial. *Acta Medica Scandinavica, 220*(4), 307.

71. Shealy, C. N., Helms, J., & McDaniels, A. (1990, December). Treatment of male infertility with acupuncture. *Journal of Neurological and Orthopaedic Medicine and Surgery, 11*(4), 285.

72. Hansen, P. E., & Hansen, J. H. (1985, September). Acupuncture treatment of chronic tension headache: A controlled cross-over trial. *Cephalgia, 5*(3), 137.

73. Shealy & Church, *Soul medicine,* 214.

74. Dhond, R. P., Kettner, N., & Napadow, V. (2007). Neuroimaging acupuncture effects in the human brain. *Journal of Alternative and Complementary Medicine, 13*(6), 603–616.

75. Feinstein, D. (2007). Energy psychology: method, theory, evidence. *Psychotherapy: Theory, Research, Practice, Training, 45*(2), 199–213.

76. Tiller, *Science and human transformation,* 119.

77. Yount, G., Qian, Y., & Zhang, H. (2005). Changing perspectives on healing energy in tradition-al Chinese medicine. In M. Schlitz & T. Amorok (with M. S. Micozzi), *Consciousness and healing: Integral approaches to mind-body medicine* (p. 424). St. Louis, MO: Churchill Livingstone.

78. Wang C., Collet, J. P., & Lau, J. (2004, March 8). The effect of Tai Chi on health outcomes in patients with chronic conditions: A systematic review. *Archives of Internal Medicine, 164*(5), 493.

79. Irwin, M. R., Olmstead, R., & Oxman, M. N. (2007). Augmenting immune responses to varicella zoster virus in older adults: A randomized, controlled trial of Tai Chi. *Journal of the American Geriatrics Society, 55*(4), 511–517.

80. Mayer, M. (2004). *Secrets to living younger longer: The self-healing path of qigong, standing meditation and tai chi* (p. 6). San Francisco, CA: Bodymind.

81. Grauds, C., & Childer, D. (2005). *The energy prescription* (p. 94). New York, NY: Bantam.

82. High technology meets ancient medicine. *Alternative Medicine,* March 2002, 93.

83. Rooke, A. (2006). *Pacemakers.* Association of Veterans Affairs Anesthesiologists (AVAA) Forum.

84. Fenster, J. M. (2003). *Mavericks, miracles, and medicine: The pioneers who risked their lives to bring medicine into the modern age* (p. 171). New York, NY: Carroll & Graf.

85. *Neuroinsights* (2006). Neurotechnology publication retrieved February 15, 2009, from www.neu-roinsights.com/pages/24/index.htm

86. Shealy & Church, *Soul medicine.*

87. Shealy, C. N. (2006). *Life beyond 100.* New York, NY: Jeremy P. Tarcher/Penguin.

CH. 5 THE CONNECTIVE SEMICONDUCTING CRYSTAL

1. Adapted from Oschman, J. (2003). *Energy medicine in therapeutics and human performance* (p. 93). Boston, MA: Butterworth Heineman.

2. Ibid.

3. Pickup, A. (1978). Collagen and behavior: A model for progressive debilitation. *Medical Science, 6,* 499. Quoted in Oschman, *Energy medicine,* 92.

4. Ho, M-W. (1999, October 2). *Coherent energy, liquid crystallinity and acupuncture.* Address to British Acupuncture Society. Quoted in Oschman, *Energy medicine,* 87.

5. Oschman, *Energy medicine,* 92.

6. McCrone, J. (2004, June 1), How do you persist when your molecules don't? *Science and Consciousness Review.* Retrieved from www.sci-con.org/articles/20040601.html

7. Chen, E. (2006, September). Are cytoskeletons the smallest electric power line to transmit electricity in the meridians? *Journal of Accord Integrative Medicine, 2*(5), 109.

8. Oschman, *Energy medicine,* 213.

9. Oschman, *Energy medicine,* 213.

10. Bruce Lipton, quoted in A. Ardagh (2005), *The translucent revolution: How people just like you are waking up and changing the world* (p. 341). Novato, CA: New World Library.

11. Savva, S. (2006, September). Biofield control system of the organism—what is its physical car-rier? *Journal of Accord Integrative Medicine, 2*(5), 112.

12. Used with permission, adapted from Oschman, *Energy medicine,* 65.

13. Ibid., 47.

14. Ibid., 46.

15. McTaggart, L. (2002). *The field* (p. 46). New York, NY: HarperCollins.

16. Oschman, *Energy medicine,* 79.

17. Ahn, A. C., Wu, J., Badger, G. J., Hammerschlag, R., & Langevin, H. M. (2005, May 9). Electrical impedance along connective tissue planes associated with acupuncture meridians. *Complementary and Alternative Medicine, 5,* 10.

18. Cho, Z. H., Chung, S. C., Jones, J. P., Park, J. B., Park, H. J., Lee, H. J., Wong, E. K., & Min, B. I. (1998). New findings of the correlation between acupoints and corresponding brain cortices using functional MRI. *Proceedings of National Academy of Science, 95*(5), 2670.

19. Tsong, T. Y., (1989). Deciphering the language of cells. *Trends in Biochemical Sciences, 14*(3), 89.

20. Used with permission, adapted from Oschman, *Energy medicine,* 79.

21. McClare, C. W. F. (1974). Resonance in bioenergetics. *Annals of the New York Academy of Science, 227,* 74.

22. Feinstein, D. (2008). Six pillars of energy medicine. *Alternative Therapies in Health and Medicine, 14*(1), 44–54.

23. I am indebted to James Oschman for this insight at the ISSSEEM conference, June 24, 2006, Denver, CO.

24. McTaggart, *The field,* 47.

25. Ibid., 48.

26. Frohlich, H. (1968). Long-range coherence and energy storage in biological systems. *International Journal of Quantum Chemistry, 2,* 641. Quoted in McTaggart, *The field,* 49.

27. McTaggart, *The field,* 49.

28. Ho, Coherent energy. Quoted in Oschman, *Energy medicine,* 310.

29. Oschman, *Energy medicine,* 72.

Ch. 6 Belief Therapy

1. Lipton, B. H., Bensch, K. G., & Karasek, M. A. (1991). Microvessel endothelial cell transdifferentiation: Phenotypic characterization. *Differentiation, 46*(2), 117.

2. Lipton, B. H., Bensch, K. G., & Karasek, M. A. (1992). Histamine-modulated transdifferentiation of dermal microvascular endothelial cells. *Experimental Cell Research, 199*(2), 279.

3. Epigenetics [Special issue]. (2001, August 10). *Science, 293*(5532).

4. Lipton, B. H. (2005). *The biology of belief: Unleashing the power of consciousness, matter, and miracles* (p. 112). Santa Rosa, CA: Elite Books.

5. Oschman, J. L. (2005). Energy and the healing response. *Journal of Bodywork and Movement Therapies, 9,* 11.

6. McCraty, R., Atkinson, M., & Tomasino, D. (2003). *Modulation of DNA conformation by heart-focused intention* (p. 6). Boulder Creek, CA: Institute of HeartMath.

7. Institute of HearthMath. (2003). *Emotional energetics, intuition and epigenetics research* (p. 1). Boulder Creek, CA: Institute of HearthMath.

8. Childre, L., & Martin, H. (2000). *The HeartMath solution* (p. 37). San Francisco, CA: HarperSanFrancisco.

9. McCraty, Atkinson, & Tomasino, *Modulation of DNA conformation,* 4.

10. Yount, G., Qian, Y., & Zhang, H. (2005). Changing perspectives on healing energy in traditional Chinese medicine. In M. Schlitz & T. Amorok (with M. S. Micozzi), *Consciousness and healing: Integral approaches to mind-body medicine* (p. 424). St. Louis, MO: Churchill Livingstone.

11. Bairoch, A., Apweiler, R., Wu, C. H., Barker, W. C., Boeckmann, B., Ferro, S., . . . Yeh, L. S. (2005). The universal protein resource. *Nucleic Acids Research, 33,* D154.

12. Moseley, J. B. (2002, July 11). A controlled trial of arthroscopic surgery for osteoarthritis of the knee. *New England Journal of Medicine, 347,* 81.

13. Gellene, D. (2008, September 11). Knee surgery for arthritis not effective, study finds. *Los Angeles Times.*

14. Vedantam, S. (2002). Against depression, a sugar pill is hard to beat. *Washington Post,* May 7, 2002, A01

15. Stein, R., & Kaufman, M. (2006, January 1). Depression drugs safe, beneficial, studies say; Suicide risk rejected, but critics question validity of findings. *Washington Post.*

16. Shealy & Church, *Soul medicine,* 182.

17. Moore, T. J. (1999, October 17). No prescription for happiness. *Boston Globe.*

18. Kelleher, S., & Wilson, D. (2005, June 26). The hidden big business behind your doctor's diagnosis. *Seattle Times.*

19. Kondro, W. (2006, March 16). Drug company experts advised staff to withhold data about SSRI use in children. *Health Canada.*

20. Duke University. (2006, March 4). Anti-depressant use associated with increased risk for heart patients [Press release]. Duke University, Durham, NC.

21. Vedantam, S. (2006, March 23). Drugs cure depression in half of patients, doctors have mixed reaction to study findings. *Washington Post.*

22. *Economist.* (2008). Hope from a pill: Disagreements over whether drugs to combat depression are worth taking. *Economist,* March 1, 2008, 84.

23. Harris, G. (2006, March 23). Panel advises disclosure of drugs' psychotic effects. *New York Times.*

24. Vedantam, S. (2006, April 12). Comparison of schizophrenia drugs often favors firm funding study. *Washington Post.*

25. *New York Times.* (2006, July 23). Our conflicted medical journals.

26. Manchikanti, L. (2007). National drug control policy and prescription drug use: Facts and fallacies. *Pain Physician, 10,* 399.

27. Olfson, M., Marcus, S. C., & Shaffer, D. (2006). Antidepressant drug therapy and suicide in severely depressed children and adults: A case-control study. *Archives of General Psychiatry, 63*(8), 42.

28. Harris, G. (2007, June 27). Psychiatrists top list in drug maker gifts. *New York Times.*

29. Shealy, C. N. (2005). *Life beyond 100* (p. 27). New York, NY: Jeremy P. Tarcher/Penguin.

30. Maugh, T. (2006, July 21). Drug mistakes hurt or kill 1.5 million each year in US. *Los Angeles Times.*

31. Motluk, A. (2005). "Safe" painkiller is leading cause of liver failure. *New Scientist,* December 8, 2005, 19.

32. Anderson, G., Hussey, P. S., Frogner, B. K., & Waters, H. R. (2005). Health spending in the United States and the rest of the industrialized world. *Health Affairs, 24*(4), 903.

33. Ibid., 903.

34. Ibid., 903.

35. Kerr, E. A., McGlynn, E. A., Adams, J., Keesey, J., & Asch, S. M. (2004). Profiling the quality of care in twelve communities: Results from the CQI study. *Health Affairs, 23*(3), 247.

36. *New York Times.* (2005, March 6). One nation under stress. Reprinted from the *Economist.*

37. *Economist.* (2005). Scalpel, scissors, lawyer. *Economist,* December 17, 2005, 30.

38. Conover, C. (2003, July). *A review and synthesis of the cost and benefits of health services regulation.* Durham, NC: Duke University Press.

39. Oxman, T. E., Freeman, D. H., Jr., Manheimer, E. D. (1995). Lack of social participation or religious strength and comfort as risk factors for death after cardiac surgery in the elderly. *Psychosomatic Medicine, 57*(1), 5–15.

40. Gander, M. L., & von Känel, R. (2006). Myocardial infarction and post-traumatic stress disorder: Frequency, outcome, and atherosclerotic mechanisms. *European Journal of Cardiovascular Prevention and Rehabilitation, 13*(2), 165–172.

41. Davidson, R. J., Kabat-Zinn, J., Schumacher, J., Rosenkranz, M., Muller, D., Santorelli, S. F., . . . Sheridan, J. F. (2003). Alterations in immune function produced by mindfulness meditation. *Psychosomatic Medicine, 65*(4), 564.

42. Murphy, M., & Donovan, S. (1988). *Contemporary meditation research: A review of contemporary meditation research with a comprehensive bibliography* (p. 1931). San Francisco, CA: Esalen Institute.

43. Dossey, L. (1996). *Prayer is good medicine* (p. 8). San Francisco, CA: HarperSanFrancisco.

44. McCraty, R. (2003). *Impact of the power to change performance program on stress and health risks in correctional officers.* Boulder Creek, CA: Institute of HeartMath.

45. Dozor, R. (2004). Integrative health clinic meets real world. In D. Church (Ed.), *The Heart of Healing* (p. 309). Santa Rosa, CA: Elite Books.

46. Ornish, D. (2004). Love as healer. In D. Church (Ed.), *The Heart of Healing* (p. 258). Santa Rosa, CA: Elite Books.

Ch. 7 Entangled Strings

1. Church, D. (2004). Journey of a Pomo Indian medicine man. In D. Church (Ed.), *The Heart of Healing* (p. 31). Santa Rosa, CA: Elite Books..

2. For catalogues of studies of distant healing, see psychiatrist Daniel Benor's database at www.WholisticHealingResearch.org and the Institute of Noetic Sciences website, specifically www.noetic.org/research/overview

3. Sicher, F., Targ, E., Moore, D., II, & Smith H. S. (1998). A randomized double-blind study of the effect of distant healing in a population with advanced AIDS. *Western Journal of Medicine, 168*(6), 356.

4. Abbott, N. C. (2000). Healing as a therapy for human disease: A systemic review. *Journal of Alternative and Complementary Medicine, 6*(2), 159.

5. Benor, D. (1990). Survey of spiritual healing research. *Complementary Medical Research, 4*(1), 9.

6. Jonas, W. B. (2003). Science and spiritual healing. *Alternative Therapies in Health and Medicine, 9*(2), 56.

7. Goswami, A. (2000). *The visionary window: A quantum physicist's guide to enlightenment* (p. 15). Wheaton, IL: Quest.

8. Goswami, A. (2004). *The quantum doctor: A physicist's guide to health and healing* (p. 62). Charlottesville, VA: Hampton Roads.

9. Ibid., 15.

10. Ibid., 62.

11. McTaggart, L. (2007). *The intention experiment: Using your thoughts to change your life and the world* (p. xx). New York, NY: Free Press.

12. Peoc'h, R. (2002, September 1). Psychokinesis experiments with human and animal subjects upon a robot moving at random. *Journal of Parapsychology.*

13. Goswami, *The quantum doctor,* 63.

14. Bruce, C. (2004). *Schrödinger's rabbits: The many worlds of quantum* (p. 90). Washington, DC: Joseph Henry Press.

15. Goswami, *The quantum doctor,* 64.

16. Nova. *The elegant universe* [Documentary]. Retrieved August 1, 2006, from www.pbs.org/wgbh/nova/elegant/everything.html

17. BBC2 (Producer). (2002, February). *Horizon* program. London, UK: BBC2.

18. Cline, D. (2003, March). The search for dark matter. *Scientific American.*

19. Swanson, C. (2003). *The synchronized universe.* Tucson, AZ: Poseidia.

20. Kaku, M. (2006). *Reading the mind of God.* Address at the International Society for the Study of Subtle Energies and Energy Medicine (ISSSEEM) conference, June 24, 2006, Denver, CO.

21. Radin, D. (2008, January). Testing nonlocal observation as a source of intuitive knowledge. *Explore: The Journal of Science and Healing, 4*(1), 25.

22. Brooks, M. (2004, March 27). The weirdest link. *New Scientist.*

23. Kim, L. (2008). *Healing the rift: Merging science and spirituality* (p. 176). New York, NY: Cambridge House.

24. Radin, D., Stone, J., Levine, E., Eskandarnejad, S., Schlitz, M., Kozak, L., Mandel, D., & Hayssen, G. (2008). Compassionate intention as a therapeutic intention by partners of cancer patients: Effect of distant intention on the patients' autonomic nervous system. *Explore: The Journal of Science and Healing, 4*(4), 235.

25. Jean Houston, quoted in the *Utne Reader.* Retrieved October 19, 2008, from http://www.utne.com/story.id=616

26. Moehring, D., Maunz, P., Olmschenk, S., Younge, K. C., Matsukevich, D. N., Duan, L. M., & Monroe, C. (2007, September 6). Entanglement of single atom quantum bits at a distance. *Nature, 449,* 68.

27. Radin, D. (2006). *Entangled minds: Extrasensory experiences in a quantum reality* (p. 1). New York, NY: Paraview Pocket Books.

28. Grinberg-Zylberbaum, J., Delaflor, M., Attie, L., & Goswami, A. (1994). The Einstein-Podolsky-Rosen paradox in the brain: The transferred potential. *Physics Essays, 7*(4), 422.

29. Bohm, D., & Hiley, B. (1992). *The undivided universe: An ontological interpretation of quantum theory* (p. 382). New York, NY: Routledge.

30. Kelly, R. (2007). *The human antenna.* Santa Rosa, CA: Energy Psychology Press.

31. Baldwin, G. S., Brooks, N. J., Robson, R. E., Wynveen, A., Goldar, A., Leikin, S., Seddon, J. M., & Kornyshev, A. A. (2008). DNA double helices recognize mutual sequence homology in a protein free environment. *Journal of Physical Chemistry, 112*(4), 1060–1064.

32. *Economist* (2005). A mirror to the world. *Economist,* May 14, 2005, 81.

33. Ibid.

34. Einstein, A., Podolsky, B., & Rosen, N. (1935). Can quantum mechanical description of reality be considered complete? *Physical Review, 47,* 777–780.

35. Radin, Testing nonlocal observation, 25.

36. Sloan, R. P., & Ramakrishnan, R. (2005). The MANTRA II study. *Lancet, 366,* 1769.

37. Marie-Louse von Franz, quoted in I. McCallum (2005), *Ecological intelligence* (p. 146). Cape Town, South Africa: Africa Geographic.

38. Quoted in L. Dossey (2001), *Healing beyond the body* (p. 199). Boston, MA: Shambhala.

CH. 8 SCANNING THE FUTURE

1. Quoted in L. Dossey (1996), *Prayer is good medicine* (p. 11). San Francisco, CA: HarperSanFrancisco.

2. Marianoff, D. (1944). *Einstein: An intimate study of a great man.* New York, NY: Doubleday.

3. McCraty, R. (2005, January). Telephone and e-mail exchanges with author.

4. Radin, D. I., Taylor, R. D., & Braud, W. (1995). Remote mental influence of human electrodermal activity: A pilot replication. *European Journal of Parapsychology, 11,* 19.

5. McCraty, R., Atkinson, M., & Bradley, R. T. (2004). Electrophysiological evidence of intuition: Part 1. The surprising role of the heart. *Journal of Alternative and Complementary Medicine, 10*(1), 133.

6. Durka, P., Ircha, D., Neuper, C., & Pfurtscheller, G. (2000). Time-frequency microstructure of event-related electro-encephalogram desynchronisation and synchronisation. *Medical and Biological Engineering and Computing, 39*(3), 315.

7. Kelly, R. (2006). *The human aerial* (p. 96). New Zealand: Zenith.

8. McCraty, R., Atkinson, M., & Bradley, R. T. (2004). Electrophysiological evidence of intuition: Part 2: A system-wide process? *Journal of Alternative and Complementary Medicine, 10*(2), 325.

9. Arden, J. B. (1998). *Science, theology, and consciousness: The search for unity* (p. 104). Westport, CT: Praeger.

10. Norretranders, T. (1998). *The user illusion: Cutting consciousness down to size* (p. 216). New York, NY: Viking Penguin.

11. Ibid., 259.
12. Zimmerman, M. (1989). The nervous system in the context of information theory. In R. F. Schmidt & G. Thews (Eds.), *Human physiology* (p. 166). Berlin, Germany: Springer-Verlag.
13. Blanton, B. (2000). *Practicing radical honesty.* Virginia: Sparrowhawk.
14. Penrose, R. (1990). *The emperor's new mind: Concerning computers, minds, and the laws of physics* (p. 574). New York, NY: Vintage.

CH. 9 WRITING "MIRACLES!" ON EVERY PRESCRIPTION PAD

1. Dillard, J. (2004). Pain as our greatest teacher. In D. Church (Ed.), *The Heart of Healing* (p. 247). Santa Rosa, CA: Elite Books.
2. Dillard, J. (2003). *The chronic pain solution: The comprehensive, step-by-step guide to choosing the best of alternative and conventional medicine.* New York, NY: Bantam.
3. Dillard, J., & Ziporyn, T. (1998). *Alternative medicine for dummies.* Foster City, CA: IDG Books.
4. Jewish Theological Seminary. (2004). *Survey of physicians' views on miracles.* New York, NY: Jewish Theological Seminary.
5. Hodge, D. R. (2007). A systematic review of the empirical literature on intercessory prayer. *Research on Social Work Practice, 17*(2), 174.
6. Astin, A. W. (2008). Students become more spiritual in college. Retrieved November 2, 2008, from http://www.pewtrusts.org/news_room_detail.aspx?id=35952
7. Woodcock, A., & Davis, M. (1978). *Catastrophe theory* (p. 9). New York, NY: Viking Penguin. Quoted in W. Miller & J. C'deBaca (2001), *Quantum change* (p. 71). New York, NY: Guilford.
8. Miller, W., & C'deBaca, J. (2001). *Quantum change: When epiphanies and sudden insights transform ordinary lives.* New York, NY: Guilford.
9. Greenfield, S. (2000). *The private life of the brain* (p. 9). New York, NY: John Wiley.
10. Pulos, L. (2007). *Advances in energy psychology and healing.* Keynote address at the Toronto Energy Psychology Conference, October 27, 2007.

CH. 10 ENERGY PSYCHOLOGY

1. Robins, E. (2004). Future cures: Cheap, fast, radical, effective. In D. Church (Ed.), *The heart of healing* (p. 281). Santa Rosa, CA: Elite Books.
2. Oschman, J. L. (2006). Trauma energetics. *Journal of Bodywork and Movement Therapies, 10,* 32–42.
3. Wells, S., Polglase, K., Andrews, H. B., Carrington, P., & Baker, A. H. (2003). Evaluation of a meridian-based intervention, Emotional Freedom Techniques (EFT), for reducing specific phobias of small animals. *Journal of Clinical Psychology, 59,* 943–966. doi:10.1002/jclp.10189
4. Wells, S. (2005, March 27). E-mail to author.
5. Baker, A. H., & Siegel, M. A. (2010). Emotional Freedom Techniques (EFT) reduces intense fears: A partial replication and extension of Wells et al. *Energy Psychology: Theory, Research, and Treatment, 2*(2), 13–30. doi:10.9769.EPJ.2010.2.2.AHB
6. Salas, M. M., Brooks, A. J., & Rowe, J. E. (2011). The immediate effect of a brief energy psychology intervention (Emotional Freedom Techniques) on specific phobias: A pilot study. *Explore: The Journal of Science and Healing, 7*(3), 255–260.
7. Rowe, J. (2005). The effects of EFT on long-term psychological symptoms. *Counseling and Clinical Psychology Journal, 2*(3), 104–111.
8. Church, D., & Brooks, A. J. (2010). The effect of a brief EFT (Emotional Freedom Techniques) self-intervention on anxiety, depression, pain and cravings in healthcare workers. *Integrative Medicine: A Clinician's Journal, 9*(4), 40–44.
9. Church, D. (2013). *The EFT manual* (3rd ed.). Santa Rosa, CA: Energy Psychology Press.
10. Russell, B. (2014). New book highlights success of clinical EFT tapping. Retrieved February 4, 2014, from http://www.examiner.com/article/new-book-highlights-success-of-clinical-eft-tapping
11. Lambrou, P. T., Pratt, G. J., & Chevalier, G. (2003). Physiological and psychological effects of a mind/body therapy on claustrophobia. *Subtle Energies and Energy Medicine, 14,* 239–251.
12. Swingle, P. G., Pulos, L., & Swingle, M. K. (2004). Neurophysiological indicators of EFT treatment of posttraumatic stress. *Subtle Energies and Energy Medicine, 15*(1), 75–86.
13. Darby, D., & Hartung, J. (2012). Thought Field Therapy for blood-injection-injury phobia: A pilot study. *Energy Psychology: Theory, Research, and Treatment, 4*(1), 25–32. doi:10.9769. EPJ.2012.4.1.DD
14. Temple, G. P., & Mollon, P. (2011). Reducing anxiety in dental patients using Emotional Freedom Techniques. *Energy Psychology: Theory, Research, and Treatment, 3*(2), 53–56. doi:10.9769. EPJ.2011.3.2.GPT.

15. Schoninger, B., & Hartung, J. (2010). Changes on self-report measures of public speaking anxiety following treatment with Thought Field Therapy. *Energy Psychology: Theory, Research, and Treatment, 2*(1), 13–26. doi:10.9769.EPJ.2010.2.1.BS

16. Jain, S., & Rubino, A. (2012). The effectiveness of Emotional Freedom Techniques (EFT) for optimal test performance: A randomized controlled trial. *Energy Psychology: Theory, Research, and Treatment, 4*(2), 13–24. doi:10.9769.EPJ.2012.4.2.SJ

17. Jones, S., Thornton, J., & Andrews, H. (2011). Efficacy of EFT in reducing public speaking anxiety: A randomized controlled trial. *Energy Psychology: Theory, Research, and Treatment, 3*(1), 19–32. doi:10.9769.EPJ.2011.3.1.SJ

18. Sezgin, N., & Özcan, B. (2009). The effect of progressive muscular relaxation and Emotional Freedom Techniques on test anxiety in high school students: A randomized controlled trial. *Energy Psychology: Theory, Research, and Treatment, 1*(1), 23–30. doi:10.9769.EPJ.2009.1.1.NS

19. Feinstein, D. (2008). Energy psychology: A review of the preliminary evidence. *Psychotherapy: Theory, Research, Practice, Training, 45*(2), 199–213.

20. Feinstein, D. (2012). Acupoint stimulation in treating psychological disorders: Evidence of efficacy. *Review of General Psychology, 16*, 364–380. doi:10.1037/a0028602

21. Feinstein, D., Craig, G., & Eden, D. (2005). *The promise of energy psychology.* New York, NY: Tarcher.

22. Whitaker, R. (2011). *Anatomy of an epidemic: Magic bullets, psychiatric drugs, and the astonishing rise of mental illness in America.* New York, NY: Random House.

23. Russek, L., & Schwartz, G. E. (1997). Perceptions of parental love and caring predict health status in midlife: A 35-year follow-up of the Harvard Mastery of Stress Study. *Psychosomatic Medicine, 59*(2), 144.

24. Oschman, J. L. (2006). Trauma energetics. *Journal of Bodywork and Movement Therapies, 10*, 32–42.

25. Marino, R. (n.d.). Emotions affect red blood cells. Retrieved February 2013 from http://www.eftuniverse.com/index.php?option=com_content&view=article&id=2481

26. Church, D. (2013). *EFT for weight loss* (2nd ed.). Santa Rosa, CA: Energy Psychology Press.

27. Church, D. (2013). *EFT for fibromyalgia and chronic fatigue.* Santa Rosa, CA: Energy Psychology Press.

28. Feinstein, Craig, & Eden, *Promise of energy psychology.*

29. Shapiro, F. (1989). Efficacy of the Eye Movement Desensitization procedure in the treatment of traumatic memories. *Journal of Traumatic Stress, 2*(2), 199–223.

30. Williams, R. M. (2004). *PSYCH-K: The missing peace in your life!* Crestone, CO: Myrddin.

31. Hall, S., Lewith, G., Brien, S., & Little, P. (2009). A review of the literature in applied and specialised kinesiology. *Forschende Komplementärmedizin/Research in Complementary Medicine, 15*(1), 40–46.

32. Testimonials at www.psych-k.com/real_results.php

33. Fleming, T. (2006). *Emotional healing with Tapas Acupressure Technique.* Presentation at the Eighth Annual International Energy Psychology Conference, May 5, 2006, Santa Clara, CA.

34. Schulz, K. (2009). Integrating energy psychology into treatment for adult survivors of childhood sexual abuse. *Energy Psychology: Theory, Research, and Treatment, 1*(1), 15–22. doi:10.9769. EPJ.2009.1.1.KS

35. Lipton, B. H. (2005). *The biology of belief* (p. 84). Santa Rosa, CA: Elite Books.

36. Church, D. (2013). Clinical EFT as an evidence-based practice for the treatment of psychological and physiological conditions. *Psychology, 4*(8), 645–654. doi:10.4236/psych.2013.48092

37. Church, D., De Asis, M. A., & Brooks, A. J. (2012). Brief group intervention using EFT (Emotional Freedom Techniques) for depression in college students: A randomized controlled trial. *Depression Research and Treatment, 2012*, 1–7. doi:10.1155/2012/257172

38. Church, D., Piña, O., Reategui, C., & Brooks, A. (2012). Single session reduction of the intensity of traumatic memories in abused adolescents after EFT: A randomized controlled pilot study. *Traumatology, 18*(3), 73–79. doi:10.1177/1534765611426788

39. Temes, R. (2006). *The tapping cure: A revolutionary system for rapid relief from phobias, anxieties, post-traumatic stress syndrome disorder, and more* (p. 140). New York, NY: Marlowe.

40. Church, D. (2014). Pain, depression, and anxiety after PTSD symptom remediation in veterans. *Explore: The Journal of Science and Healing* (in press).

41. Brattberg, G. (2008). Self-administered EFT (Emotional Freedom Techniques) in individuals with fibromyalgia: A randomized trial. *Integrative Medicine: A Clinician's Journal. 7*(4), 30–35.

42. Bougea, A. M., Spandideas, N., Alexopoulos, E. C., Thomaides, T., Chrousos, G. P., & Darviri, C. (2013). Effect of the Emotional Freedom Technique on perceived stress, quality of life, and cortisol salivary levels in tension-type headache sufferers: A randomized controlled trial. *Explore: The Journal of Science and Healing, 9*(2), 91–99. doi:10.1016/j.explore.2012.12.005

43. Church, D., & Palmer-Hoffman, J. (2014). TBI symptoms improve after PTSD remediation with Emotional Freedom Techniques. *Traumatology* (in press).

44. Stewart, A., Boath, E., Carryer, A., Walton, I., & Hill, L. (2014). Can Emotional Freedom Techniques (EFT) be effective in the treatment of emotional conditions? Results of a service evaluation in Sandwell. *Journal of Psychological Therapies in Primary Care* (in press).

45. Hodge, P. M., & Jurgens, C. Y. (2011). A pilot study of the effects of Emotional Freedom Techniques in psoriasis. *Energy Psychology: Theory, Research, and Treatment, 3*(2), 13–24.

46. Lee, J.-H, & Kim, J. W. (2013). *Randomized controlled trial for the evaluation of the effects of EFT-Insomnia (EFT-I) for the elderly* (Master's thesis). Kyung Hee University, Korea.

47. Lee, J.-H, Suh, H.-U, Chung, S.-Y, & Kim, J. W. (2011). A preliminary study for the evaluation of the effects of EFT-I (EFT program for insomnia) for insomnia in the elderly. *Journal of Oriental Neuropsychiatry, 22,* 101–109.

48. Church, Pain, depression, and anxiety.

49. Stapleton, P., Sheldon, T., Porter, B., & Whitty, J. (2011). A randomised clinical trial of a meridian-based intervention for food cravings with six-month follow-up. *Behaviour Change, 28*(1), 1.

50. Church, D., & Wilde, N. (2013, May). Emotional eating and weight loss following Skinny Genes, a six week online program. Reported at the annual conference of the Association for Comprehensive Energy Psychology (ACEP), Reston, VA.

51. Hartung, J., & Stein, P. (2012). Telephone delivery of EFT (Emotional Freedom Techniques) remediates PTSD symptoms in veterans: A randomized controlled trial. *Energy Psychology: Theory, Research, and Treatment, 4*(1), 33–42. doi:10.9769.EPJ.2012.4.1.JH

52. Stein, P., & Brooks, A. J. (2011). Efficacy of EFT (Emotional Freedom Techniques) provided by coaches vs. licensed therapists in veterans with PTSD. *Energy Psychology: Theory, Research, and Treatment, 3*(1), 11–17. doi:10.9769.EPJ.2011.3.1.PKS

53. Fox, L. (2013). Is acupoint tapping an active ingredient or an inert placebo in Emotional Freedom Techniques (EFT)? A randomized controlled dismantling study. *Energy Psychology: Theory, Research, and Treatment, 5*(2), 15–28.

CH. 11 YOUR HAPPY GENES

1. Isles, A. R., & Wilkinson, L. S. (2008). Epigenetics: What is it and why is it important to mental disease? *British Medical Bulletin, 85,* 35–45.

2. Higgins, E. S. (2008). The new genetics of mental illness. *Scientific American Mind,* June 2008, 41–47.

3. Stuffrein-Roberts, S., Joyce, P. R., & Kennedy, M. A., (2008). Role of epigenetics in mental disorders. *Australian and New Zealand Journal of Psychiatry, 42,* 97–107.

4. Binder, E. B., Bradley, R. G., Liu, W., Epstein, M. P., Deveau, T. C., Mercer, K. B., ... Ressler K. J. (2008, March 19). Association of FKBP5 polymorphisms and childhood abuse with risk of posttraumatic stress disorder symptoms in adults. *Journal of the American Medical Association, 299*(11), 1291–1305.

5. *Economist.* (2006). Learning without learning, *Economist,* September 23, 2006, 89.

6. Poulter, M. O., Du, L., Weaver, I. C., Palkovits, M., Faludi, G., Merali, Z., Szyf, M., & Anisman, H. (2008). GABA receptor promoter hypermethylation in suicide brain: Implications for the involvement of epigenetic processes. *Biological Psychiatry, 64*(8), 645–652.

7. McGowan, P. O., Sasaki, A., Huang, T. C., Unterberger, A., Suderman, M., Ernst, C., ... Szyf, M. (2008, May 7). Promoter-wide hypermethylation of the ribosomal RNA gene promoter in the suicide brain. *PLoS One, 3*(5), 2085.

8. Haeffel, G. J., Getchell, M., Koposov, R. A., Yrigollen, C. M., Deyoung, C. G., Klinteberg, B. A., ... Grigorenko EL. (2008, January). Association between polymorphisms in the dopamine transporter gene and depression: Evidence for a gene-environment interaction in a sample of juvenile detainees. *Psychological Science, 19*(1), 62–69.

9. Oberlander, T. F., Weinberg, J., Papsdorf, M., Grunau, R., Misri, S., & Devlin, A. M. (2008, April). Prenatal exposure to maternal depression, neonatal methylation of human glucocorticoid receptor gene (NR3C1) and infant cortisol stress responses. *Epigenetics, 3*(2), 97–106.

10. Kawai, T., Morita, K., Masuda, K., Nishida, K., Shikishima, M., Ohta, M., Saito, T., & Rokutan, K. (2007, October). Gene expression signature in peripheral blood cells from medical students exposed to chronic psychological stress. *Biological Psychology, 76*(3), 147–155.

11. Cole, S. W., Hawkley, L. C., Arevalo, J. M., Sung, C. Y., Rose, R. M., & Cacioppo, J. T. (2007, September). Social regulation of gene expression in human leukocytes. *Genome Biology, 8*(9), R189.

12. Karssen, A. M., Her, S., Li, J. Z., Patel, P. D., Meng, F., Bunney, W. E., Jr., ... Lyons, D. M. (2007, December). Stress-induced changes in primate prefrontal profiles of gene expression. *Molecular Psychiatry, 12*(12), 1089.

13. Smoller, J. W., Rosenbaum, J. F., Biederman, J., Kennedy, J., Dai D., Racette, S. R., Laird, N. M., . . . Slaugenhaupt, S. A. (2003, December). Association of a genetic marker at the corticotropin-releasing hormone locus with behavioral inhibition. *Biological Psychiatry, 54*(12), 1376–1381.

14. Kim, L. (2008). *Healing the rift* (p. 122). New York, NY: Cambridge House.

15. Selye, H. (1974). *The stress of my life: A scientist's memoirs.* New York, NY: Van Nostrand Reinhold.

16. Dusek, J. A., Otu, H. H., Wohlhueter, A. L., Bhasin, M., Zerbini, L. F., Joseph, M. G., Benson, H., & Libermann, T. A. (2008, July 2). Genomic counter-stress changes induced by the relaxation response. *PLoS One, 3*(7), 2576.

17. Ornish, D., Magbanua, M. J., Weidner, G., Weinberg, V., Kemp, C., Green, C., . . . Carroll, P. R. (2008, June 17). Changes in prostate gene expression in men undergoing an intensive nutrition and lifestyle intervention. *Proceedings of the National Academy of Sciences, 105*(24), 8369.

18. Koenig, H. (2007). *Spirituality in patient care.* Philadelphia, PA: Templeton Foundation Press.

19. Cohen, S., Janicki-Deverts, D., & Miller, G. E. (2007, October 10). Psychological stress and disease. *Journal of the American Medical Association, 298*(14), 1685–1687.

20. Weil, A. (2007). How panic hurts the heart. *Dr. Andrew Weil's Self Healing Newsletter,* December 2007, 2.

21. Thaker, P. H., Han, L.Y, Kamat, A. A., Arevalo, J. M., Takahashi, R., Lu, C., . . . Sood, A. K. (2006, August). Chronic stress promotes tumor growth and angiogenesis in a mouse model of ovarian carcinoma. *Nature Medicine, 12*(8), 939–944.

22. Marini, S. C. (2008). *Spirituality and immunity* (Unpublished monograph, p. 4). Philadelphia, PA: Marini.

23. Crute, S. (2008). The best medicine. *AARP: The Magazine,* March/April 2008, 62.

24. Gehring, W. J. (2005, May–June). New perspectives on eye development and the evolution of eyes and photoreceptors. *Journal of Heredity, 96*(3), 171–184.

25. Kiecolt-Glaser, J. K., Gouin, J. P., Weng, N. P., Malarkey, W. B., Beversdorf, D. Q., & Glaser, R. (2011). Childhood adversity heightens the impact of later-life caregiving stress on telomere length and inflammation. *Psychosomatic Medicine, 73*(1), 16–22.

26. O'Donovan, A., Epel, E., Lin, J., Wolkowitz, O., Cohen, B., Maguen, S., . . . Neylan, T. C. (2011). Childhood trauma associated with short leukocyte telomere length in posttraumatic stress disorder. *Biological Psychiatry, 70*(5), 465–471.

27. De Weerth, C., van Hees, Y., & Buitelaar, J. K. (2003). Prenatal maternal cortisol levels and infant behavior during the first 5 months. *Early Human Development, 74*(2), 139–151.

28. Entringer, S., Epel, E. S., Lin, J., Buss, C., Shahbaba, B., Blackburn, E. H., Simhan, H. N., & Wadhwa, P. D. (2013). Maternal psychosocial stress during pregnancy is associated with newborn leukocyte telomere length. *American Journal of Obstetrics and Gynecology, 208*(2): 134.e1–134. e7. doi:10.1016/j.ajog.2012.11.033.

29. Veenhoven, R. (2008, September). Healthy happiness: Effects of happiness on physical health and the consequences for preventive health care. *Journal of Happiness Studies, 9*(3), 449–469.

30. Fowler, J. H., & Christakis, N. (2008, December 4). Dynamic spread of happiness in a large social network: Longitudinal analysis over 20 years in the Framingham Heart Study. *British Medical Journal, 337,* 2338.

31. Champage, F. A., & Meany, M. J. (2007). Transgenerational effects of social environment on variations in maternal care and behavioral response to novelty. *Behavioral Neuroscience, 121,* 1353–1363.

32. Hayashi, T., Urayama, O., Kawai, K., Hayashi, K., Iwanaga, S., Ohta, M., Saito, T., & Murakami, K. (2006). Laughter regulates gene expression in patients with type 2 diabetes. *Psychotherapy and Psychosomatics, 75*(1), 62–65.

33. Kaliman, P., Alvarez-Lopez, M. J., Cosin-Tomas, M., Rosenkranz, M. A., Lutz, A., & Davidson, R. J. (2014). Rapid changes in histone deacetylases and inflammatory gene expression in expert meditators. *Psychoneuroendocrinology, 40,* 96–107.

34. Yount, G. (2013). Energy healing at the frontier of genomics. *Energy Psychology: Theory, Research, and Treatment, 5*(2), 35–40. doi:10.9769.EPJ.2013.5.2.GY

35. Fraga, M. F., Ballestar, E., Paz, M. F., Ropero, S., Setien, F., Ballestar, M. L., & Esteller, M. (2005, July 26). Epigenetic differences arise during the lifetime of monozygotic twins. *Proceedings of the National Academy of Sciences, 102*(30), 10604.

36. Harper, L. (2005). Epigenetic inheritance and the intergenerational transfer of experience. *Psychological Bulletin, 131*(3), 340.

37. Dias, B. G., & Ressler, K. J. (2014). Parental olfactory experience influences behavior and neural structure in subsequent generations. *Nature Neuroscience, 17*(1), 89–96.

Ch. 12 Soul Medicine as Conventional Medicine

1. Eccles, J. (1991). *Evolution of the brain: Creation of the self.* New York, NY: Routledge.
2. Shealy, C. N., & Church, D. (2006). *Soul medicine* (p. 74). Santa Rosa, CA: Elite Books.
3. World Health Organization. (2002). *WHO Traditional Medicine Strategy 2002–2005.* Geneva, Switzerland: WHO.
4. Barnes, P., Powell-Griner, E., McFann, K., & Nahin, R. (2004, May). *Complementary and alternative medicine use among adults.* CED Advance Data Report 343.
5. Frenkel, M., Ayre, E. A., Carlson, C., & Sierpina, V., (2008, May/June). Integrating complementary and alternative medicine into conventional primary care: The patient perspective. *Explore: The Journal of Science and Healing, 4*(3), 178.
6. Elder, C. R., Gullion, C. M., DeBar, L. L., Funk, K. L., Lindberg, N. M., Ritenbaugh, C., . . . & Stevens, V. J. (2012). Randomized trial of Tapas Acupressure Technique for weight loss maintenance. *BMC Complementary and Alternative Medicine, 12*(1), 19.
7. University of Illinois, Chicago. (2006). The paradox of increasing genomic deregulation associated with increasing malignancy. Retrieved June 10, 2008, from www.mechanogenomics.com
8. Hubbard, B. M. (2005). Bringing god home. In D. Church (Ed.), *Healing Our Planet, Healing Our Selves* (p. 11). Santa Rosa, CA: Elite Books.
9. World Future Society. (2007). *Forecasts for the next 25 years* (p. 7). Bethesda, MD: World Future Society.
10. Shealy & Church, *Soul medicine, 43.*
11. Connor, S. (2003, December 8). Glaxo chief: Our drugs do not work on most patients. *Independent.*
12. Kelleher, S., & Wilson, D. (2005, June 26). The hidden big business behind your doctor's diagnosis. *Seattle Times.*
13. Ibid.
14. Vedantam, S. (2006, April 12). Comparison of schizophrenia drugs often favors firm funding study. *Washington Post.*
15. Grauds, C., & Childer, D. (2005). *The energy prescription* (p. 15). New York, NY: Bantam.

Ch. 13 Tapping a World of Healing

1. Church, D., Geronilla, L., & Dinter, I. (2009, January). Psychological symptom change in veterans after six sessions of EFT (Emotional Freedom Techniques): An observational study. *International Journal of Healing and Caring, 9*(1).
2. Church, D. (2010). The treatment of combat trauma in veterans using EFT (Emotional Freedom Techniques): A pilot protocol. *Traumatology, 16*(1), 55–65.
3. Church, D., Hawk, C., Brooks, A., Toukolehto, O., Wren, M., Dinter, I., & Stein, P. (2013). Psychological trauma symptom improvement in veterans using EFT (Emotional Freedom Techniques): A randomized controlled trial. *Journal of Nervous and Mental Disease, 201*, 153–160.
4. Karatzias, T., Power, K., Brown, K., McGoldrick, T., Begum, M., Young, J.,...Adams, S. (2011). A controlled comparison of the effectiveness and efficiency of two psychological therapies for post-traumatic stress disorder: EMDR vs. EFT. *Journal of Nervous and Mental Disease, 199*(6), 372–378.
5. Schulz, K. (2009). Therapists' views on integrating energy psychology in work with survivors of childhood sexual abuse. *Energy Psychology: Theory, Research, and Treatment, 1*(1), 15–22.
6. Mollon, P. (2008). *Psychoanalytic energy psychotherapy: Inspired by thought field therapy, EFT, TAT, and seemorg matrix.* London UK: Karnac.
7. Church, D. Yount, G., & Brooks, A. J. (2012). The effect of Emotional Freedom Techniques (EFT) on stress biochemistry: A randomized controlled trial. *Journal of Nervous and Mental Disease, 200*, 891–896.
8. Boath, A., Carryer, A., & Stewart, A. (2013). Is Emotional Freedom Techniques (EFT) generalizable? Comparing effects in sport science students versus complementary therapy students. *Energy Psychology: Theory, Research, and Treatment: 5*(2), 33–43.
9. Church, D. (2010). The effect of a brief EFT (Emotional Freedom Techniques) self-intervention on anxiety, depression, pain and cravings in healthcare workers. *Integrative Medicine: A Clinician's Journal, 10*(4), 40–44.
10. In Corvallis, suddenly there came a tapping. *Oregonian,* June 18, 2007.
11. Achenbach, J. (2007). Golfers "tap" into psychology. *Golfweek,* March 25, 2007, 60.
12. Church, D. (2009). The effect of energy psychology on athletic performance: A randomized controlled blind trial. *Open Sports Sciences, 2,* 94–99.

CH. 14 MEDICINE FOR THE BODY POLITIC

1. Feinstein, D. (2008) Energy psychology in disaster relief. *Traumatology, 141*(1), 124–137.
2. U.S. Centers for Disease Control and Prevention (CDC). Retrieved from www.cdc.gov
3. Ibid.
4. Retrieved August 1, 2006, from health.dailynewscentral.com/content/view/0001907/49
5. Grille, R. (2005). *Parenting for a peaceful world.* New Zealand: Longueville.
6. Kim, L. (2008). *Healing the rift* (p. 127). New York, NY: Cambridge House.
7. Hoek, H. W., Brown, A. S., & Susser, E. (1998, August). The Dutch famine and schizophrenia spectrum disorders. *Society for Psychiatric Epidemiology, 33*(8), 373–379.
8. Levitt, S. D. (2006), *Freakonomics: A rogue economist explores the hidden side of everything* (Rev. ed.). New York, NY: Morrow.
9. Raine, A., Brennan, P., & Mednick, S. A. (1994). Birth complications combined with early maternal rejection at age 1 year predispose to violent crime at 18 years. *Archives of General Psychiatry, 51*(12), 984.
10. Odent, M. (2006). The long term consequences of how we are born. *Journal of Prenatal and Perinatal Psychology and Health, 21*(2), 187.
11. Peter G. Peterson Foundation. (2013). *Americans spend over twice as much per capita on healthcare as the average developed country.* Retrieved February 24, 2014, from http://pgpf.org/Chart-Archive/0006_health-care-oecd
12. Working together for a healthy USA. *Fortune,* February 5, 2007, S2.
13. E-mail to author, February 3, 2007.
14. *New York American,* June 20, 1909.
15. Photo courtesy of Yannis Behrakis/Reuters.
16. Johnson, C., Shala, M., Sejdijaj, X., Odell, R., & Dabishevci, K. (2001). Thought field therapy —soothing the bad moments of Kosovo. *Journal of Clinical Psychology, 57*(10), 1237.
17. Feinstein, Energy psychology in disaster relief.
18. Feinstein, D. (2006). Keynote address at the Association for Comprehensive Energy Psychology (ACEP) Conference, May 6, 2006, Santa Clara, CA.
19. Cool, L. C. (2004). The power of forgiving. *Reader's Digest,* May 2004, 94.
20. Retrieved August 1, 2006, from www.emdrhap.org/aboutus/ourefforts/middleeast.php
21. Sakai, C., Paperny, D., Mathews, M., Tanida, G., Boyd, G., Simons, A.,...Nutter, L. (2001). Thought field therapy clinical application: Utilization in an HMO in behavioral medicine and behavioral health services. *Journal of Clinical Psychology, 57*(10), 1215.
22. Feinstein, D., Craig, G., & Eden, D. (2005). *The promise of energy psychology.* New York, NY: Tarcher.
23. Cane, P. (2000). *Trauma healing and transformation* (p. 10). Santa Cruz, CA: Capacitar.
24. Ibid., 61.
25. Feinstein, Energy psychology in disaster relief.
26. Houston, J. (2000). *Jump time: Shaping your future in a time of radical change.* New York, NY: Tarcher/Putnam.

CH. 15 TEN PRINCIPLES OF EPIGENETIC MEDICINE

1. Schakut, A. (2005). The biomarker benefit. *Economist Intelligent Life Report,* Summer 2005, 106.
2. Medicine without frontiers. *Economist Technology Quarterly,* September 17, 2005, 37.
3. Alsever, J. (2006). The gene screen. *Business 2.0,* October 2006, 110.
4. *United Press International.* (2007, January 24). New nanotechnology is announced, in *Science Daily.*
5. Swallow the surgeon. *Economist,* September 6, 2008, 27.
6. Fischbach, A. (2005, August 1). YMCA customizes program to prolong exercise habits. *Associated Press,* quoting a U.S. study published in the *European Journal of Sports Science* (2003).
7. Collinge, W. In R. Kelly (2000), *Healing Ways* (p. 159). New York: Penguin.
8. Purohit, S., & Yeats, W. B. (1970). *The ten principal Upanishads* (p. 80). London: UK.
9. Weil, A. T., & Snyderman, R. (2002). Integrative medicine: Bringing medicine back to its roots. *Archives of Internal Medicine, 162,* 397.
10. Mountainview Consulting Group. (2008). Integrating primary care and behavioral health services (p. 8). American Psychological Association, Bureau of Primary Health Care, Managed Care Technical Assistance Program.
11. Laje, G., Paddock, S., Manji, H., Rush, A. J., Wilson, A. F., Charney, D., & McMahon, F. J. (2007, October). Genetic markers of suicidal ideation emerging during citalopram treatment of major depression. *American Journal of Psychiatry, 164*(10), 1530.

12. Holsboer, F. (2001, July). CRHR1 antagonists as novel treatment strategies. *CNS Spectrums, 6*(7), 590–594.

13. Weil & Snyderman, Integrative medicine, 397.

14. Weil, A. (1995). *Spontaneous healing: How to discover and enhance your body's natural ability to maintain and heal itself* (p. 226). New York, NY: Knopf.

15. Ibid.

16. Pearson, C., Fugh-Berman, A., Allina, A., Massion, C., Whatley, M., Worcester, N., & Zones, J.; National Women's Health Network. (2002). *The truth about hormone replacement therapy.* Roseville, CA: Prima.

17. Shealy, C. N. (2005). *Life beyond 100* (p. 37). New York, NY: Jeremy P. Tarcher/Penguin.

18. Shealy, C. N. (1999). *Sacred healing: The curing power of energy and spirituality* (p. 102). Boston, MA: Element.

19. Siegel, B. (1988). *Love, medicine, and miracles: Lessons learned about self-healing from a surgeon's experience with exceptional patients.* New York, NY: Bantam.

20. Retrieved February 10, 2009, from www.teleosis.org

CH. 16 PRACTICES OF EPIGENETIC MEDICINE

1. Epigenetics [Special issue]. (2001, August 10). *Science, 293*(5532).

2. Shealy, C. N. (2005). *Life beyond 100* (p. 36). New York, NY: Jeremy P. Tarcher/Penguin.

3. Pear, R. (2004, December 31). Social security's latest obstacle: Life expectancy. *New York Times.*

4. Working together for a healthy USA. *Fortune,* February 5, 2007, S2.

5. American College of Emergency Physicians. (2006). *Seconds save lives.* Washington, DC: American College of Emergency Physicians.

6. Mountainview Consulting Group. (2008). *Integrating primary care and behavioral health services* (p. 8). American Psychological Association, Bureau of Primary Health Care, Managed Care Technical Assistance Program.

7. Johansson, J. E., Adami, H. O., Andersson, S. O., Bergström, R., Holmberg, L., & Krusemo, U. B. (1992, April 22). High 10-year survival rate in patients with early, untreated prostatic cancer. *Journal of the American Medical Association, 267*(16).

8. Sukovich, W. (2006). New surgical trends in treating low back pain. *Martha Jefferson Hospital Clinical Front,* Spring 2006, 1.

9. Weil, A. (2006). *Dr. Andrew Weil's Self Healing Newsletter,* July 2006, 4.

10. Ibid., 6.

11. Church, D. (2014). *EFT for Back Pain* (2nd ed.). Santa Rosa, CA: Energy Psychology Press.

12. Swartz, S. (2005). Managing menopause. *Santa Rosa Press Democrat,* January 18, 2005, D1.

13. Lewis, T., Amini, F., & Lannon, R. (2000). *A general theory of love* (p. 221). New York, NY: Random House.

14. Ibid., 222.

15. Barrett, B., Muller, D., Rakel, D., Rabago, D., Marchand, L., & Scheder, J. C. (2006, Spring). Placebo, meaning, and health. *Perspectives in Biology and Medicine, 49*(2), 178.

16. Channick, S. (2006, January 18). Have physicians given up bedside manner in the quest for money? *HCD Health.*

17. Shealy, *Life beyond 100,* 44.

18. Micozzi, M. (2005, March 23). *Frontiers of Healing Forum.* Institute of Noetic Sciences, Petaluma, CA.

19. Krames, E. (n.d.). *Pain medicine—Using the tools of the trade.* Pacific Pain Treatment Centers, San Francisco, CA. Retrieved September 1, 2006, from www.painconnection.org/ MyTreatment/ support_krames_0403.asp

20. Ibid.

21. Blanton, B. (1996). *Radical honesty* (p. 241). New York, NY: Dell.

22. Pearsall, P. (2002). *The Beethoven factor.* Charlottesville, VA: Hampton Roads.

23. Pearsall, P. (2004). The Beethoven factor. In D. Church (Ed.), *The Heart of Healing* (p. 125). Santa Rosa, CA: Elite Books.

24. Bahan, W. (1988). *Spirit of sunrise.* Denver, CO: Foundation House.

25. Bruce, E. (2002). *Shaman, M.D.: A plastic surgeon's remarkable journey into the world of shapeshifting.* Boston, MA: Inner Traditions.

26. Gould, S. J. (1994, October). The evolution of life on earth. *Scientific American.*

27. Crick, F. (1994). *The astonishing hypothesis: The scientific search for soul* (p. 3). New York, NY: Scribner.

Index